Books of Merit

ALSO BY NELLIE McCLUNG

Clearing in the West
Sowing Seeds in Danny
Purple Springs
Painted Fires
All We Like Sheep
Be Good to Yourself
Flowers in the Living

The Stream Runs Fast

Nellie McClung, 1920

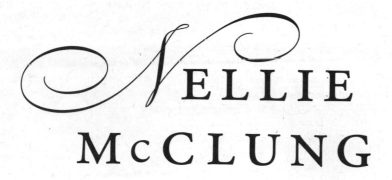

NELLIE McCLUNG

THE STREAM RUNS FAST

My Own Story

Thomas Allen Publishers
Toronto

Library and Archives Canada Cataloguing in Publication

McClung, Nellie L., 1873-1951
The stream runs fast : my own story / Nellie McClung.
ISBN 978-0-88762-306-6
1. McClung, Nellie L., 1873-1951.
2. Feminists—Canada—Biography.
3. Authors, Canadian (English)—20th century—Biography.
I. Title.

PS8525.C52Z475 2007   305.42092   C2007-904404-2

Cover image: Library and Archives Canada

Published by Thomas Allen Publishers,
a division of Thomas Allen & Son Limited,
145 Front Street East, Suite 209,
Toronto, Ontario M5A 1E3 Canada

www.thomas-allen.com

The publisher gratefully acknowledges the support of
The Ontario Arts Council for its publishing program.
The Ontario Arts Council is an agency of the Government of Ontario.

We acknowledge the support of the Canada Council for the Arts, which
last year invested $20.1 million in writing and publishing throughout Canada.

We acknowledge the Government of Ontario through the
Ontario Media Development Corporation's Ontario Book Initiative.

We acknowledge the financial support of the Government of Canada through the Book
Publishing Industry Development Program (BPIDP) for our publishing activities.

11 10 09 08 07   1 2 3 4 5

Ancient forest friendly: printed on 100% post-consumer recycled paper

Printed and bound in Canada

Contents

Introduction

JANUARY FIRST, 1943, was not just another day. It was not only the first day of a new year to me, but it was the first day of a new era. The old molds had suddenly broken and I knew that on the highway of life I had come to a wide place on the road.

Hitherto I had done certain things on each day of the week, circumstances driving. Now I was free. Nothing mattered. I could stop and stare, dawdle, dream or drift, do anything I wished or—nothing. The books had closed. I could not comprehend it all at first. I felt as stripped and bare as the old horse with his harness gone!

I became acutely sensitive to my surroundings; the old familiar objects became doubly dear. The sun, sea and sky were mine now to enjoy. I listened to the robins busy with the arbutus berries, and filling the air with excited conversation like women waiting for the store to open for a bargain sale. They were getting ready for their long trek south, and were putting in one good meal before they started. . . . The sun was running over the green fields playing strange tricks with the trees on the headlands. The green fields here at the coast, fed by the winter rains, cheat the gloomiest day and make it impossible for anyone to feel sad. Everything that I saw that day as I looked out of my window had a merry look, even the washing on the line under the bare cherry trees made a gay show-ing of color and graceful billowings. The yellow jasmine that had now reached the window sill smiled at me, with its dainty golden stars, and I smiled back.

What had I to be so glad about?

My world was at war. The doctors tell me I'm washed up and fin-ished. I can no longer drive a car, work in the garden or travel, must avoid crowds, eat sparingly, observing one general rule: "If you like it, avoid it." What had I to be so glad about?

But I am glad and my heart sings. Having loved this present world, known its joys and enjoyed its pleasures, I can now do a bit of free-wheeling, and besides, I have a great treasure bestowed upon me, one that was never mine before. Now I have Time, a full issue, as long as it lasts. I feel like Scrooge on that beautiful sparkling Christmas morning when he, too, found something very precious.

Time! Blue-misted, rainbow-hued Time, tanged by the salt Pacific breeze—twenty-four hours a day to use as I wished. I have lost space and speed but won Time, and now I can actually summer-fallow my mind, and it needs just that after these long active years. Like the impatient prairie farmer, I have cropped it too steadily, forcing it to yield. Now I can construct a new life on a new pattern. For the first time in my life I can disregard the clock and the calen-dar, and write as I please.

One dark memory assails me in this matter of writing. Hitherto I have done my best work when I have had a few good, lively interrup-tions. When I began *Clearing in the West* I did the first third in my usual hit-and-miss manner, working at odd times, and running a house at the same time. I remember I used to set the alarm clock to remind me to turn on the oven for the next meal, and always in the back of my mind I promised myself that some day I would have a real chance at writing, when I had nothing else in the world to do. I often indulged in that pleasant dream and told myself that I had never really had a fair chance.

Later in that year, 1934, all the conditions were perfect. I had no concern with meals. I took no outside engagements. I had a round table in an upper room in another woman's house. The lighting was good, the windows were too high for me to see out, I had piles of paper, a dozen sharpened pencils and not a thing in the world to do but write. For two terrible days I sat looking at the paper with my mind as dry as a covered bridge, not an idea stirring. It gave me a queer panicky feeling. I wondered if this really could happen to me. Did I really have to carry weight to be able to run at all? I kept thinking of a dozen things I wanted to do, every one of which seemed far more important than finishing my book. I wondered what I could say by way of explanation. Would I really have to admit that it wasn't in me to write any more? But my mind warmed up at last and I finished the book. Now I am going to continue the same story, my own story. This time I write with a sense of urgency, poignant but not unpleasant. In the back of my head I can hear the old tune we sang at Sunday School: "Work for the Night is Coming" . . .

It is strange about Time. One day I was no more conscious of it than I was of the air I breathed. There was plenty of time, days and days, running in and out, thousands of them. Then all at once some place there jangled a warning bell.

Writing is not like any other kind of work. There is a fervor in it that overcomes fatigue or even pain. It is a fire in the blood, a shot in the arm. It holds us when life begins to ravel, just as all the earth gathers itself into the brief brightness of Indian Summer before the stillness of winter falls. I wonder if it is the desire to be remembered? Miss Millay spoke for all of us when she wrote:

> "Stranger pause and look
> From the dust of ages,
> Lift this little book
> Turn its battered pages;
> Read me, do not let me die;
> Search the fading letters, finding
> Steadfast in the broken binding
> All that once was I!

Women at your toil,
Women at your leisure,
Till the kettle boil
Snatch of me your pleasure.
Where the broom straw marks the leaf
Women quiet with your weeping
Lest you wake a workman sleeping
Mix me with your grief!"

This may not be a noble reason for writing. It may be just one cut above the people who carve their names on park benches, but it is real and dominant in all of us. But this is not my only reason for writing this book.

I have seen my country emerge from obscurity into one of the truly great nations of the world. I have seen strange things come to pass in the short span of one lifetime, and I hasten to set it down while the light holds. People must know the past to understand the present and to face the future. The British people endured their trials because they have their roots in history.

In Canada we are developing a pattern of life and I know something about one block of that pattern. I know it for I helped to make it, and I can say that now without any pretense of modesty, or danger of arrogance, for I know that we who make the patterns are not important, but the pattern is.

That night, when it seemed that I might be going out with the tide, I knew I had no reason for feeling cheated, for I had had a good innings and a long run. I had warmed both hands before the fires of life.

I had been paid my wages in the incorruptible coin of loyal friendship and love, and the sense of life's continuity comforted me more than the drugs the young doctor had administered for my relief. Even in the shaded light of the room, the drama of life was proceeding, clear and decisive, and I knew that all was well with the world—the nurse was knitting a little shirt . . .

I thought, by some strange freak of memory, of the Tenmarq wheat the Mennonites had brought to Kansas from Russia in 1873, the year I was born, and how it is now going back to Russia to seed its scorched fields. There it is again, the great circle of life, nothing lost, nothing without meaning; sixteen gallons of wheat hand-picked by poor peasants, whose names no one remembers, now going back in a great convoy of ships to feed a nation.

As my brain cleared, I had a great longing to live. There was good mileage in me yet, and there were so many things that I wanted to do and had always been so sure that I would do. I did not want to leave one good word unwritten, one good story untold. I would have worked harder if I had known that life could be so soon over. I always knew that our spiritual forces were not keeping pace with our mechanical development. It is so easy to destroy and so hard to build up. The challenge of the new world never lay so heavily upon me and never did time seem so inexorable. There is a new world to be built and it must come in the hearts of the people. We have to see it before we can build it. Armies can stop wars, but only the Truth can make men free. Miracles are happening everywhere; new processes, new methods, new materials. Men were never so clever and never so needy. The age of plenty is here, if only the heart of man can be prepared, and he can be made to see that what hurts one nation hurts all. What a time to be alive! And what a poor time to die. So I lived.

"Without Regret" is the name I would like to have chosen for this book. There is something light and gallant about the phrase which appeals to me, reminiscent of that great passage in one of Walt Whitman's poems, where he speaks of his admiration for animals because they are not sorry or repentant for anything they have ever done, nor do they ever weary one with their apologies or excuses. I have been reading over my diaries which I have kept since 1912, and my scrapbooks, and it has been rather an overwhelming task, but I am glad that I have kept everything, and so in these I have an honest record of my activities with both the praise and blame which came to me, but the reading of them has been a task which leaves me shaken at times.

I have been accused, attacked and maligned. Once I was burned in effigy (which I had entirely forgotten until I read the Party's apologies in one of my scrapbooks). I have been caricatured, usually as a mosquito or other disagreeable insect, under the caption of "Calamity Nell." I have engaged in hot controversies, been threatened with violence and with libel suits, but on the other side of the ledger I have been stoutly defended by many good friends, known and unknown. I have had songs and poems written to me and I've had my name in lights. I have had and still have many loyal and faithful friends, who have known me long and still love me. I have always been rather proud of my enemies too, for I have never desired the approval or even the tolerance of the people whose interests run contrary to the public good, the people who believe if they are happy and prosperous, all's well with the world. I have never indulged in hating people and am glad to remember that I could attack opinions without feeling any bitterness towards the people who held them. But still I cannot look back without regret. I can see too many places where I could have been more obedient to the heavenly vision, for a vision I surely had for the creation of a better world.

But I hope I am leaving at least some small legacy of truth

The Stream Runs Fast

1

Manitou—1896

WHEN I WROTE the last sentence of *Clearing in the West* in 1935, I had every intention of continuing the story, as soon as we were settled in our new home at Lantern Lane, six miles from Victoria. But the new life, in this quiet neighborhood, with its delights of field and flower, its mellow climate, and the long season for sowing and reaping, its new trees and flowers, and the easy pace of living fascinated me, so instead of writing about the past, I wrote two books about this pleasant habitation of the blessed. I knew I had a story to tell of other days, a story of Canada and its march of progress, but the days were golden with sunshine and full of lark song, and the drone of bees. The lotus flower had cast its spell upon me, and I was sure that there would always be time to write. I was like the beauty parlor operator, at whose hands I once received a check-over, lasting two or three hours, during which time we discussed many problems of this world and the next. She had given me a fascinating picture of her matrimonial adventures, three all told, with another one pending, with interesting pictures of the many jobs she had held in between. When I was leaving she asked me if I would mind telling her how I made my living—if it was a fair question. I considered it was a fair question and told her I was a writer. She expressed an eager interest, and said she wished she had known, "for you know," she said wistfully, "that's what I've always planned on doing myself, when I am incapacitated for everything else."

Clearing in the West ended in the approved manner. The two young people stood on the rear platform of a "mixed" train and saw the sun break through the dark shoulder of a rain-cloud and knew that "tomorrow would be fine."

One hundred and one miles southwest from Winnipeg, Manitoba, lay the little town of Manitou, set in the hollow of the rolling grove-dotted prairie and there we lived for the first fifteen years of our married life. It had first been called "Manitoba City," by some unimaginative person, but this was changed to "Manitou" long before our arrival. Five grain elevators, painted red, along the track, bore evidence to the fertility of the soil. The railway station, also painted red, stood at the bottom of the long Front Street, whose slope was sufficient for sleigh riding when the street was covered with snow; but the youngsters had better and safer hills and so left Front Street to its legitimate sober traffic.

We had the one drug store in Manitou and our living quarters were four rooms up the long stairway at the south side of the grim gray building. They were hot in summer and cold in winter, but we did not know that and it would not have mattered if we had known, for to us they were everything the heart could desire. The parlor and dining room, divided by an archway, hung with golden brown chenille curtains on an oak pole, were in front, and from their windows we looked down on the street, a wide dirt road, with tying posts for the farmers' teams when they and their wives went into the store to do their "trading"; and that was not entirely a word left over from the posts of the Hudson's Bay, where Indians traded skins for flour and blankets. Our people brought in eggs and butter, and sides of bacon home-cured, and sometimes dressed chickens to the butcher shop.

Immediately beside our store was the Farmers' Store, some sort of a loose co-operative, whose proprietor worked in his shirt sleeves, protected by brown paper cuffs, but on Sunday wore striped trousers and a Prince Albert coat, and took up the collection in the Methodist Church, with a flower in his button-hole all the year round (geraniums covered the bleak stretch from November till May).

I bought my first set of "good" dishes from him, blue willow pattern. We bargained a bit first, according to custom, but on my third visit he wrote the price on a piece of paper, shading it with his hand, as he would a match on a windy night, and let me see the magic figures. I had a feeling that this was a special price to me only, and for this moment only, and that was surely good salesmanship. I thought of it today, when wiping the last vegetable dish, complete with lid, the other fifty-four pieces having taken the unreturning way.

The suave proprietor had many good stories to his credit. One of these concerned the mean woman of the district who sold him a four-pound stone in the middle of a crock of butter, receiving twenty-five cents a pound for it, and received it back the same day in a caddy of tea at sixty cents a pound. The story is a legend now and has been told in many forms, and no doubt has happened in many places.

Wes and I had about four dollars between us when our trip was over, but the rent was paid for the month and the down payment was made on the furniture. The local furniture dealer charged us 2 per cent a month interest, just to make us hurry with the payments, and no doubt kept a watchful eye on the furniture. We felt rich and secure in our four little square rooms above the drug store and have many happy memories of their kindly walls. I loved every dish and every pan and thought nothing could be more beautiful than the satin-striped wallpaper on the parlor and dining rooms, one stripe plain and one flowered. The centre table had a cover of Irish crochet, with raised pink roses, given to me by Minnie Smith, one of my pupils whom I taught in Treherne. The boys around town had given us a parlor suite, upholstered in Turkish design, each piece a different color. A hanging lamp was suspended from the high ceiling and was raised and lowered by manipulation of two chains ending in gold acorns; the shade, of frosted glass, was patterned in wild roses and morning glories and was finished with glass fringe which jingled when Adam McBeth's dray passed below on the street.

We had two pictures framed in oak, lovely sepia pictures of farm-houses set in hilly country that ran to the sea, with cows on the meadows and curving roads leading to their rustic gates. We have them yet and they are still beautiful. The long windows had Nottingham lace curtains in a fern pattern, hanging from oak poles. We had two Brussels rugs and a fine oak dining table and chairs, which are still serving at a cottage at Matlock on Lake Winnipeg. They may burn, but they will never wear out. In the kitchen we had a good, square, black stove (a grim-faced bit of furniture compared with the painted ladies of today), but it had a good deep firebox and a fine oven and gave us assurance, and so did the drug store boxes and a good pile of wood in the back yard. Lumber was plentiful and there was no such thing as fuel conservation, so we burned the boxes lightheartedly, just as the farmers burned their straw piles—this was in 1896.

Some of my cooking experiments took queer turns, and on Wesley's suggestion I went to see Mrs. Cassin to find out how to cook an apple pie so the lower paste would be as light as the upper. He had boarded at the hotel before we were married, and liked Mrs. Cassin's cooking; her instructions improved my technique, but there were still lapses—such as lumpy gravy and the taste of soda in my biscuits.

One day a book agent came to see me about buying a cook book. The price was $3.00 and that was real money, but I must have been hitting an all-time low, for when Wes came in he cast his vote in favor of the purchase and produced the money. I thought he was just a bit too enthusiastic, but I did not analyze his motives too closely. I had no intention of being an apologetic cook so I welcomed the book and have leaned heavily on it all these years. It is called *Breakfast, Dinner and Supper* and now in its second binding is as good as ever, though some of its pages show definite traces of struggle. The Preserving section and the Home-Made Candy are as full of history as an old tree. Cook books come and go; they are endorsed and guaranteed and "tested in our own laboratories," but when I want to know the whole truth on Pickling or how to stuff a Hubbard squash, I go to my fine old book with its blue oil cloth binding. I have never found it wanting. In its pages there are many interesting annotations, and it has long served as a loose-leaf scrap book, revealing much of the intimate life of our family. The first page bears an inscription in a widespread, wiggly hand, containing the information that this book was "presented to Mrs. R. W. McClung by her daughter, Florence McClung, in the year 1907" (which was the first year Miss McClung was at school). A yellowed sheet torn from a scribbler, bearing the nail mark where it was hung on the kitchen wall, contains the record of how the four eldest McClung children raised money for the Fresh Air Fund. Jack has fifty cents to his credit for making the highest marks in Grade Seven; Paul evidently contributed the same amount, but earned in a different way. His was the gilded coin of worldliness, earned by carrying wires from the station to the Cassin house, on the occasion of the Johnson–Jeffreys fight. Whether this contribution was made at the dictates of Paul's conscience or not I cannot remember; it may have been. For at that time Paul had the worthy desire to be a missionary. However, his zeal for the foreign field weakened after he had ridden around for a couple of days on Adam McBeth's dray. He said missionaries might not always have horses, and besides, they wouldn't be meeting trains every day. However, Paul came through with another contribution, which was good, honest, sweat-of-the-brow money, ten cents for weeding Willie Wyley's garden. Florence sacrificed ice-cream cones to the amount of twenty cents, and earned another five cents—so the record states—for going to the Baptist picnic. This item is a bit puzzling, for let no one think that the Baptist picnic was not a joyous affair. It is believed that there was a denominational feud between Florence and her friend, Margaret Chalmers, on the subject of sprinkling vs. immersion, and this five cents was paid in an effort to heal the breach between these two militant defenders of the faith.

Now I see I am getting ahead of my story. That's what comes of looking backward. Memory telescopes the past. The distant hills are seeming nigh. My hope is that the readers of this book have the same fine disregard for chronology that I have, and will be content to go in and out and find pasture.

2

Humble Beginnings

A COUPLE OF WEEKS after our marriage a first-class salesman came to town carrying an impressive attaché bag, in which reposed the prospectus of a new magazine. He was a pleasant, engaging young fellow who would have done for a Charles Dana Gibson model. The new magazine about to break over our quiet lives was called *Town and Country*, and it would carry each month pictures and sketches of the leading people in one of the more important country towns. Manitou had been chosen for Volume 1, Number 1, and the young man had been advised to see me and enlist my services; the company, he said, was anxious to use native writers. . . .

I liked the sound of that. I never had been called a native writer before. It had a patriotic appeal, and I even subscribed for the magazine. Someone must show faith in the venture. Five dollars was the subscription price. The young man was apologetic about taking a subscription from me, though he told me everyone taking part must subscribe. It was a pure formality, he said. There would be expenses to be met . . . He was glad I was willing to undertake the assignment—that's what he called it. He said writers were the great interpreters of a country. What Dickens did for London, and Scott for Scotland, he believed I could do for southern Manitoba. "We want you to hold a mirror up to this country; or perhaps a microscope," he said, "and you must feel free to write as you please. No one wants bare facts; no one is satisfied with bare facts; we want to light candles of imagination in the minds of our people. . . ."

I did not tell all this to Wes. He had a blunt way of puncturing some of my beautiful balloons, and the worst of it was he was generally right. Very rarely have I had the satisfaction of saying to him: "I told you so." Many years after, Robert E. Knowles defined Wes in a brief sentence: "That man of yours," he said, "can do a lot of washing in a very few suds." So I held my peace but worked hard. I interviewed people, walked miles, dug into the newspaper files in the office of the *Manitou Mercury*, making elaborate notes and dreaming great dreams of what a native writer can do for a community.

I had no difficulty in getting the old-timers to talk. They blossomed out under my rapt listening, and I soon saw that every house had a story. I got the lowdown on the family rows, hot off the griddle. Many of the people in Manitou had come from the same part of Ontario, and I found out that they had long memories for old sins and old sorrows. One thing bothered me. I had to do indirect advertising for the business firms, for of course, like all up-to-date magazines, we had to depend on advertising for our revenue. Our expenses would naturally be heavy, for we were going to use the best of everything. We were going to make our province known far beyond our boundaries.

It was not so easy, for example, to make the Ice Cream Parlor and Confectionery sound attractive, where the fly-paper hung from the ceiling far into the autumn, and the proprietor, big, fat, lazy Bill Summers, had to be sent for by the Post Master to empty his box. Bill had an excellent excuse for this. He said he knew that all his letters were bills, and he never did like bills, and besides he knew what he owed the wholesale as well as they did, and he knew when he could pay them a ——— sight better, so they could save their stamps. Bill's ad in the paper ran on and on from one season to the next. Behind the shop he lived with his cat and dog and a boxful of paper-bound books, which he read over and over again. Dirty, happy, unmolested. He had what he wanted. Ease, romance, and his own thoughts.

Of course, that would not do for *Town and Country*, but I found a keen enjoyment in tracing the evolution of the indolent, leisure-loving fellow who ate his own candies and let the world pass him by. He came from a family of hustlers, who worked the clock around, stark, prosaic, grim-faced, hard-handed people. Bill was the youngest of the family and the others had no respect for him at all, and said he would die in the poor house; but they were wrong about that. I quoted a verse of "The Lotus Eaters" when I went into his store once to buy canned salmon, and he welcomed it like an old friend. Then he told me about his mother, who died when he was four years old. He remembered how tired she always was, and how she longed for time to read. "The Summerses were all slave drivers," he said, "and drove her to death. Perhaps you've heard of people being 'born tired.' Well, that's the way I was born, and when I got the money left to my mother by an uncle, I bought this business and settled down. In fact, I flopped down, and spread out my feet. I'm only sorry Uncle Bill didn't peg out in time for my mother to use the money. She and I could have had a good time here. I suppose you've heard that I'm lazy. I am. Lazy but happy."

The day I went to interview him he did not answer the store bell, but I could see the back of his head over the top of his barrel-chair in the room behind, so I went in. He was sound asleep and gently snoring with the big black and white cat on his knee, and a brown spaniel asleep on his feet, and in his hand a copy of Marie Corelli's *Romance of Two Worlds*. I tip-toed out. I was afraid that Mr. Summers' story would not do for *Town and Country*. Something told me that I was not on the right track, but the going was pleasant and I went on.

I got many a good story about the "younger sons" who were sent out of England to be out of the way. One of these I wrote later under the title "Permission" in the volume of short stories called *The Next of Kin*, which was published during the First World War.

We were fortunate in having in that neighborhood many English and Scotch families, whose resolute determination to succeed in this new country against all the hardships of isolation and the severities of our winter climate called forth our admiration. They brought a great contribution to our lives; something more beautiful than even their Chelsea potteries and highboys, tapestries and crested silver. From them we heard much of the Royal family and their influence on the people of Britain. To us, so far away, hard-working and unromantic people as we were, the Royal family with its numerous dependents seemed like a heavy financial load, but in our British people, steeped in the traditions of the past, we saw something of the coherence and strength of the British form of government.

The new magazine never saw the light of day, and the young man with the bright vision faded away, and I did not see him again for many years. But I never regretted the time I had spent getting material for *Town and Country*, for I felt it was not wasted. I really did learn something about the people of the community, and got a glimpse of their hopes and fears and their ambitions for their children. Being a young country, most of the people were young, even these tired farm-women who pleated their aprons as they talked to me. Hope and ambition kept them on the rails; the hope of a new house or even a pump in the kitchen, if only the rain would come at the right time and the frost keep off. I found out that the women who were making a quilt or making a rug had a brighter outlook than the women who had no hobbies. Something that they could work on from day to day, something that they could be proud of, lightened their burdens. I remember one good sentence which had a whole story behind it. One woman told me quite frankly about a quarrel she had with her husband, which, fortunately, did not come to an open break. "I would have left him that time," she said, "but I had two hens setting and I knew he would never think to feed them!" Even though the young man with the bright smile was gone and my five dollars gone with him, I kept watching for stories and began keeping a record, not exactly a diary, but a book which I find very useful now. I began to pay more attention to my reading, even trying to analyze short stories, in an attempt to discover the technique. I remember how diligently I pored over Bret Harte's "The Luck of Roaring Camp," trying to see how he produced the effect on his readers. I even dug out the books we used at the Collegiate. I studied again an excellent book on English Composition. It gave examples of good prose with explanatory notes; somewhat in the style of Arthur Quiller-Couch's *Art of Writing*. The book has disappeared long ago, but some of these literary gems remain with me.

One, from *The Mill on the Floss*:

"The boat reappeared, but brother and sister had gone down in an embrace never to be parted, living over again in that brief moment all their lives, since first they joined their little hands in love, and roamed the daisy fields together."

That, and the oft-quoted and sometimes ridiculed passage from *Dombey and Son* about the "golden water on the wall" carried me to Heaven's gate. Neither of these passages would be accepted by a modern short story group, but their place in Literature is safe for all that.

3

Genesis

MANITOU had three doctors in 1896, and they were very important to us for a drug store was really a drug store then, whose chief reason for being was the making up of prescriptions. Our front windows contained show bottles, green, red and blue, standing about three feet high, and beautiful to behold, though prone to freeze when the weather turned cold. I was somewhat disillusioned when I found the contents were made from Diamond dyes and water from the pump, but nevertheless they made a dignified insigne of an ancient profession.

Dr. Moore was the old doctor, beloved of many, a genial, kindly man with many degrees and great dignity. He signed his prescriptions with his name and often quoted a Latin phrase and its translation: "In this manner was a cure effected." Then there was the young doctor, a graduate of Manitoba Medical College, Harry Cook, whose father was an Anglican missionary, and the third doctor, who had recently arrived from Cypress River on the Glenboro line, was Dr. R. W. MacCharles, a Dalhousie man from Cape Breton. He was tall and broad-shouldered, with graying hair. He had all the reserve of his Scotch ancestry, but when I met him in the store and noticed his keen blue eyes and his finely-shaped capable hands, I declared that he would be the McClung family doctor, if and when a doctor were needed.

Wes and I agreed on the subject of raising a family. We were going to have six. That is, of course, some time in the future. The future does not bother anyone until it begins to turn into the present, so I was quite philosophical about the prospect.

But there came a morning in October when I was not sure that I wanted any breakfast, and I felt dizzy. A possibility not entirely pleasant suggested itself: I had read of lovely ladies growing deadly pale, and fainting at inopportune times, and I knew what it meant in fiction, but it just couldn't be—I was bilious, that was all; and anyone could be bilious. I had been staying in too much. I must get out and walk more.

In about three weeks, after tramping the roads and drinking lemonade and taking soda to settle my stomach, all to no effect, I was feeling pretty low in my mind. On October 20th, my birthday, I walked out the three miles to my old district. I had often walked this road and knew every foot of it. I knew I would feel better if I could sit on the moss-grown stone in the coulee where I often sat when I was coming back from Hazel School to my boarding house, and where I had dreams—such noble dreams—of being a writer. It was a bright, crisp day, with high, white clouds drifting against the ground wind. From one field I could hear a thrasher at work, with its familiar shaking rhythm that made me ache for something that was gone. Perhaps it was my far-off youth, I was twenty-three that day, but the years are long to the young.

The day was so beautiful it hurt like an old tune. I could hear the geese going south, with that keening cry that always tore at my heart even when I was a child. Flocks of prairie chicken fed on the yellow stubble and then winged their way over to the straw piles, whirring then floating, then whirring again. Beside me a stunted rose bush waved its crimson haws slowly as a curling wind went by. Little warm winds passed over my face, coming from nowhere. I had often met these welcome little gusts as I was returning home from Hazel

School, which stood on the wheat land above, and I had imagined them to be the contribution of some kindly hollow which absorbed in the daytime more sunshine than it needed, but held it until nightfall and then released it to comfort some tired man or woman coming home from work. Everything was the same as it used to be, the sky, the clouds, the sounds, the tawny grass in the coulee dripping and bending, and yet nothing was the same. For my stomach was sick, and I saw no beauty anywhere. I was lonely as a lost dog, and felt cheated, too, for Wes had gone to Winnipeg that day without me. We had counted on this trip to the city, on my birthday, and now I could not go. How could anyone travel with a stomach like mine? We had planned to stay at the Leland Hotel, and go to the Bijou Theatre at night to see a play. I loved to see a play and had seen but few . . . how I had looked forward to being in our seats early, not to miss that dazzling moment when the lights go down in the pit, conversation ceases, and the crimson velvet portieres are folded back by invisible hands, and then slowly and noiselessly the curtain rises on the scene of enchantment!

And I had planned to wear my nice blue dress, trimmed with passementerie, and have my hair done at a hairdresser's. But here I was in a tweed skirt and jersey, my old coat and dusty shoes, sitting huddled in misery on the shady side of a cold gray stone, sorrier for myself than I had ever been before. Then I grew resentful, not because I was going to have a baby, and not because I was afraid of pain or minded the prospect of losing my lead pencil figure either. I weighed an even hundred pounds. No one can raise a family without putting on some flesh, and anyway, older women looked better when plump. But why had not something been found to save women from this infernal nausea? What good was it? If it had been a man's disease, it would have been made the subject of scientific research and relieved long ago. But women could suffer; it kept them humble! I had heard about the curse of Eve, and here it was in full measure. But what useful purpose did it serve? Life at that moment looked like a black conspiracy against women. If God ordained that the race was to be perpetuated this way, why had he thrown in this ugly extra, to spoil the occasion? It was not like God . . . who paints the wayside flower and lights the evening star, . . . who tempers the wind to the shorn lamb and notices the fall of the sparrow.

That terrible description of a sick stomach as told by Mulvaney in *Soldiers Three* exactly described mine, but when I thought of it, I grew sicker. . . . I was too miserable to go across the fields to see my good friend Clara, who lived in the yellow farmhouse, not half a mile away. I did not want to see anyone.

Women had endured too much and said nothing. I certainly was not going to be meek and mild and resigned. Women should change conditions, not merely endure them, and I was positive something should be done. I remembered with particular bitterness hearing the men in our neighborhood joke about Mrs. Jim Barnes who got her husband to move the stairs in their little log house every time another baby was coming. She said it made her feel she had a new house, and it became a joke up and down the neighborhood. I remember on my first visit to Brandon, when I was riding on a load of wheat, hearing Mrs. Barnes' brother-in-law shout to the other men: "The stairs are on the move again!" And one of them shouted back in a great burst of laughter: "That's fine! I hope it's twins!" When I thought of it now, it cut like a knife. I could see Mrs. Barnes, a pallid, overworked little Englishwoman, homesick, and old at thirty. They already had more children than their little house could hold. Two little ones had died, but these husky brutes, strong as young bulls and with a similar mentality, could laugh and actually find a cause for merriment in the poor woman's pain. I cursed them now with a horrible Irish curse, which came from some dark morass of memory. . . . Then suddenly I found myself crying, not for myself but for all the overburdened inarticulate women of the world. . . .

That pulled me up with a start, and I wiped my eyes hastily. Tears were not the remedy. Women had cried too much already. The sun was getting low, and the sunshine pale and cold when I started back. I was not in a hurry, no one was waiting for me, and that was a strange sensation. Mother had always been watching for me when I lived at home, and had an irritating way of welcoming me in by saying: "What kept you?" I thought of her now with a lump in my throat, and wished I could hear her say it. I was alone now, in a new and rather terrifying world. It seemed like ten years since I used to ride the sorrel horse into Manitou and tie him to the hitching post in front of the Farmers' Store. Many years afterwards when I read D. H. Lawrence's gripping story entitled "The Woman Who Rode Away," it brought back this chill pale afternoon when my heart was troubled. It was a low moment in my life; surely a climacteric, when the eyes that look out of the windows are darkened. Many bewildered women have gone down this same dark road.

When I reached Front Street I had no desire but to gain the long stairway and get under cover. Suddenly I saw Dr. MacCharles walking towards his office, and an impulse came to me. Here was one person I could talk to, the logical person, the deep well in whom the secrets of all hearts were safe. I was still in a raging mood and I wanted to get a few things said. All that I remember about his office was that the walls were of new lumber, and there was a volume of Burns' poetry in a plaid silk cover on his table.

I sat down in the patient's chair, and he sat across the table and listened. He let me talk it out, showing no surprise, but I could feel his interest. People were passing the window but they seemed to belong to another world. When I stopped, he began, unhurried and sure, yet not too sure. His tweedy, Scotch way of speaking was comforting. His words were not so much addressed to me as all womankind. He said women did bear the heavy burden of reproduction, and he had often wondered about it, too. Certainly it was not fair. No one could say it was fair, but then there are many things in life which are not fair. Human justice is something we have to work for. It does not come ready-made; women have all the human diseases and then a few of their own, while they are not as strong physically as men, they are stronger to endure. Undoubtedly, women are better patients than men, and every doctor knows it. That the race has survived and is improving is proof of women's fidelity and fortitude. He said the nausea I was going through was due largely to nerves, for naturally the beginning of a new life make great psychological demands, but I would soon feel exceptionally vigorous. Medical science, he said, is only in its infancy. There will be great discoveries; some diseases have been conquered, and others will be. Not once did he tell me that I had a good man, and was young, strong and healthy and really had no reason to be disturbed. His silence on this subject was a compliment to my intelligence, and I certainly was in no mood to have platitudes flung at me.

I do not know exactly how he did it, but I know that once again I was a member in good standing in the human family, and more than that, he made me feel that I was one of the standard-bearers of the race, pledged to its protection and continuance. Any little inconvenience suffered by me would be small dues for me to pay for membership in this greatest of all societies.

There began one of the enriching friendships of my life, which, happily, has continued to this day.

When I came out of his office the sun had gone down, but its last rays made violet and rose edges on the clouds above the town, mellowing the stern reality of the unpainted houses. There was a hint of winter in the air, bracing and cheering. I went up the covered stairway with one driving desire. I wanted to eat. I'd had nothing since morning, less than nothing. I lighted a fire in the square, black stove and cooked myself a good meal of bacon and eggs, and fried two slices of bread in the bacon fat, with a gay disregard of the evils of fried food. I made a good brew of coffee too, with thick cream, and opened a jar of strawberries.

Before I went to bed I went out on the back verandah to have a look at the night. (This nightly observation came of being farm-bred, and accustomed to that nightly round of the stables to see that all was well with the stock.) On that night I could only look up at the stars shining bright in a chill October sky. Very pleased I was to see them smiling down on me, with a new friendliness, and I knew what it was. The stars in their courses were not more a part of God's great plan of creation than I.

As I listened to the faint night sounds, the distant bark of dogs, the rumble of wagons, women calling in their children, I could hear again over and above it all, the honking of wild geese, but their cry now was not one of longing or pain; it was a hymn of high adventure. They knew where they were going. They were travelling "on the beam." Then came back to me Bryant's confident words:

"He who, from zone to zone
Guides through the boundless sky
    thy certain flight,
In the long way that I must tread alone,
Will lead my steps aright!"

We had a very good time that winter. My sister-in-law, Eleanor McClung, came out and stayed a month with us and we also had a visit from Florence McLean, the well-known Scottish singer, for whom our Florence is named. By putting a stretcher in one corner of the kitchen we could accommodate a guest. I remember with great pleasure the nights we spent skating at the rink, and the miles I walked along the prairie roads. I was determined that I would do all I could to give the baby a good mind and a strong body.

The economic aspect of having a baby had no fears for us. Doctors were modest in their fees—twenty-five dollars covered everything, and there were no hospital fees, for no one went to a hospital for a little thing like having a baby, and there was no fee for the anesthetist, for no anesthetic was used, except when something went wrong. The practical nurse charged one dollar a day and had to be spoken for several months in advance. Then she wrote your name on the calendar above her kitchen table, and that was a solemn contract. She stayed with you for nine nights and then, if everything was all right, came in the morning and went home at night for another two weeks. It was all very simple and satisfactory.

In my spare time I studied mathematics, especially geometry. Edgar Burgess, the Principal of the school, often brought over a few deductions and we spent many a happy hour working them. I also began to do puzzles from the *Detroit Free Press*, and won honorable mention and subscriptions, and I read poetry.

The two boys who worked in the store, Herb, my young brother-in-law, and Charlie Hasselfield, one of my former pupils at Hazel School, had their meals with us, and how I combined literature and cooking is still bright in my memory and I hope in theirs. They had an early dinner and I read to them while they were eating. Herb said he liked to hear me read. It took his mind off my cooking, but Charlie was loyal to his old teacher, so it was two against one. In the drug store we carried a good stock of books and I remember particularly the pleasure we had in Bret Harte's short stories and poems. Sometimes to vary the exercise we did a bit of memorizing. One good one remains, immortal in its beauty. It is Bret Harte's "Tribute to Dickens"—

> "About the pines the moon was slowly drifting,
> The river sang below,
> The dim Sierras, far beyond, uplifting,
> Their minarets of snow.
>
> "The roaring camp-fire, with rude humor, painted
> The ruddy tints of health
> On haggard face and form that drooped and fainted
> In the mad race for wealth."

There is enough beauty in that poem to carry anybody over a meat-pie with a tough crust.

The first time I went home after I was married I brought a box of drugs to my mother, having now a connection, by marriage, with the British Pharmacopoeias, which I called familiarly the "B.P." I was somewhat ashamed of the home-made remedies still used by my family, and felt it my duty to lift them into higher realms of healing where there would be fewer charms and more chemistry. My mother believed tea leaves was the best remedy for burns. But in my superior wisdom I produced a fine big bottle of carron oil, explaining to her that while cool tea leaves would undoubtedly be soothing, and would keep out the air, they could not possibly heal a burn. Mother listened to me and thanked me for the oil, and told me she knew that limewater and sweet oil shaken together was good for burns, but was glad to know the proper name. As long as she kept house the brown bowl remained for the tea leaves! And now tannic acid is recognized. So again the old remedy scores!

I brought resinol too, to replace the Balm of Gilead salve—which she made each year out of the sticky buds in early spring, combined with mutton tallow and a few drops of carbolic acid. But that remedy was too firmly established to be changed. She did express approval of the tube of lanoline, but she held to her belief that the real wool off the sheep's back, lightly washed and kept wrapped, is still the best remedy for grass cuts—a few strands of it wrapped around the injured toe is not only a salve but a bandage. Beef Iron and Wine for a spring tonic did not get much of a welcome. It was too easy to take, and therefore was not to be depended on like the one she made herself from a prescription given many years ago in the Medical Department of the *Family Herald*.

No doubt each generation feels itself wiser than the one before, and remembering how I regarded my parents has made me charitable to the many evidences of this in my own family. I have received much correction at their hands and have taken it. I knew they too would learn. The stern old world has pounded many lessons into proud young hearts, and so the old play goes on. Only the players change!

I wish I might worthily portray the social life of our little town in that remote day when no telephone or radio broke the stillness of our lives. I remember how ceremoniously we called on each other, duly observing days and hours. Mrs. R. W. McClung was at home on the first and second Tuesday, from three to five, and had cards engraved with that information. So the first and second Tuesday was the time to have the four rooms, including hall and stairway, as clean as mortal hands could make them. Although the calls were brief, I knew how sharp-eyed the callers were, and if there was a cobweb on the ceiling, they would see it, though they would not be so rude as to lift an eye in that direction.

I prepared for my first calling day with great thoroughness. I swept and dusted. I polished the black stove, legs and all. I put out fresh stand covers, removed the fur from under the bed, and put out the best marseilles bed spread—colored spreads were unheard of. I washed and ironed the pillow shams, and carefully adjusted them on the wooden bar. The pillow shams were one of my prized possessions, and were one of my wedding presents. On one was embroidered a beautiful child asleep on a pillow of roses, on the other the same child awake, still buttressed with roses and the inscriptions read: "I slept and dreamed that life was beauty" on number one, and on number two—"I woke and found that life was duty!"

I washed the morning-glory lamp shade and polished the gold acorns. I washed door knobs, polished floors, straightened pictures, made the table small, and put on a white linen cloth embroidered in violets. This embroidered tablecloth was my own effort, and I hoped nobody would look at it too closely.

To Mrs. Ruttan, who was my guide, and friend, I went for final instructions. What should I give my callers to eat on this first day? She said a cup of tea and a piece of wedding cake was the correct thing, but that looked pretty skimpy to me, so I added some homemade candy, and still the table looked bare, but Mrs. Ruttan held firm. I must remember that the ladies were only calling—it was not a party.

But having cooked for threshers, I had a fear of running short, and so made a loaf of sandwiches, cutting them so thin and so small they looked foolish. But I knew that a thick sandwich would constitute a social error. I balked at cutting off the crusts though—that was the McCurdy strain in me that "could'na thole the waste." I was very glad that I had the sandwiches, for the callers came that first day in such numbers that if my good friend, Mrs. MacNamara, hadn't gone down the back stairs and across lots to her own house to bring me a full-sized chocolate cake, the news might have gone abroad that the bride had failed to provide enough food.

Altogether I have happy memories of that first day. Even the mournful remark of the dismal old lady who looked me up and down and said with a sigh, "I'm glad to see that you are wearing your wedding dress. Wear it while you can." Poor old dear, she made her contribution to the gaiety of our little town too, by her sad forebodings. Her face should have been furrowed with care, for her mind ran continually on death and sorrowing. She saw warnings in the clouds, and heard wailing voices in the winds. But her brow was calm and unwrinkled, and her cheeks as smooth as a calla lily. Sorrow was becoming to her, as moonlight to the lady in the beautiful song. She never missed a funeral and became an authority on procedure. To end the picture and make it complete, she wrote obituary verses.

4

The Family

OUR FIRST BORN arrived in the gray dawn of June 16th, when the scent of wild roses came down the village street, carried on the dewy breeze of morning. It was at a time of great heat but there had been a cooling rain in the night, and so the hour of Jack's arrival bore that odor which is dear to every prairie dweller—that good earthy smell when the rain has laid the dust. This bit about the scent of roses is all hearsay on my part. I was not noticing anything except the handsome young stranger who had come with the dawn; his round pink head covered with soft, silky brown hair, tight little ears and doubled up fists covering his eyes; his perfect finger nails, and his regular breathing—that was the sweetest sound I ever heard. He came with a cry of distress, but that was soon hushed when he found he was among friends. There was a white and blue lined cradle ready for him, with white blankets and a down pillow. But I wanted him beside me in his white shawl; I think that was the most exquisite moment I have ever known!

Before the week was over his two grandmothers had arrived. My mother-in-law was ecstatic in her praise of the baby's beauty. She said she had never seen such a beautiful child. My mother, who already had ten grandchildren, was more conservative. "The child," she said, "is well enough. We should all be thankful that he appears normal and healthy; looks do not matter; and children change greatly anyway. If he is as good as he looks he will do very well." But she was really pleased when she knew the child was to be called John Wesley. Among her ten grandchildren "John" had only been given as a second name, and I knew it was her favorite name.

I have a vivid memory of the first night we were left alone with the baby. I was all right until I heard Mrs. Law's footsteps going down the stairs. The baby was asleep in his cradle, and I assured Mrs. Law that I would get along all right. But when the darkness settled in, and the streets grew quiet, I began to be afraid. What would I do if he should suddenly take sick? He might have colic, or even a convulsion.

I pretended I was asleep. I did not want Wes to know I was frightened. Then suddenly we clutched each other's hands in the darkness. He was worse than I was. We were almost afraid to breathe. The baby slept on. He might not have been so composed if he had known he had two fraidy-cats to take care of him.

But he grew and thrived and every day absorbed us more. Talk about the influence parents have on children! It is nothing to the way children change their parents! My heart was always tender towards children, and I would do anything for their pleasure and comfort. I was brought up in the tradition that a mother who neglected her baby was the lowest form of sinner. One woman in our neighborhood was branded for life when it became known that she had made no preparation at all for the child who was coming. She said she did not think it would live. She might better have robbed the collection plate or killed a policeman on duty. But a new responsibility came to me after Jack was born, as I thought about him and his future. All children now were my children. I remembered the story in *Uncle Tom's Cabin* about the colored woman who was ordered by her cruel mistress to wean her own baby so she could nurse the white child, and how, when her own baby cried, she was compelled to leave it in the cabin, where its cries could not be heard in the house. It had shocked me when I read it years before. Now it filled me with rage. I wanted to do something about it.

Women must be made to feel their responsibility. All this protective love, this instinctive mother love, must be organized some way, and made effective. There was enough of it in the world to do away with all the evils which war upon childhood, undernourishment, slum conditions, child labor, drunkenness. Women could abolish these if they wanted to.

I determined to join the W.C.T.U. It was the most progressive organization at that time, and I determined that I would stir the deep waters of complacency. It could be done in one generation. These flashes of the crusading spirit often assailed me. I wanted to raise a family who would be like the Booths, and scatter the darkness of humanity, and light the candles of freedom in the dark places of the world. But a good hard streak of Scotch caution told me my first job was to raise a family, and give them sound bodies and sound minds and cheerful memories, not rolling the sins of the world on them at too early an age. Let them have all the fun in life that I could give them. I knew what a heritage a happy childhood can be. I had had one. I believe my devotion to the Dickens' stories saved me from a fatal error. I remembered that awful woman, Mrs. Jellyby, who was intent on saving the population of Ballyaboolaga, while her own children had to shift for themselves.

In the course of time Florence was born, one cold January morning. We had moved out of the four rooms over the drug store to accommodate our increasing family, and rented a house opposite the Orange Hall. We put in two Klondike heaters downstairs and made grated openings in the floors to let some heat come into the bedrooms, and there, as the rising sun was struggling to pierce the thick frost on an eastern window, Florence Letitia McClung lifted up her voice and wept. Outside it was fifty-two degrees below zero. But the Klondike heaters were gorged with wood, and diligently tended by one Alice Foster, a fine-looking girl from a farm, who knew all about stoves and their ways. I have no recollection of any discomfort, but I do remember how that child gave tongue. Jack, one year and eight months old, a good walker but not yet talking, stood still and listened, with a great wonder in his eyes. The house, which was a poor old shell, carried every sound. Then he ran to his clothes box where his own modest wardrobe was kept, and began to pitch out his belongings like a badger digging a hole. When Alice brought up the news, I was sure Jack, generous and provident, was offering his all on the altar of brotherly love, but Alice thought he was preparing to leave.

For six weeks the thermometer stayed around forty degrees below zero, and the old house cracked with frost. But the good provider I had married fulfilled his promise to feed me and keep me warm, me and my offspring, many or few, and after all these years I must say the obligations have been faithfully met.

In less than another two years Paul joined our family, one snowy November morning at an early hour, Dr. MacCharles and Mrs. Law again seeing me safely through. With three children now, I remembered the old rhyme which I had often heard, relative to this matter of family increase:

> "When you have one,
> You can take it and run,
> When you have two,
> Perhaps you can do.
> But when you have three,
> You stay where you be."

Jack, being the eldest, assumed responsibility early. He did his best to shepherd his sister when she was able to run about. He got into a fight one day with Alec Macnab, who lived across the street, and who had said Florence's face was dirty. When I went out to quiet the disturbance, and heard the cause, I ventured the opinion that Alec had not misstated the case. Miss McClung's face was all he needed as evidence to prove his statement. Jack gave me a look of exasperation and said: "But that's none of his business." I talked to him afterwards and he explained: "I could tell her her face is dirty, or you could tell her, and that would be all right. We would be telling her so she would wash her face. But Alec flung it at her to make little of her."

Another day he was scolding a boy who had kicked our dog, and the boy said in his own defense: "You stepped on Jim's tail one day and hurt him just as bad as I did." Jack was indignant. "I stepped on his tail by mistake. You kicked him on purpose. A dog knows the difference. I did not hurt his feelings, and you did." I began to think there was some virtue in the hours I had spent in working mathematical problems before he was born. With three children under four years old, I did not spend much time studying world happenings, but I did read poetry to them, believing they would get the rhythm of it, even if they did not understand it. I loved to hear them repeating snatches of it before they went to sleep. They loved Eugene Field's:

"Sleep little pigeon and fold your wings,
Little blue pigeon with velvet eyes,"

and, of course, "Winken, Blinken and Nod" and "Little Orphan Annie."

Another prime favorite was the story about the little boy who was so fond of sugar and ate so much of it that he melted and ran away at last. The tragedy of his latter end did not depress them at all.

"He ran away like melted butter,
When before the fire it is put to warm,
And the ducks and the drakes ate him up in the gutter,
And that was the end of Sugary Sam."

The picture of Sam in his final dissolution was well-thumbed and worn.

I am convinced it is just as easy to bring up three children as one. They bring each other up, really. No one could be busier than I was, when I had only Jack. He was on my mind both night and day. Now that I had three to think of, it was really easier, and in all this I had the assistance of Alice Foster, who deserves to have a whole book written about her alone. I had her for twelve years and depended on her as I did on my own right arm.

Alice was so patient with children and so wise in handling them, I always knew she would marry a widower with a family of small children. Character is destiny. And I could see Alice heading into some dead woman's place and filling it nobly. Some man, probably a minister, recovering from his loss and just beginning to take notice, would be sure to see her as the answer to his prayers. Eight small children was the allotment I gave her.

Alice trained for a deaconess and went to the Gower Street Church in St. John's, Newfoundland, and there she met a Methodist minister.

"Please note," she wrote in announcing her engagement, "that Sidney has only three children. You said eight, but you were always a bit free-handed." I knew the answer to that one too, but I did not say it. I sent a letter of sincere congratulations to Sidney, and told him his judgment was excellent, and I record with pride that Alice named her first boy "Paul" and her first girl "Florence," so it would seem that she, too, had pleasant memories of the years we spent together.

5

_____

Town Hall Tonight

THESE ARE MAGIC WORDS which often changed the monotony of our lives into the lilting rhythm of waltz-time. Manitou had the name of being a good show town, which means we all rallied to the call when the word went forth that some concert party, dance, or magician was coming. Our population being then, as now, about nine hundred, we, the footloose and show-minded, could fill the hall, so I think we got every attraction that, in the early nineties, ever took to the road.

And how we enjoyed them! Harold Nelson, and his Shakespearean players, the Cosgroves, with Marietta LaDell, Jessie McLaughlin, Edith Miller, Edith Sutherland, Nanny Strachan and Gavin Spence, the Swiss Bell Ringers—the beautiful Palmatier sisters, the Jubilee Singers, the Webling sisters, and our own George Rutherford and Minnie Ruttan.

I can recapture the feeling of rapture as we walked to the hall, carrying our coats on a fine spring or summer evening. The fine weather did not mean the end of the concert season for us. Far from it. No doubt the entertainers preferred warm weather and we were never too busy to come.

The hall may have been a drab little place, with nothing but a raised platform and coal oil footlights, but when the blinds were drawn and all the lamps lighted and the audience assembled, no opera house that I have ever been in gave out a greater feeling of high expectancy. We dressed in our best for these great occasions. We wore no hats. Brides wore their wedding dresses. Mrs. Gordon Bradley, our best local singer, always wore a red flower in her black hair. There were opera wraps which closely resembled piano drapes but no remarks were made. We were too happy to be catty. The opening hour was eight o'clock, and if the artists "obliged" with encores, the performance lasted well into the night. Then there were refreshments for the performers, and the committee, and bouquets of garden flowers. Manitou was a good show town, and we were proud of our good name.

Let no one think that our entertainment was all made for us. We had concerts of our own; school concerts and flag drills and Indian club swinging; plays and cantatas by young people's societies; Christmas concerts with Santa Claus coming down from the loft on a rope, to the loud acclaim and gasping surprise of the believers. I still have a pang when I think of the night Bert Crane forgot to take his gloves up with him, and the rope burned his hands, but he distributed the presents and made pleasant remarks to the "Sixes and Under," who never knew their kind benefactor had suffered an injury.

One of the real events was the visit of the poetess E. Pauline Johnson, who for two nights filled the Methodist Church with an admiring audience. Pauline was at the zenith of her power and beauty, at that time having recently returned from her triumphal tour of England. The night was bitterly cold, but the Church was overflowing. Pauline's advertising had shown only the Indian girl in her beaded chamois costume and feather headdress, so when a beautiful young woman in white satin evening dress came out of the vestry door and walked to the platform, there was a gasp of surprise from the audience. Pauline smiled at us reassuringly, knowing what was in our minds.

"I am going to be a white woman first," she said in her deep voice, "the Indian part will follow." Then she told us about her home, "Chiefswood," at Brantford on the Grand River, built by her father, of black walnut from his own land—land given by the British Crown to the Brotherhood of the Six Nations, founded over four hundred years ago by Hiawatha.

She told us about her recent visit to England, and her encounters with some of the well-intentioned but clumsy efforts to smooth over the fact of her Indian blood.

"My dear," said one short-sighted countess, raising her lorgnette, "your skin is really very clear and white, and yet you say your father is an Indian." Pauline acknowledged the fact, and the countess blundered on: "Really," she said, "I would not have known it." But before the interview was over, the Mohawk Princess scored. She blandly asked her interrogator if it was true that she was of pure white blood, at which the countess snorted in indignation. "Of course I am," she said—to which Pauline murmured politely:

"I would never have known it!"

I remember the rhythm and charm of her voice as she recited a poem about the Grand River,

"Here, impossible romances
Indefinable sweet fancies
    Cluster round
. . .
And the perfume of some burning
Far-off brushwood ever turning
    To exhale
All its smoky fragrance dying
In the arms of evening lying
    Where I sail."

Languorous, picture-making poetry, not much meaning in it, but it was surely pure music on her lips.

In the second part of the program the grand lady was gone and a lithe Indian girl took her place, telling us stories of her people, and

their battle for existence. I remember especially the story of Ones-
imo, who made love to a white man, and then stabbed him to free
her Indian lover. I think Pauline must have been an actress of great
power, for I can still recall the great moment in this story. So real was
the cold duplicity of the heroine, that the mother of the young man
who had agreed to drive Pauline to her next engagement frantically
appealed to him to have nothing to do with this treacherous woman,
and Pauline, like the good trouper she was, added that story to her
repertoire.

On the day following her recital, my sister-in-law and I called on
her at the hotel, but that calm, simple sentence tells nothing of our
state of mind. She was the first great personage we had met, and we
knew it was a time for white gloves and polished shoes. However,
at her first word, we felt at home with her and for an hour we sat
entranced in the best parlor of the Cassin house, with its old-gold
plush chairs under us, and the enlarged photographs and deer heads
looking down on us, oblivious of everything but this charming,
friendly woman. She told us of her first efforts to sell her poems,
and how proud she was when she first saw her verse in print.

We tried to remember our manners; we knew a call must not drag
on into a visit. Then we asked her if she would come for dinner with
us the next day, which was Sunday. She would and did, and no one
ever had a more gracious guest. She told us about the old Mohawk
Church, where she worshipped when she was at home. It was the
first church in Ontario and in it was the Bible which Queen Anne
had given to the congregation in 1701.

The afternoon went by on silken wings. Cold winds blew down
Front Street in Manitou; we were still living in the four rooms above
the drug store, and the shutters creaked in the blast, but we were living in another world, touching the hem of our own romantic past.

Unfortunately for me, I never saw Pauline again, though in her
last illness, which lasted for two years, it was my great privilege to
write to her and receive letters from her in reply. She died in Vancouver on March 7th, 1913, and was buried on her birthday, March
10th, from Christ Church.

From her friend, Jean Stevenson, I heard about her funeral, and the honors paid her. Representatives were present from every organization in the City. Lady Tupper led the Imperial Order of the Daughters of the Empire, and on the casket, in purple drape, showing the royal blood of the deceased, was a pall worked by the Pauline Johnson Chapter of the I.O.D.E. The Capilano tribe, whose legends Pauline has immortalized, was officially represented by Chief Matthias, in full regalia, who followed directly behind the bier, while drawn up along Georgia Street a long line of silent Red men "stood immobile all through the service and until the funeral cortege had passed on the way to the cemetery." Flags on all public buildings hung at half-mast, and the following telegram was received by Mayor Baxter from H.R.H. the Duke of Connaught, then Governor-General of Canada: "Kindly express to the friends of the late Pauline Johnson my very deep regret at the news of her death."

Fortunately, Mrs. Stevenson has preserved many of her letters, which reveal her strength and sweetness of character and her profound wisdom. Never once did Pauline falter in her loyalty and devotion to her own people, even when she stood on London Bridge, and looked at the glories of the greatest city in the world, she saw it through the eyes of her people.

"It is a far cry from a wigwam to Westminster," she wrote. "And London seems a strange place to the Red Indian whose eyes still see the forest trees, even as they gaze across the Strand, and whose feet still feel the clinging moccasin even among the scores of clicking heels that hurry along the thoroughfares of the pale faces."

She compares what she sees and hears in St. Paul's with the rites and ceremonies of her own people. Instead of the altar lights, flared the camp fires on the Onondega "long house," and the resinous scent of the burning pine drifted across the fetid London air. "I saw the tall, copper-skinned firekeeper of the Iroquois council enter, the circle of light flung fitfully against the black surrounding wood. None so regal, so august, as he. His garb of fringed buckskin and ermine was no more grotesque than the vestments worn by the white preachers in high places."

I wonder what will be the place assigned to her in Canadian literature in the future. Will her melodious verse survive? She left only three slim volumes of poems, but I do not believe we have any poem that sings more sweetly than her "Paddle Song." I still remember the spell it put upon me when first I read it:

"After the cataract comes the calm,
We've raced the rapid; we're far ahead
The river slips through its silent bed,
    Sway, sway,
As the bubbles spray
And fall in tinkling tunes away."

This poem, I am glad to note, is still in one of the School Readers, which augurs well for its immortality.

Now for a happy coincidence.

As I was writing these words, I interrupted the writing to listen to a school broadcast, and was delighted to hear a soft-voiced teacher telling her class the legend of the young chief, who went forth into the woods to expiate the sin of having begotten twin sons. She gave Pauline the credit of having received the legend from old Chief Capilano, and preserving it in beautiful words. The children loved the story and the teacher promised to tell them another legend the next day. I could easily believe that in some bright meadow in the Elysian fields, gay with Indian paint-brush and shooting star, Pauline and her people were happily listening, glad to know that their wisdom and their love of truth was still revered and cherished upon earth.

I must take one other memory of the old Town Hall out of "Time's careless keeping."

Its timbers will always be sacred to me for it was there that my daughter Florence and I joined the Dickens' Fellowship. And it was not a simple initiation of paying a fee and signing a card and receiving the right hand of fellowship. We were initiated as the Indians conduct their ceremonials, by a test of hardihood, but I must begin at the beginning.

Across the road from our house stood a little weather-beaten dwelling whose occupants came and went frequently. It seemed to harbour a strange contagion of impermanency, though it was an honest enough little house with its L-shaped walls and lean-to kitchen. At the time of which I write its tenants were a Mr. and Mrs. Vander and their three children. The father was a meek little man with a Byronic face, who spoke beautiful English and read from the classics. The mother went out working by the day, a tired draggled woman, who accepted her lot in life without complaint. The family consisted of three handsome children, the eldest girl had a gift for music and art, which won for her an honorable place in the local school. She had her father's gift for language and one day defined her family in these words:

"Father gives us amusement and instruction but mother feeds and clothes us. I like them equally well, according to my mood and my needs. We couldn't very well get on without them. I think I like father a little bit better than mother, for I'm often sorry for mother and being sorry for people does not make for loving."

There was a scarcity of teachers in the Manitou District at this time, and when I discovered that Mr. Vander had once taught in a boys' school, I thought we might be able to get a temporary certificate for him and get him installed in one of the country schools. I knew he could teach well if he wanted to. His wife was more enthusiastic than he when I went over and made the suggestion. When I mentioned the usual salary of fifty dollars a month, I could see that he was not impressed.

"We're doing very well as we are now," Mr. Vander began. "My time is quite well taken up teaching the children, supplementing the rather sketchy teaching they are receiving in your Canadian schools. Frankly I believe in leaving well enough alone."

Mrs. Vander interrupted in her quiet way.

"I could employ my time, too, looking after their needs, but where is the money to come from if I stopped working, Frederick? I do not really enjoy working in other people's houses."

"It's all a bit of a bore," said Frederick, "but if you can get permission for me to teach and persuade the school to take me, I will sacrifice my own desires and take it." His brown eyes beamed on me then, fortified by his own high resolve.

We got the school and permission came from the Department and Mr. Vander was duly called for by one of the trustees and was taken out, the ten miles to his school. Mr. Vander's term of employment was exactly two weeks. The youngest girl came over to tell me. Her tone was one of complete detachment; she was the perfect reporter who gave the facts, uncolored by her own opinions.

"My father has returned. He will not go back."

I went over to interview the unwelcome prodigal.

"I left your school," he said in his most melodious voice, "not without regret. My reasons were entirely psychological, and you, being a Canadian, may find them difficult to understand. The people in that district are too utterly ignorant. I could never hope to reach them."

"You went there to teach the children," I said. "And if their parents are ignorant, that is all the more reason that their children should be taught. I know the people out there, and they are good decent, hard-working people. I'm sure they were kind to you and willing to give you the best they had."

He settled himself more comfortably in his chair and bowed his head.

"Mr. Vander," I went on, "you should try to grow up and assume some responsibility. You left that school because you wanted to come back to that easy chair where food and lodging are provided by your wife's efforts. Have you no pride?"

"Pride!" He caught at the word eagerly. "Yes, madam, I have pride. I have pride of ancestry, nationality and tradition. I am proud of my heritage of English literature and if you and my wife will

refrain from interrupting me I will take you into my confidence.
I have a plan to help my fellow men, an infinitely better plan than
this teaching scheme, one into which I can put my whole heart."

He was off on his magic carpet, leaving the cares of the world
behind him, and strangely enough he was able to make us listen.

His plan was, in brief, to give readings from Dickens' *A Christmas Carol* two days before Christmas. He would make his own tickets and send the children out to sell them:

AN EVENING WITH DICKENS — THE CHRISTMAS CAROL
Interpreted by Frederick T. Vander,
late of Drury Lane, London
Manitou Town Hall
Admission by Ticket Only

That cold December night came down in the best Manitoba
tradition, a windy night, with stars hanging low in a sky of cold
steel. A cold night never held any of us in if we wanted to go out so
the McClung family was represented by three members—Jack,
Florence and myself. The head of the house had a curling game at
the rink and pleaded his case by saying that he must have exercise.
Jack would have gladly gone with his father, but I coaxed him to
come with us with the argument that the literary arts must be encouraged, and everyone should hear the *Christmas Carol* at least once
a year.

The hall was a draughty place, heated by one stove in the middle
of the room. A straggling audience occupied the zone around the
stove and a fair pile of firewood promised a continuance of heat.
(The newspaper said in its account of the gathering that "the intelligence of the audience made up for the smallness of its numbers.")

Promptly at eight o'clock the Interpreter, Mr. Frederick T. Vander, in evening dress, came out from the back room with a copy of
the *Christmas Carol* in his hand. He was in good voice and looked
like a perfect Bob Cratchet. He even had the white scarf inside his
coat with its fluttering white ends. I resolutely put aside the opinion

I had of him as a husband and father and settled down to enjoy the performance.

"Marley was dead," he began, and we were off. Let the wind blow, let the tin roof crackle and buckle, we were listening to an immortal tale. The little man knew how to present his story. He played all parts with equal facility; he was Scrooge, tight-fisted and wizened, harsh of voice and hard of heart; he was the timid little clerk trying to warm himself at the candle. He was the fog that came pouring into every chink, "making the houses across the street into mere phantoms." And how well he did the nephew all in a glow of good fellowship who came in to wish old Scrooge a merry Christmas!—which he defined as—"A kind forgiving charitable time . . . when men and women open their shut-up hearts freely and think of the people below them as fellow passengers to the grave, and not another race bound on other journeys!"

So intent were we on the story that no one noticed that the fire was burning low and it was not until the knocker on the door changed to Marley's face that someone on the outer fringe of the audience came forward and mended the fire noisily. The Interpreter glared at the interruption but resumed the story. The caretaker of the hall, Mr. Miller, roused to his duty by this alien hand laid on his stove, reasserted his authority by piling in more wood and more wood, and soon the crackling of the stove joined the rumbling of the tin roof. The audience stretched their chilly hands to the warmth and went adventuring on the high seas where grizzled men raised their voices in praise of Christmas.

It was not until the Second Spirit entered that we began to feel sudden draughts across the floor as certain members of the audience drifted out. Each time the door opened a blast from the Arctic Circle smote us. Then, by sign language, we urged Mr. Miller to greater efforts.

About ten o'clock when Scrooge and the Spirit of Christmas Present went through the streets and saw "The brightness of the roaring fires in kitchens where preparations for the Christmas dinner were going on and tantalizing smells of turkey and sage came through the doors as happy children ran out to meet their cousins arriving"—it was then I missed my first born who had noiselessly departed, but Florence stayed on. She was drawn as far into her coat as she could get and had gathered her feet under her for warmth.

We lost another detachment when the Cratchets sat down to the goose, and the young Cratchets crammed spoons into their mouths lest they should shriek for goose before their turn came to be helped.

By the time the last Spirit had taken Scrooge to see his grisly ending, the wind had risen to new heights, and not only the tin roof, but the timbers of the hall creaked and groaned, and made strange and threatening noises. The audience were all around the stove now and the Speaker was with us too. He had put on his overcoat and mittens.

We looked in vain for Mr. Miller, but it appeared that he had gone, and evidently had taken the last of the firewood with him, so there we were at the end of our resources, but not the end of the story.

We saw it out; we stayed until the end, which came about eleven; and in spite of the cold and the burned out fire, the crackling roof and the bitter wind that found out every crack in the old Orange Hall, in spite of everything, we felt the thrill of the awakened soul of Ebenezer Scrooge, as the magic of Christmas ran in our veins, setting at naught the discomfort of the hour.

Since then, many many times we have heard the story told in the golden voices of John and Lionel Barrymore, heard it in warm rooms brightened by wood fires, with plates of apples waiting for us, and the fragrance of coffee on the air. But it was on that cold night in the old Orange Hall in Manitou that Florence and I, numb to the knees, really entered into the magic circle of the Dickens' Fellowship, and we felt ever since that we have the right to gather with the faithful wherever they are.

Ad astra per aspera.

6

Social Life

COLLIER'S "History of England," studied by public school children in my day, was a fairly dull recital of wars, conspiracies and the misdeeds of kings, but there were paragraphs—all too few—which bore the byline "Social Life of the People." I knew them by heart. They were emerald islands in a dull grey sea. In these meagre records we learned that the early Britons dyed their skins with a purple herb called woad. We were not told why they did it, but it seemed a good idea, like painting Easter eggs. They made clothes of the skins of animals. They put greased paper in their windows before they had glass, and there were some really exciting paragraphs which had to do with blood bonds and "shield maidens" who hurled the javelins, and brave hunters who took their swords in their teeth and went into the sea to do battle with the walrus and sea lion. Not much was said about the women, but we were pretty sure that they were left to do all the uninteresting work. The men hunted, fished and fought, doing a little cattle rustling as opportunity offered, while the women tanned the skins, made the clothes, and mucked around on the earthen floors, raising the family in their spare time. Later they learned to weave and spin. The Spear and the Spindle division runs back into the gray shades of the ancient days.

Now I wonder if in one hundred years the people will be interested in the social life of the people of my generation. When people are living on food put up in pellets which can be carried in their vest pockets, and travelling through the air and communicating with each other at will with distance annihilated, it may be that they will like to read of a time when the pace of life was slower and the struggle for existence a day to day matter, involving real effort and considerable ingenuity. Far be it from me to wish that the hands of the clock should ever turn backward, but one cannot help wondering in what direction the human soul will develop, when it is free from the burdening cares which make up the battle for existence.

Perhaps we have emphasized the importance of work too much, but we knew no other way of living, so we have made a virtue of it. We speak of basic industries and we know that what happens on the farms, in the mines and in the lumber woods, happens to the race. There is not a public man today that does not pay his tribute of praise to the worker. The "little people" we call them now, "who carry the load." Goldsmith sounded this note in his "Deserted Village," when he wrote:

"Princes and lords may flourish or may fade,
A breath can make them as a breath has made,
But the bold peasantry, the nation's pride,
When once destroyed can never be supplied."

On the farms before electricity and labor-saving devices lightened their loads, women's work obsessed them. Their hours were endless, their duties imperative. Many broke under the strain and died, and their places were filled without undue delay. Some man's sister or sister-in-law came from Ontario to take the dead woman's place. Country cemeteries bear grim witness to the high mortality rate in young women.

I wrote a story about one of these in 1914. I remember the date because we had just come to Edmonton and I had an attack of quinsy, which laid me up for a week. This gave me time to catch up on my reading. In a country paper I read of the death of a farmer's wife, aged thirty-three, who left "six small children to mourn her loss." The obituary closed piously with the words: "Thy will be done."

I did not believe that it was the will of God that had taken away this young mother and decided I should write something about it and because I wanted the story to be told many times, I wrote it in verse, knowing that the beat of words, even ordinary words, carries far, like music across water. I have no illusions about my skill as a writer of poetry, but the story I wrote about Jane Brown certainly went far and wide, and was recited at many Women's Institutes, socials and other gatherings, and was copied in hundreds of newspapers. It is nearly thirty years since I wrote about Jane, but even in the last year I have had several requests for copies.

The worst feature of life on the farm for women in that period was the lack of household help. Water was carried in and carried out. The women had access to no laundries, no bakeries, and I knew homes where there was not even a sewing machine. I remember very well the first ready-made dress I saw. A daring woman, Mrs. Bill Johnston, sent to Montreal for it and sent the money, fifteen dollars, mind you, and the neighbors cheerfully prophesied that she would never see the money again or the dress either. But the dress came and even the doubters had to admit it was a good-looking dress, and could be made to fit by "boning the body." The owner declared that she had enough bones of her own, and she was going to wear it just as it was. She liked a soft-fitting dress.

The first evidence of co-operation among the farmers that I remember was the inauguration of "beef-rings," and I regret that I am not able to record its origin. It may have been sponsored by the Department of Agriculture. The head of the beef-ring had a chart, showing how the meat could be divided. One animal was killed each week, and the farmers shared the meat. The people who got a sirloin roast one week would get stewing beef off the neck the next week, and the whole scheme worked without a hitch. But the coming of the automobile changed all our habits. The farmer with a car drove into town for his meat, and his groceries, too, so the little store languished, not able to meet the competition which the city stores offered. Other changes came too. The young people, having tasted the delights of driving into town with dinner at a hotel and a dance at the Masonic Hall, began to rebel at the "twenty-five hour day" on the farm, and dream of nice clean jobs in town. The trek from the farm began, with devastating effects on agriculture. But the stores in town, and particularly the banks, benefitted by the advent of good, smart, industrious country boys.

Looking back at it all now, I am convinced that the gloomy home atmosphere drove out more young people than their distaste for the long hours and the endless chores. Many a farmer, finding his years of labor sitting heavily on him, sank into a bog of surliness. They felt their long years of heavy work had given them the right to be disagreeable. They seemed to resent youth with its gaiety and love of fun. The colts in the pastures, kicking up their heels, kittens playing over a wood-pile; children, shouting over a game of "pom-pom-pullaway" in the school yard brought no smiles to these sour faces. Who was to blame?

The settlement of a new country takes a heavy toll, and one generation is bound to suffer. Education did not keep pace with the settlement, and children—especially the boys who were big enough to work—did not attend school even when the school came. Perhaps they went for a few months in the winter, but they were shy and backward, ashamed of their ignorance and the teachers were not always wise or tactful. These big lads did not like school, naturally. No one likes to appear at a disadvantage. When they grew older they knew they had been cheated out of something. This frustration took different forms in different people. In some it blossomed into a wholesome concern for the education of their own children. Others, not so fortunate, sank into a morass of resentment against society in general. They were the sour-faced ones whose boys left home as soon as they could.

In the first school in which I taught, one of the men of the district tried to keep his boys from going to the lake to skate, which surely was an innocent and inexpensive form of entertainment. He was afraid they might start to go into the little town, and there be tempted to spend money. I remember his words of complaint to me when I pleaded for the boys.

"When I was their age," he said bitterly, "I never left the farm, but these two young scamps go out of the house three times for every once they come in!"

I met these big boys many places, and my heart was heavy for them, and heavier still when I learned later how the Finnish people had solved that problem with their Continuation Schools. We could have had something of this nature if we had valued education as highly as the Finns value it, but in a new country everyone is in a hurry to get ahead. Education, they believed, could wait, but in all human history nothing waits. The stream runs fast. We cannot help the past, but we need not repeat its mistakes!

7

The Winds of the World

THE WINDS OF THE WORLD began to blow as the nineteenth century came to an end, and they even found their way into our placid existence. I do not think our newspapers carried much world news, or if they did we were not interested, so the South African war came on us unexpectedly. There always had been trouble with the Zulus, an indefinite term to us, signifying black men with earrings who carried spears. Hadn't we read and recited a poem about a surprise attack on our gallant men as they slept their honest sleep on a mountain side in Africa? "While close on front and either flank the live black crescent crept." In my first acquaintance with this poem, I thought that the live black crescent was some deadly tropical insect.

The South African war assumed a very serious aspect when our young men were recruited, and went. To us there seemed to be no good reason for fighting the Boers, who had worked their own land and minded their own business, people much like ourselves who had battled with flood and storms, stone bruises and chilblains. We had all read Olive Schreiner's "Story of a South African Farm." Paul Kreuger's picture in the newspaper showed him to be an honest, rugged old fellow, closely resembling, with his square face and chin whisker, many of the faces in my father-in-law's ordination picture.

We certainly could not feel any enmity to a man who looked like Dr. Morley Punshon.

We wondered what the war really was about. Was it the gold of Johannesberg and the diamond mines of Kimberley that had kindled all this flame of conquest? And in this uneasy suspicion we were not alone, for the news trickled through that one of the younger British statesmen, Mr. Lloyd George, a Welsh Baptist, had stoutly defended the Boers and been mobbed in Birmingham when he tried to speak.

I had been reading Prescott's *History of Mexico*, and I could not keep from wondering if we were not carrying on the same sort of conquest that Cortez carried on in the sixteenth century, when life was more barbarous. He was set at his task with the full blessing of the Church, steeped in the belief that the end justifies the means and that good can come from evil. The wholesale slaughter of the Aztecs was easily condoned when their gold and precious jewels went back to Spain to enrich the Mother Church. At our Epworth League meetings we debated these questions freely.

Meanwhile in Canada the tide of patriotism rose. Everyone was singing a new song called "The Soldiers of the Queen," which fanned the flame of Imperialism, and Kipling's "The White Man's Burden" made the soaring climax of many an address. It gave the whole business of war the high purpose of a Crusade and threw a glamor around the fighting man. We were not fighting for anything so cheap and corruptible as gold. We were paying our debt to the underprivileged, though perhaps ungrateful people of the world.

> "Take up the White Man's burden,
> Send forth the best you breed,
> Go bind your men to exile
> To serve your Captive's need,
> To wait in heavy harness
> On fluttered folk and wild,
> Your new-caught sullen people,
> Half devil and half child.

Take up the White Man's Burden
And earn his old reward—
The blame of those ye better,
The hate of those ye guard,
The cry of hosts ye humor
(Ah slowly) toward the light.
'Why brought ye us from bondage
Our loved Egyptian night?'"

There were other verses enlarging the theme of the white man's duty to "the lesser breeds without the Law," as he phrased it in his great Recessional, written in 1897.

Looking back at it now I remember how much we depended on Kipling. His words had a ring of Old Testament authority. We would have been happier about the war in South Africa if we had known that ten years after the end of hostilities Great Britain would hand back the country to the South Africans, and that the Union of South Africa would become one of our great allies.

Some glimpse of this settlement came to us in another one of Kipling's poems called "Kitchener's School," in which he tells something of the British plan of colonization. It is addressed to the people of the Sudan:

"He (Kitchener) has gone back to his city,
Not seeking presents or bribes
But openly asking the British
To buy you Hakims and scribes.
Knowing that you are forfeit by battle
And have no right to live,
He begs for money to bring you learning
And all the English give.
It is their treasure—it is their pleasure,
Thus are their hearts inclined,
For Allah created the English mad—
The maddest of all mankind.

They do not consider the meaning of things,
They consult not creed or clan;
Behold they clap the slave on the back
And he ariseth a man.
They terribly carpet the earth with dead
And before their cannons cool
They walk unarmed by twos and threes
And call the natives to school."

This poem is probably one of Kipling's greatest contributions to the work of Empire building, for it touches the vital spot which marks the difference between the colonization done by Britain and that of some other countries that are much in our minds today.

But I must get back to my story and remember I am not writing a tract on colonization, but a story of plain people.

January 22nd, 1901, was a dull cold day in Manitou, Manitoba, with icy flakes of snow riding in on the wind that came out of the north west. A sullen sky threatened that the night would come down early. Horses hitched to sleighs stamped impatiently as the cold settled down on them, and the women in the stores waiting for the men to complete their business saw the short afternoon dulling into night, and anxiously wished to be on their homeward way.

Suddenly the news broke!

Thomas Atkinson, the C.P.R. operator, took the message from the wires. Mr. Atkinson had been listening to the talking wires all day and knew that trouble was brewing. Four days before he had heard that all was not well at Osborne House. But there were no magic air channels then to carry the news to the men on the roads or the women in the farmhouses, and so the blow fell in country places with tragic suddenness.

Mr. Atkinson swung around in his swivel chair and despatched a messenger to the Fire Hall, the School, and the Presbyterian Church. Then he walked out into the small waiting room and lifted his hand for silence and announced—"The Queen is dead." Instinctively the men removed their hats.

In ten minutes the bells began to ring, hurriedly, noisily, their rusty notes jarring each other in their discordant passage, Andy Martin pulling the rope at the Fire Hall, John Logan at the School. But when the news reached the Presbyterian Church, August Henneberg with true Presbyterian forethought, knew what to do. August knew that tidings of sorrow were not expressed with a loud jangling of bells. So from the church steeple came a measured tolling, solemn and dignified, and soon the other bells steadied and grew calm.

The streets filled with people, the roads leading into Manitou were dotted with sleighs. Chores or no chores, the people came in to see if it were really true.

When Blake Hewitt, late of Iowa, came in he went at once to the Farmers' Store, dropping his horse's halter shanks to make them believe they were tied. Mr. Robinson, the proprietor, who had removed his brown paper cuffs, stood inside the door talking to a group of customers. "What's all the excitement?" Mr. Hewitt asked. Mr. Robinson's voice was solemn and deep. "Queen Victoria is dead," he said. "The Queen is dead," Mr. Hewitt repeated, "so that's why the bells were ringing. I thought something was wrong."

Mr. Hewitt's listeners might not have noticed the words or seen anything objectionable in them, but unfortunately for Mr. Hewitt there was in the Farmers' Store at that moment, Mrs. John Farnicombe, whose mother had been one of Queen Victoria's ladies-in-waiting. Mrs. Farnicombe still had the bonnet given by Her Majesty to her mother.

In telling of the incident Mrs. Farnicombe said her blood seemed to turn to water as she heard what he said; her head swam; her knees grew weak. She could not believe her ears. He thought something was wrong, and the terrible man was gone before she rallied. Gone like Judas, Mrs. Farnicombe said—gone into the night! Oh how she wished she had withered him with a look. He thought something was wrong, indeed!

Mrs. Farnicombe, torn with indignation, told the story to groups of people in the store and on the street, and at last made her way to see her friend Mrs. Bamford who lived in a little white house near

the Presbyterian Manse. Mrs. Bamford was everybody's friend, a
sweet-faced old lady with white hair and brown eyes. It was believed
that she belonged to one of the titled families of England and had
been disinherited because she had eloped with her father's coach-
man. But as she and her husband had never become confidential with
the neighbors on this point, the matter was not definitely known. If
she ever regretted her choice and longed for the marble halls she had
left, she gave no sign, but continued to live happily and serenely.
From her we heard many beautiful stories of the Royal Family; their
kindness and courtesy, their consideration for other people.

When the news of the Queen's death was borne out across the
fields in the rusty note of the bells, it fell upon our hearts with a stab
of personal bereavement. She was more than a ruler to us. She was a
legend, a tradition—the embodiment of maternal affection, goodness and piety. My mother had seen her once when she came to
Dundee, and "had been almost near enough to touch her mantle."
As a child I firmly believed that the Queen, in her generosity, had
given us the twenty-fourth of May for a holiday at considerable
inconvenience to herself, and that we must ever keep it in grateful
remembrance.

On that dark January day when the bells were tolling for her I
felt that I should do what I could to pass on my love for her to my
children. Jack was the only one big enough to understand so I took
him out with me. I wanted him to remember the solemn notes of
the bells, the sad faces of the people, and he still remembers it—tho'
he was not yet four years old.

On our way home we went in to see Mrs. Bamford. I told him the
Queen had been as sweet and kind and lovely, with the same shiny
white hair and beautiful hands. Mrs. Farnicombe came in while we
were there, hot with raging anger because of a dreadful man who
had made light of the death of the Queen. She related the conversation dramatically. "He said it, Mrs. Bamford," she cried tearfully,
"'I thought there was something wrong' were his very words, as if
the death of our Queen were not the greatest calamity we could
suffer. . . . A wretched, ignorant foreigner, my dear, without hope

or God in the world; with no reverence, no sanctities, and he would dare to speak of her thus, lying cold in death."

"Hush dear," Mrs. Bamford said soothingly, "my daughter will serve us a cup of tea and we will all feel better. Do not be so sure that Mr. Hewitt meant any disrespect. The Queen would be the first one to defend him. She once defended a boy who pointed a pistol at her, and the demented man who struck her on the head and crushed a lovely bonnet. When they were ordered to be flogged, it was the Queen herself who saved them. She won respect by being worthy of it, my dear, not by demanding it."

Before we left, Mrs. Bamford had an explanation to cover Mr. Hewitt's words. "I think you have misjudged Mr. Hewitt," she said to her friend, "without meaning to do so. You were under the strain of deep emotion and read into his words a meaning of your own. Are you sure he didn't say—'I thought there was something wrong' meaning 'I knew there was something wrong.' That, my dear Mrs. Farnicombe, would make his words entirely innocent, and that is what I prefer to believe. That is what Her Majesty would wish us to believe, and I think it would be wise to say no more about it."

And there was no more said about it. The Queen's deputy had spoken.

8

Strong Women

THE FIRST TIME I felt the stirrings of ambition to be a public speaker was at a W.C.T.U. Convention in Manitou in 1907. This was a great event for our little town—seventy-five delegates from all parts of the Province, with morning, afternoon, and evening meetings, was an undertaking to challenge all our resources. I do not remember how it happened that the Convention came to Manitou. I had not been a delegate up to that time, but I had been a member of the organization, and I was simply thrilled when I was asked to give the address of welcome on behalf of the local unit. I began my preparations at once. I got a new dress, navy blue and white striped voile trimmed with narrow white Valenciennes lace; a white leghorn hat with red velvet flowers. I was determined to be as easy as possible on the eye. Years afterward I heard Carrie Chapman Catt say when she was not sure of her speech she always got a new dress, but if she knew she had a good speech, any dress would do.

In spite of the new dress I had some anxious moments when I contemplated the task of welcoming the delegates. What could I say that hadn't been said many times before? I had a clear idea of some of the things I would not say. I would not run into statistics like some temperance speakers I had heard, nor would I tell them how many loaves of bread a man could buy if he never drank beer. I knew vaguely why people drank. It answered something in their blood, some craving for excitement and change. Hadn't I turned round and round myself to enjoy a moment of dizziness, a blotting out of the old familiar landscape? I knew it was foolish, bad, and dangerous, and yet it had a charm.

I knew the lives of these country people, with their disappointments, long hours, and gray monotony; and I felt that we must give them something rather than take something away. We must be like the pack rats who never steal but merely make an exchange.

Prohibition is a hard-sounding word, worthless as a rallying cry, hard as a locked door or going to bed without your supper. It could never fire the heather, and yet the heather must be fired. People had to have something which would take them out of themselves; the church has given many a real vision of God and His plan for the world. But even the church often presents a dour face, with its locked door and musty smells. I often thought of the Salvation Army when they came to Brandon in 1885, with their color, warmth and band music. How they drew the lonely country boys into their barracks and set them singing the Gospel hymns. They knew the drawing power of coffee and sandwiches and the beat of a drum, the compelling power of rhythm, and light and warmth and friendliness. They knew how to fight the powers of evil, and we, the temperance women, would have to make our cause attractive. We must fight fire with fire.

I never doubted for a moment that this could be done, for I knew we had all the arguments. No one could deny that women and children were the sufferers from the liquor traffic; any fun that came from drinking belonged to men exclusively, and the men themselves would be the first to admit that. I saw in my easily stirred imagination, that life for both men and women could be made much more attractive with recreation grounds, games, handicrafts, orchestras, folk dances, better houses, better farms; new hopes for a new world. I was well away on the wings of fancy as I drafted out a speech of welcome for the delegates.

I was not the only person who prepared for the coming of the seventy-five. The two paper hangers were busy for a month preceding the event, papering and painting spare rooms. House cleaning went on apace, curtain stretchers were borrowed and lent and lay on green lawns. The air throbbed with the beating of carpets, and the dressmakers never had the pins out of their mouths. Manitou was going to show them how a convention should be managed.

Even ladies must eat, so the Manitou hostesses prepared. They filled crocks with lemon biscuits for they had a reputation for keeping well. In the drug store we knew that lemon biscuits were being produced, for the real heart of a lemon biscuit comes from the five cents' worth of oil of lemon and the five cents' worth of citrate of ammonia—(these provide the rising and the flavor, otherwise it is just a plain beaten biscuit). To Mrs. August Henneberg belonged the credit of bringing in the recipe from somewhere in the States, or maybe she made it up, for Mrs. Henneberg was a lady of original ideas; and I know she was the first to think of splitting the squares and putting in wild strawberry jam.

The Convention met in June, just after the school term, the leafiest, greenest time of the year—with field crops rippling in the sun and wild roses in bloom on the roadsides. The opening meal was served at one o'clock. The trains passed at Manitou at noon and the reception committee, with white bows on their watch chains, lined the sidewalk and delegates were shown to their billets. Then everyone went to the old Orange Hall where the banquet was served. The Hall was scrubbed into a state of cleanliness not known before and the long tables were a sight to remember. Everything had been prepared in advance and the only hot dish was the scalloped potatoes. In that abundant time there was cold chicken, sliced or jellied; pink sugar-cured hams stuck with cloves; and molds of head cheese on beds of lettuce garnished with hard-boiled eggs; lemon pies whipped up in mounds of white meringue and stippled with orange and brown—from the two minutes in a hot oven; ice cream in freezers; and cakes which make a mock of us now in this strictly rationed time. Will I ever forget those dishes of creamed potatoes—made with real cream and served with ripe cucumber pickles clear as amber and sweet as honey? Why do I write of these things on this day of 1943, when I should be telling a sober and serious story of my country's past, revealing, if I can, the mind of my people?

No doubt this hearty fare had something to do with the success of the address of welcome which followed the banquet. It is easy to talk to people who have come together for a three-day holiday. It is quite likely that there is no person else who remembers that speech, but I remember it. I remember the effect it had on me. For the first time I knew I had the power of speech. I saw faces brighten, eyes glisten, and felt the atmosphere crackle with a new power. I saw what could be done with words, for I had the vision of a new world as I talked. I was like the traveller who sees through the mist the towers of the great city. It was not ideas I was giving them exactly, but rather ferments—something which I hoped would work like yeast in their minds.

That was a long time ago as we reckon time, but it does not seem long. I still remember that my head was lighter than my heart when it was all over, for I knew that I was committed to a long fight and a hard one. Still the vision has never faded. There is a land of pure delight ahead of us, a land of richer fruitage and brighter sunshine, even though the way may be long and hard and dangerous. That Better Country has fired man's imagination since time began.

War had no place in our thoughts then. We were too civilized for war we thought. We believed the enemies we had to fight were ignorance, greed, intolerance and boredom.

It is easy to see why we concentrated on the liquor traffic. It was corporeal and always present; it walked our streets; it threw its challenge in our faces! We were worried then about Jennie Gills who was one of our members. Jennie was "expecting" again, and her husband had celebrated the last occasion by getting roaring drunk and coming home with the avowed intention of killing Jennie and the new baby.

There were other homes too, across whose portal the shadow of the trade had fallen. In a little town the currents run deeply and we knew each other's sins and sorrows. We knew about the men who cashed their wheat tickets and spent most of it over the bar, forgetting to bring home the children's shoes. Elsewhere I have written the story of the woman and her little girl who were disappointed in their trip to Ontario. Oh no, there was nothing fanciful about the evils of intemperance with its waste of money as well as its moral hazards. It was ever before us. And we remembered Gladstone's words concerning the ease with which he could pay the national debt if he had a sober England.

We believed we could shape the world nearer to our heart's desire if we had a dry Canada and that, we felt, would come if and when women were allowed to vote. We did not believe that women would ever become drinkers. We argued, subconsciously, that women have more resources within themselves, more outlets for their energies, and so did not need this false exhilaration. I remember the first time I saw an intoxicated woman—the daughter of one of Winnipeg's best known families, in a box at the old Bijou Theatre. She interrupted the play and had to be removed. Her lapse from sobriety rather upset my theory that people drink to relieve the monotony of a drab life. How could life be drab for this girl, in a city, with a great house full of servants, plenty of money, books, music, companions, youth and beauty? She had not found her place in life surely. But when we achieved our ambition—the full emancipation of women—there would be work for her, work which would lift her out of herself.

So ran my dream.

About this time, that is soon after the Convention, the powers of darkness showed their hand and the stock of the Women's Christian Temperance Union soared to a new high. In Carman, a small town between Manitou and Winnipeg, a vote on local option was coming and the liquor interests were afraid they would be defeated, for at that time women who had property in their own name could vote in municipal matters. And in Carman there were enough of these to swing the vote. The Conservative Government of Manitoba was appealed to by the Interests—couldn't they think of something? It would never do to let one town carry local option. The Government had resourceful advisers and they had a plan. They would quietly, and without any flourish of trumpets, disfranchise the women.

When the voting day came and the women went out to vote they found their names were not on the list—no woman could vote—by Order in Council. I would like to have been there that day. There followed a reaction which frightened the powers, and from end to end of Manitoba a new movement began which ran like a prairie fire before a high wind. If the present Government would not give us a vote there was just one thing left for us to do. We would change the Government, and that is what we did, though it took a little time.

It was a bonny fight—a knock-down and drag-out fight, but it united the women of Manitoba in a great cause. I never felt such unity of purpose and I look on these days with great satisfaction. We really believed we were about to achieve a new world. Now we had the key to the treasure house of life for we could send our own representatives to Parliament.

I believe we might have reaped a great harvest if the blight of war had not blown its poisonous breath over the world.

It is just as well that we did not foresee the day when a woman member of the Federal House would say, in her first interview after she had been elected to the seat left vacant by her husband, that she had helped to elect her husband in his campaigns—not by her speeches but by her ability to shake up a good cocktail. How indignant we were! Surely it was not for this that we had struggled to get votes for woman. We felt betrayed and cast down. We felt that the House of Commons needed a lot of things more than it did another cocktail shaker. Many were the letters that I wrote in imagination to the lady in question, but I was always glad that I had not sent them. Then one day in Ottawa I met her—a dainty, gentle woman, beautiful as a Dresden shepherdess. To connect her with any phase of the evils of intemperance became an absurdity. I thought of James M. Barrie's tender words regarding the woman who swore and so put herself outside the pale of respectability in Thrums—"There was no wickedness in her words," wrote her historian, "she swore like a child who had been in ill company." Mrs. Black and I talked about the wild flowers of Canada and she gave me some of her exquisite drawings. When we parted she said, impulsively, "I've always wanted to know you. I knew you would improve on acquaintance." I gathered from that innocent remark that Mrs. Black had probably been writing letters to me too, in her mind, but the mellowing years had dulled our differences and we laughed together like two old friends.

I have a copy of her book *My Seventy Years* with a friendly inscription from her and her collaborator, Elizabeth Bailey Price. It is a fascinating book, revealing the writer with frankness and sincerity, untainted by egotism, and showing in many an instance the mischievous delight she took in shocking the complacent, which no doubt explains her first interview.

She tells the story in her book about a Missionary meeting she was asked to address in London in 1916. George Black, her husband, was then Commissioner of the Yukon and also the commander of the Yukon Infantry, and while in London she was feted and honored and in great demand as a speaker. She had confined her observation to the Yukon and its beauties, not venturing into the political or religious field. On arrival at the Church house she was ushered to the platform where there were many clergymen and Bishops who eyed her suspiciously. The Bishop of London, in his preliminary remarks, mentioned all the speakers but Mrs. Black. When at last her turn came to speak she received a few curt words from His Lordship who said, "I believe Mrs. Black is what is called a sourdough, and she will speak a few words."

The lady from the Yukon was not accustomed to such oblique treatment, so she began—"My Lord chairman. If this is the way you treat women who are asked to speak, I do not wonder that suffragettes go around with axes over here." Then she spoke of religion and the influence that marriage has in deciding a women's religion. "I am an Anglican," she said, "because I married one. If I had married a Fiji Islander, I would probably be eating a missionary today instead of talking to missionaries."

This, to come from a sweet-tongued gentle little person with the face of a Madonna, must have created a sensation at the Church House.

Before I leave this part of my story I must pay my tribute to the brave women of the W.C.T.U. Looking back at our life in the small town I see we owed much to the activities of the W.C.T.U. and these initials, I hasten to explain, stand for "Women's Christian Temperance Union," and not "Women Continually Torment Us," as some have believed.

It was the W.C.T.U. who planned debates, and spelling matches, and ran a reading room, wherein the Review of Reviews, and *Scribner's* and *McClure's* magazines could be read, along with the *Family Herald*, the *Witness* and others.

They were a resolute band of women, these early Crusaders, and I am always glad I met them and fell under their influence at an early age.

A composite picture of the leaders at that time would show a tall, thin woman with her hair parted in the middle and waved back into a bun at the back of her well-shaped head, a crisp white frill at her neck fastened with a cameo brooch, a hunting case watch pinned on her left shoulder, secured by a gold chain around her neck; black henrietta cloth dress, black stockings, and a white handkerchief, a white bow of ribbon, probably tied on the watch chain; clear eye, a light hand with cakes, and not afraid of anything!

The rank and file of the sisterhood sometimes had fears! For the W.C.T.U. was never in any danger of inheriting that "woe" which is pronounced against those "of whom all men speak well." Little Mrs. Durban found that out the day she joined, and went home wearing the bow of white ribbon. Mrs. Chisholm of Winnipeg had given an address in the Methodist Church, and under the spell of her eloquence, Mrs. Durban had paid her dollar, signed the pledge and had the bow pinned on her.

But when she got home, her husband, James Durban, being a man of the world, engaged in the fuel business, saw danger in this innocent little white bow. He knew it might endanger his trade with the Ellis House, licensed to sell malt and spirituous liquors. Once every week Mr. Durban delivered fuel to the Ellis House, and got his money "right on the nail."

This being in the nineties when men were masters of their own house, James Durban commanded his wife to lay aside her white ribbon bow and go no more to the meetings of the W.C.T.U. and Mrs. Durban obeyed. But that was not the end. Mrs. Durban still paid her dues, still considered herself a member of the society pledged to rid the world of the curse of alcoholism, but she worked behind the lines. She made cakes for the socials; made candy for the Band of Hope; minded Mrs. Brown's two children on Monday afternoons, when she led the singing at the Loyal Temperance Legion. There were other unseen members who worked quietly for peace sake, but were all part of the Maginot Line of defense against the invader. The W.C.T.U. had tact as well as courage.

The W.C.T.U. trained young orators and reciters, and gave medals for the winners, and people travelled long distances to attend these gatherings. They also got permission to give temperance talks in the schools, and studied charts and diagrams to make their lessons "stick." They explained the circulation of the blood, and the effect of alcohol on the stomach, and showed why athletes do not drink even mild intoxicants, and had the children figure out how many pairs of boots and little red sleighs a man could buy with the money he spends on a daily glass of beer. At the Band of Hope, they gave badges and pins, and taught the children a marching song of which the refrain was: "*Tremble King Alcohol! We will grow up!*" They did grow up—these young people—and it looked like victory, for there were definite signs that the evils of intemperance were being curtailed.

Then came the war and the Band of Hope boys went out to fight for democracy and some did not return—and some of these who did were shattered and disillusioned and embittered, and King Alcohol did not tremble any more! Not even when women received the vote! Other societies came into being and the W.C.T.U. found its ranks thinning, though it has never rested from the conflict.

There are only two left of the Old Guard—Mrs. Ruttan who lives in Winnipeg and Mrs. Clendenan in London, Ontario. The others are gone—Mrs. Chisholm, Dr. Youmans, Mrs. Hislop, Mrs. Best, Mrs. Gordon, Mrs. Vrooman, Mrs. McClung (my mother-in-law), Mrs. Stewart, Mrs. Dolsen and many more. They are all gone. But their memory is still vivid in hearts made better by their presence.

9

The Flavor of a Hymn

WRITER in the "Canadian author" this month (that is October, 1943) contributed a kindly biographical article dealing with my literary work, which he entitles "Nellie McClung—Crusader." In it he says that my didactic enthusiasm has marred my art. "Some of her stories are sermons in the guise of fiction. There is the flavor of the Sunday School hymn and the Foreign Mission Board in some of her work."

I hope I have been a crusader, and I would be very proud to think that I had even remotely approached the grandeur of a Sunday School hymn. I have never worried about my art. I have written as clearly as I could, never idly or dishonestly, and if some of my stories are, as Mr. Eggleston says, sermons in disguise, my earnest hope is that the disguise did not obscure the sermon.

It has always seemed strange to me to find people speaking in a more or less condescending way of Sunday Schools, and Mr. Eggleston's remark regarding Sunday School hymns has caused me to examine some of the hymns which live in my memory. Some of the greatest poets of our time have contributed to the Children's section of the hymn book. I think of that hymn which begins:

"Hushed was the evening hymn,
The temple courts were dark,
The lamp was burning dim
Before the sacred Ark,
When suddenly a voice divine
Rang through the silence of the shrine."

I would be a very proud Woman indeed if some line of mine should ever appear in such good company.

I remember once in a discussion at a Canadian Authors' Convention when I had been asked to speak on "The Writers' Creed" I took the position that no one should put pen to paper unless he or she had something to say that would amuse, entertain, instruct, inform, comfort, or guide the reader. I was assailed with particular vehemence by one of my fellow members who is a writer of novels—she cried out in disgust: "Who wants to write books for Sunday Schools? I certainly do not."

No doubt she was thinking of her art. I was able to assure her that her books were safe; I remember the fifty-five books which were sent to Northfield School in the early '80's—a free gift from a country church in Ontario because we had started a Sunday School. Among the number was *Ivanhoe*, *The Talisman*, *Swiss Family Robinson*, *Children of the New Forest*, and a *Life of Livingstone*. We all read all of them, and perhaps I got my predilections towards Sunday School libraries from this circumstance. My friend the novelist could not know what they meant to us. She had no way of knowing. The Sunday School libraries supplied a need long before the era of lending libraries.

There is no doubt that environment has much to do with our character and our outlook on life. I often think of the gamble our family and other families took when we left the security of Grey County, with its church and school and friendly neighbors, and took our westward way to the wide reaches of an unknown country. What would have been our fate had no one cared for our mental and spiritual well being? It was not the financial interests of the country who cared for us. The machine companies were interested in us as customers only. They did not hesitate to sue the settler if he could not make his payments on their tariff-protected machines. They even went so far as to seize his cattle and horses. The higher institutions of learning, the universities had no thought for us. Why should they? They had their own classes. Extension courses had not been considered. There were no correspondence courses. But the church had a care for the outposts and sent us missionaries to instruct us, and books—books that warmed our hearts, that brought us pictures of far places, that pushed back the walls of loneliness, that opened golden doors, and created for us a sense of fellowship with the wide world, of which we had seen so little.

No one knows what books can mean except those of us who have been hungry for them.

I have often wondered at the scorn with which many excellent people speak of the church and its work. It cannot all be ignorance. Have they no sense of the dramatic? Can they not see the heroism of the men and women who give their lives to the spiritual needs of their fellow men? It is not an easy life the church offers, but it appeals to the best in human nature.

Just a few days ago two visitors come to see us—one a retired banker and the other a minister. The banker introduced the minister with these words: "As a rule I do not think much of preachers, most of them seem like sissies to me, being a hard-boiled business man, but I make an exception in the case of Mr. White. He's a real man, even if he is a preacher." We assured him he need not apologize for his friend or his friend's profession. We were honored by his presence.

The contrast between the two men was interesting. They were about the same age and probably had started life under similar circumstances, but their ways had diverged. The banker had been apprenticed in a small town bank in his boyhood, had handled money, and kept a ledger and became proficient in business procedure, and in time became the manager of a bank in a prairie town, with power to make loans or refuse them—opened his bank at ten, when the day was far spent on the farms, closed at three while the ordinary man worked on; and so had acquired the unmistakably superior air of the man to whom other men must come, hat in hand, asking for favors.

Meanwhile the young minister had worked his way through college, served on mission fields, done various things to raise money— sold books or maybe Fuller brushes, done without many things which the bank boy had as a matter of course. Walked while the banker drove. But he had helped to shape society, and had changed lives for the better. He had helped to build Canada. He had never known, and never would know the material security of the banker, but he had something in the twinkle of his eye and his friendly attitude towards all men, which showed his life had acquired another dimension.

I wonder if we are not getting a new consciousness of human values in this present struggle. I rather think we are, and I do not think that the church is going to be the loser.

In 1933 Hitler shared the opinion of the bank manager that most preachers were sissies and it would be an easy matter to destroy the church. He used even harsher words—"The church is hollow and rotten," he said, "it's day is gone." But the Quisling press in Norway later wrote sorrowfully: "The Christian front is the most difficult of all to conquer." And here is a statement by the great Albert Einstein, a Jew, who had no love for the Christian Church—"When National Socialism came to Germany, I looked to the universities to defend freedom, knowing they had always boasted of their devotion to the cause of truth. But no—the universities were immediately silenced. Then I looked to the great editors of the newspapers, whose flaming editorials in days gone by had proclaimed their love of freedom. But they, like the universities, were silenced in a few short weeks. Only the churches stood squarely across the path of Hitler's campaign for suppressing truth. I never had any special interest in the church before, but now I feel a great affection and admiration, because the church alone has had the courage and persistence to stand for intellectual truth and moral freedom. I am forced thus to confess that what once I despised I now praise unreservedly."

It comforts me now to remember the part the churches have played in the making of this country. How they have held together the neighborhoods with their Christmas concerts, picnics, girls' and boys' camps in later years, and the weekly services, rain or shine!

No doubt they have looked insignificant to the "intellectuals." They could see only little groups of people meeting in unattractive buildings to read words written hundreds of years ago and singing "like a mighty army moves the church of God." These little groups did not look much like an army, to the enlightened ones who believed God could be better glorified by a round of golf on a lovely Sunday morning, than sticking around teaching other people's children. But the remnant went on, quite happily, services were held at the usual hour and children were taught the deathless stories of the Bible and New Testament, and they were taught to sing, as the minister's wife played on the wheezy organ:

"Yea, though I walk through Death's dark vale,
    Yet will I fear no ill
For Thou are with me and Thy rod
And staff—they comfort still."

Pretty sombre stuff for children! What did they know of Death's dark vale?

Not much, not then, but in a few short years those children became soldiers, sailors and nurses, men and women in dangerous places, men on rubber rafts, in lifeboats, in the snows of Kiska, in the mud of Italy; they knew about Death's dark vale; and they knew fear, but again they sang the hymns they had learned in Sunday School, and found comfort as the horrible darkness of night came down on them.

How proud I would be to know I had written one sentence, or taught a lesson in Sunday School, which even for a moment comforted one of these brave people!

10

My First Story

THE ACTUAL BEGINNING of my serious writing began under the encouragement of Mrs. J. A. McClung, my husband's mother. It was in Manitou, soon after the birth of Paul, when she came to visit us. One morning she came out to the kitchen where Alice and I were at work on the weekly washing, with a magazine in her hand.

"*Collier's* has a short story contest particularly for unknown writers," she said, "and I think you should send in one. You can write. . . . It seems like a great chance."

Operations stopped while the announcement was read. But how could I ever get a story done?

"Alice and I will look after the house if you will go right now and get at it."

"I could not do it today," I said—"there's the Church Tea—I have to see about Florence's dress . . ."

My mother-in-law held firm.

"Trifles—all of them"—she said. "If you wait until you are ready to write, you will never write. Don't you know that conditions are never perfect? Life conspires to keep a woman tangled in trifles. Well now Alice and I are in charge—so you are free. How long do you need?"

"If I could have one free day, I believe I could write a story," I said. "I have been thinking of one."

So I went to the den. It was too cold upstairs. I think this was in November, 1902.

By night I had written the first Watson story—afterwards the first chapter of *Sowing Seeds in Danny*.

The next day I re-wrote it in ink, on foolscap—the announcement said writing would be acceptable if plainly legible. The next day I mailed it, and as the months rolled on, nothing more was heard.

I began then to write short articles and stories for Dr. W. H. Withrow of the Methodist Sunday School Publications, and from him I received some encouragement, and some small cheques.

In the following March, I got one day a letter from *Collier's*—and this too arrived on wash day—I remember hastily drying my hands on the roller towel before opening it.

It said my entry had not won a prize but it was held to the last, having passed all the preliminary readers. It was rather too juvenile for their purpose—but it was "a delightful story, with humor, and originality."

Then, acting on impulse, I sent the story to Dr. Withrow, and again the waves of silence broke softly over it. In June, 1905, it again came to the surface. This time a letter came from one "E.S.C." who told me he had found the manuscript in a forgotten file—read it, and been impressed by it. He had shown it to two people (one was Jean Graham) and they shared his opinion. It had "vitality, humor, and originality." The Watson family were real people, and he would like to know more of them—"You should go ahead with this," he wrote, "and make it into a book."

I shall never forget the radiance that shone around me that day. I had not a doubt in the world about my ability. Of course I could write more—now that I had this assurance. "E.S.C." was, I found, Mr. E. S. Caswell of the Wm. Briggs Publishing Company, and he became my patient, wise, encouraging counsellor. As I wrote I sent my chapters to him until I became so absorbed in the story, I pushed on to the conclusion. I wanted him to get the impact of the whole story.

It was finished in June, 1906, and Mr. Caswell was enthusiastic. However, I found out afterwards that the head of the publishing department of the Briggs Company did not share in this opinion. He said the book was "a feeble imitation of Mrs. Wiggs," and would not take it unless an American publisher could be found.

Mr. Caswell, after some delays, caused by the loss of the manuscript, got the attention of Doubleday, Page & Company, who accepted the book for publication; and in 1908 *Sowing Seeds in Danny* appeared, and became the best seller of the year in Canada, and did very well in the U.S.A. too.

The success of *Sowing Seeds in Danny* led me into a new field of adventure. I gave public readings from it. My mother-in-law was again to blame. She had a project in Winnipeg which needed money—the W.C.T.U. Home for Friendless Girls, called the Williard Home, and one day the possibility that people might be induced to pay to hear me read from the new book caused her to telephone me at Manitou. I told her it would never do, no one would come— but I also knew from the first second that I would do it. She had a way with her—that gentle, soft-spoken woman; she had the strength of the meek—the terrible meek, who win by sweetness and gentle persuasion and the brushing away of all arguments as only the meek can.

I got a new dress, a soft blue; I had my hair done at a hairdresser's, and a manicure and facial. My first excursion into the aromatic world of Applied Beauty! I even had a little rouge to tone up my pale complexion. The operator put it on, without bothering to ask me, and I had to admit it was an improvement on the rose-leaf from a summer hat, hitherto used by me for the purpose. I was learning.

I knew I could make myself heard and I knew I would not forget my piece. Anyway, being my piece I could carry on, but Grace Church, Winnipeg, is a large auditorium to fill and I feared the forbidding prospect of empty seats. Mrs. Chisholm, President of the W.C.T.U., introduced me. There were three solos by Winona Lightcap, always a favorite, so the audience could not feel cheated. I remember too that Sir Daniel and Lady McMillan sent me two dozen red roses from Government House and that the women who sponsored it were pleased. I was glad when it was over. My part wasn't very good and I knew it. It sounded like Friday afternoon in a country school.

In a week I had a letter from Will J. Green, Secretary of the Y.M.C.A. in Brandon, asking me to repeat the program in Brandon, and please name my fee. I wrote back asking twenty dollars—I was sure that would close the correspondence. No one would pay me twenty dollars. But Mr. Green wrote back that the fee was a modest one, and he named the night.

To reach Brandon, I passed through Wawanesa, and the prospect of a few days there on my return lightened my gloom. It went off fairly well. I felt more at home. Again that Fall I was invited to perform. This time it was at Roland, Manitoba, and that was a memorable visit, for there I met Virginia, and Virginia was worth an effort on anyone's part.

Virginia and her mother, who lived on a farm a few miles from Roland, entertained me, and as my train did not leave until afternoon the next day there was no need for us to cut short our visit that night. And so the three of us had a long evening. I loved to look at Virginia—eighteen years old, with dark curly hair, eyes the color of damson plums, dimples and a set of teeth that would be the delight of the toothpaste advertisers. Virginia's mother had the bewildered look of a hen that has brought forth a duckling, and sees it sail away leaving her behind frantic with anxiety.

While Virginia built up the fire in the kitchen, her mother had a chance to talk to me, about her, which she did in a whisper. "I wish you would advise Virginia, she is so strong-minded, and outspoken. I'm worried about her. Men do not like strong-minded women, and Virginia says such plain things. She's not one bit ladylike. I don't know what will become of her. Marriage is woman's only safety, and Virginia will not have me always. I am sixty, and a woman's life is pretty well over by sixty. . . . Virginia took over when her father died, and she has run the farm—my boy wouldn't stay—he went to the city. . . . She'll be all alone here when I'm through. . . . I just have the two, and Virginia is so outspoken I'm afraid people will talk about her. A young girl has to be careful, especially one who has no father."

Virginia and her mother were as far apart as two women could be. The mother, a frail-looking little shell, made an appeal to one's pity. Her hands fluttered as she talked and her thin lips quivered. I wondered what had sapped her courage.

After Virginia had fed us on jellied chicken, home-made biscuits, wild cranberry jelly, and coffee, the family conference began.

"Mother and I wanted to have you stay here, because we need some one's advice. We have a problem—or at least mother thinks it is a problem."

Virginia presented the case with precision. "Mother thinks I should get married, and I think so too, but I am more careful than mother and think ahead. There's a young man who lives a mile from here, who wants to marry me. He's a good fellow, tall, blonde, the right age, and good looking. In fact I like him real well. But I certainly will not live in his house. It is built on the high bank of a creek, beautiful for scenery, but no place for children."

Her mother threw me a glance which plainly said—"What did I tell you?"

Virginia went on. "I told him I was not going to take the chance. He could be careless with his children if he liked, but he couldn't be careless with mine—"

"Has he children?" I asked, slightly bewildered.

"No," said Virginia, unruffled, "not yet. But he will have if I marry him—and he is hesitating. Says his mother chose this place and it is full of childhood memories and all that . . ."

"Don't you think," her mother said to me, "that all discussions of children should be left until after marriage? It isn't quite delicate. I was married very young, and I knew nothing. I was a very innocent young girl. Girls were innocent then."

Virginia reached over and patted her mother's thin hand. Her own was strong and brown. The two hands told volumes.

"You learned everything the hard way, Mother," Virginia said soothingly, "I look ahead and Mrs. McClung will tell you I am right.

I wouldn't get married at all if I did not want children, and I am not going to fret my heart out with anxiety. I know what those kids of mine would do—they'd climb fences, or crawl through—they wouldn't know danger and I couldn't watch them. I'd be busy in the house with most likely a new baby, or one coming."

"Oh Virginia, what will Mrs. McClung think of you! I cannot bear to hear such talk," her mother cried in real distress.

I did what I could to allay her mother's fears. Virginia was a fore-shadowing to me of what women could be—strong, independent, courageous, outspoken, never confusing innocence and ignorance. She looked out at life and met its challenge. And where did she get this? Certainly not from her mother, I thought, but maybe it was. Life has a way of keeping the balance.

Years passed. I wondered about Virginia and the house on the creek's bank. One night after a lecture in Grace Church, I saw some people near the door waiting to speak to me. Then coming down the aisle I recognized Virginia. No mistaking the sparkling dark eyes and flashing smile. Virginia, a little older, even more lovely—Virginia carrying a red-cheeked baby with the same radiant vitality.

I greeted her warmly—and hurriedly asked her if the creek had dried up or changed its course.

She shook her head—"A new house," she said, and motioned to someone behind. Another red-cheeked, dark-eyed baby was carried up the aisle by a tall blonde young man with a well-tanned face.

"You may as well meet the whole family at once," said Virginia. "We came in to Winnipeg to show you how we are prospering. You know it's five years since we saw you, but twins count up fast."

"Virginia," I said, looking at the bright-eyed babies—"they would take first prize in any baby show."

"They did," she said proudly—"and just hold on a minute." She snapped her fingers over her shoulder, and I felt I was in a dream when I saw coming down the aisle, dressed alike, in Red River overcoats, two little boys—with blonde curls showing under their blue caps.

"Meet the troops," Virginia said, and the two blue caps were removed from the blonde heads as if by one motion. "George and Dan are three, and the little girls are six months old—all sound in wind and limb."

"Four beautiful children—so soon," I said. "Why, Virginia, you're only twenty-three or twenty-four now—you have your family!"

"That's what you think," said Virginia!

If I were writing fiction, I would end this pleasant story right here; with its further development merely indicated. But this is not really the end of the story.

The first time I returned to Winnipeg after we moved to Edmonton, I spoke at a Sunday night service in Grace Church, and as I greeted the friends who came to speak to me I wondered about Virginia. She would be the first person in the neighborhood to have a car, and drive it, and a drive to Winnipeg would be nothing to her. So I was not surprised to see her, and her husband coming down the aisle, each with a little boy about three years old by the hand. Then I was confused.

When the first words were over I raised the question which was in my mind. "I thought the babies were girls, Virginia," I said, "I must have been mistaken."

"What babies do you mean?" she asked. "We are right out of babies now. We have two girls."

There was a flurry from behind, and two miniature Virginias, wearing Red River coats and white woollen caps, stood before me, and one of them said, "She means us."

"But how did you get so big all at once?" I asked them, as we shook hands.

"We're only five," they said. I couldn't tell them apart, but that did not matter. They seemed to speak in unison. "But we're not big," they said, "George and Dan are big." And then I saw, coming to speak to me, two tall boys—George and Dan, in long pants and lumbermen's jackets—blue-eyed and handsome—straight as young trees.

"Six children," I said, looking in admiration at this remarkable group. "Virginia, you knew what you were talking about."

Then I heard about the new house and the silo, and the new farm machinery, and Virginia's aunt from Ontario who had come out to live with her mother; and their plans for the boys—they were getting more land for the boys who would go to the Agricultural College when they were old enough.

Virginia and her family belonged to that abundant rolling prairie of south-western Manitoba, with its poplar groves, and great wheat fields; its fine farm buildings, and intelligent people. Already the good work of the Manitoba Agricultural College was showing, and the Experimental Farm at Morden had demonstrated that roses and flowering shrubs, and even fruit trees will grow, with proper care.

No one can write about this part of the country without paying tribute to the foresight of Sandy Stevenson of Nelson, north of Morden, who grew the first apples in Manitoba.

He planted a shelter belt of trees, leaving only the south side open to the sun, and there he experimented with hardy apples and succeeded. That is in itself a thrilling story of one man's triumph.

I remember the first box of home grown apples I saw, exhibited on the railway station platform at Morden, for the travelling public to view. We looked on their shining faces with reverence. To us, it was a historic event.

Of course the Manitoba winters are cold, but they are honest winters, and on an honest winter one can depend. They will not deceive you in February by false signs of Spring which bring up the sap from the roots of a tree before its time, or stir the hens to thoughts of maternity. So the apple trees can be strewn with straw to catch the snow and the chances are good that the snow will shelter the roots from frost until it is time for all the processes of Spring to begin.

Then comes the first notes of the meadow lark, and the blue anemones carpet the pastures and headlands, and the whole country-side comes alive almost overnight. The umber furrows steam—the willows redden—the hens break out of their winter silence and the cattle leave the straw stacks to search for grass. Bright sunshine reveals the ravages of winter, the dustiness of the curtains, the window smears, the smoke-blackened ceiling, and house-cleaning comes up like thunder.

"We'll hurry with the house," the women say—"so we'll be ready to plant when the fields are dry."

It makes me homesick to think of it. I want to go back. That was, and always will be, my country. I was one of the children who found the pussy willows, and listened for the first meadow lark, and made little channels with a hoe to let the spring water find its way to the creek, and ran swift as rabbits when the word went round that the ice was going out of the Souris, and cried if we missed it!

I lay on the grassy banks in summer, and saw castles in the clouds, and dreamed great dreams of the future. I built my own raft to carry me down the creek—a raft which sometimes held, and sometimes sank—I never knew why, but it was all fun. These I remember.

I walked the dusty roads to school in summer, and faced the wintry winds in winter, and I knew the sting of frost, and the horror of being lost in a blizzard—these are but vagrant memories which gave to life the richness of contrast. No one can enjoy warmth who has not known cold, nor companionship who has not known loneliness.

It is a hard country, these prairie provinces, which called to themselves the sturdy of many lands. A land of quick growth, incredible growth, in its rich black soil, sudden changes of weather and killing frosts, when the gardens and fields are at their shining best. Over a smiling blue sky can roll a storm cloud edged with silver, from which can fall hailstones that batter the crops back into the earth. A farmer's financial status can be reversed in twenty minutes.

But we who grew up with the prairie remember her purple twilights, her phantom breezes, the smell of burning leaves, the ripe tints of autumn, the slanting snow. When I want to recall that feeling of security which then was mine, I think of the times I watched the snow falling gently in a criss-cross pattern between our house and the Methodist Church, as I stood at the den window, knowing that the children were all safely in, and doing their homework on the dining room table. I could see them through the open door, Jack, Paul and Florence. Jack was there, in an advisory capacity. Homework was no burden to him, but he stayed to help the young seekers after truth. The snowy nights were the occasions of reading aloud too, and while we never denied them the delight of sleigh-riding or skating on the fine nights, we loved the comfort of the storm, which held them at home. I knew what the Psalmist meant when he wrote "She is not afraid of the snow for her household!"

11

The First House

THE YEAR 1900 was a most important one for the McClung family, for it was then that we bought a house. It was a house with a history too, and when we apply that phrase we know it means human heartburnings. Happy is the house and happy the family that has no history.

The house was built by two young English brothers who lived in Canada a few years, and then went home to England and married two sisters from their own village. The two young women were typical English girls with clear skins, bright brown eyes full of wonder, pink cheeks and soft voices. The young men had told them great tales of prosperity in Canada and no doubt, the two girls thus wooed and won by the romantic young ranchers with wide hats and high boots had been envied by all the girls in their village. So no matter what came after, the sisters had had their hour of romance.

Their disillusionment began soon after their arrival. The "horse ranch" turned out to be a livery stable which was not paying great dividends. However their shock was not as bitter as that of Katrina in Sally Salimen's great story of the Aaland Islands, for these brides really had a house to live in. But it was a shock when they found that there were no servants and but little money for household needs and that the two men were not concerned about their complaints.

However, the two little brides struggled on bravely with wood fires and hard water and tried to learn Canadian ways, assisted by the neighbors who knew that their lot was not going to be an easy one. The two brothers were of that well-known Old Country type who expect a women to be so overpoweringly glad that she had found a husband she will never ask for more. Perhaps the fault is not in the individual but in their long line of ancestors, male and female, who have believed without question in the dominance of one sex.

Soon the pink cheeks began to fade and the pretty dresses grew shabby and the bright eyes were often dimmed with tears. The women were seldom seen outside their own home. Evidently the two young men thought that woman's place was the home, but they managed to have a good time themselves, dressed well, never missed a horse race and could always find enough money for their own pleasures. The families increased as the years rolled on and to the credit of the two young mothers the children were always well cared for.

After one of the big harvests the children began to talk about a trip that they were going to have to England. It was going to be the most wonderful trip that anyone had ever had, and in the best boat that ever sailed the seas, and everybody was going to have new dresses and new hats. It was during this period of high hopes that I first made the acquaintance of the families. New life seemed to come into the faces of the two women and the children wore their old clothes without complaint, thinking of the new dresses and coats that would be theirs when they went home to see their grandparents.

The trip was always placed one season ahead. In the spring they decided to go in the fall when the fruit would be ripe and they could all get roasted chestnuts. In the fall the spring would be a better time—the children must see the hedges white with May—daffodils and gilly-flowers in bloom. When this had gone on for two or three years the women stopped talking about it and one day the house was for sale. The families divided and moved away.

(I have lived long enough now to know the end of the stories I have touched upon in these pages—if stories can ever be said to end.

So I will cut into the future here to give additional information concerning the two families. Better days came to them, for the two women developed into good managers and good citizens and the second generation has done very well. Some of them now are filling important places in the teaching profession. The friend who brought me up-to-date on these matters had an explanation. "You see," she said, "the virtues of the mothers are sometimes visited upon the children, too . . .")

The house had a fine square of ground, which we proceeded to plant in potatoes to break up the grassy sod. And what a crop we had of Early Rose and Wee MacGregors! Then we planted a hedge of caragana to divide the lawn from the vegetable garden, and by the generosity of the neighbors who supplied the slips, we put in a lilac hedge on the east and north of the house.

In 1925 I visited Manitou and the lilacs were in bloom and in full fragrance, and I thought I had never seen lilacs so beautiful. They gave me the exalted feeling of the man who dug a well beside the road, even though he knew he would not return that way.

That was the first house we owned and it will always have a place in our affections. It had high ceilings and large rooms, a fine big farmer's kitchen, no conveniences and many architectural flaws, including a trap door to the basement. But we were not critical. It was ours.

The great day came when we got a carpet for the living room and dining room—a Brussels carpet made in Toronto and sent out to measurement. When we saw the great bulk as big as a sea serpent arrive on Adam McBeth's dray and laid down on the floor, we wondered would we ever get it spread out and fitted into the corners. Strangely enough, it did fit, perfectly, and its beauty made us glad. The ground color was a beautiful golden tan with great wreaths of flowers and scrolls dominated by one bright brown and orange speckled lily, exotic and wonderful like nothing any of us had ever seen. But I know now that it was a trigidia, that strange blossom that blooms but for a day. It's just as well I didn't know that this was "the mystic flower that dies in an hour" for being Irish and superstitious it might have darkened the great pleasure I felt, and made me apprehensive of disaster. I am not blaming the trigidia for what happened to the carpet but disaster overtook it in the first month of its life.

Fortunately we had one Epworth League social at our house, when the carpet was laid, and the two rooms were resplendent in their new curtains, wallpaper and paint.

But there came a night at the end of June, a heavy, thunderous night with racing clouds edged with white, when even the dog and cat were uneasy. It had been a blistering day of heat, but after sundown these ominous clouds rolled over the sky, and at ten o'clock, the cyclone struck us.

We put out all the lights, and waited in the kitchen, which was on the east and south of the house, away from the storm. The roar was deafening, and the lightning was continuous. When I opened the door into the dining room the wind slammed it back. But I saw the blinds standing straight out from the window frames—window glass in splinters on the floor and torrents of water pouring in, pictures dangling on their hooks, chairs overturned. When the storm was over there was a foot of water on the carpet, and our best books riding on it!

Wes was the most philosophical of all of us. "I never did like that spotted lily!" he said. The next day Manitou wandered about looking at the wreckage. Old Mr. Ross, having reached the years of retirement, and still being strong and active, accepted the mission of looking for lost articles, and spent the whole summer at it. One of the teachers, whose trunk had been blown away with the summer kitchen of her boarding house, was considerably embarrassed more than once, when the old man met her, and presented some article of underwear on his stick—and she, poor girl, walking out with her beau. It was painful to have to admit ownership! People were more easily embarrassed in the early nineties than they are now.

The day after the cyclone hot winds blew, and a bright sun shone and the waters dried, the glass was restored to the windows, and the carpet survived and lived out its days; every lily gleaming bright.

In this house Horace was born, in the early hours of a June afternoon. Paul, aged five, had been sent to school with Jack and Florence to have him out of the way and came back at four bursting with the news. Someone had told him on his way home. He raced upstairs, had a look at his young brother, expressed satisfaction, and took to the street. He rang all the doorbells in our neighborhood, and gave out the bulletin:

"It bin a boy. If it bin a girl, we would a called her Lizzie!"

Mrs. Sharpe, Mrs. Dales, Mrs. Chalmers, Mrs. MacTavish, Mrs. McNamara, Mrs. Turnbull, Mrs. Jones and Father Duffy were all responsive, and expressed their pleasure, but I fear the announcement brought no answering gladness from a couple who lived around the corner. They had no children and were annoyed by the children's shouts as they played in the long summer evenings. They had told us that they could not enjoy their evenings until the children were called in for the night, and so had to stay up late to get their reading done and then slept late. Their theme song, if they had had one would be: "Young Fry—Stay Away from Our Door." Paul knew this too, but in his overflowing gladness, wanted everyone to rejoice with him. So that doorbell was rung too. I would have liked to see my young son make his announcement at that house. Paul had a head of thick brown curls, and was wearing a badly crumpled Buster Brown suit and was no doubt fairly grimy, it being late in the afternoon. But it was a great moment and he still remembers it. And when I asked him about it he said: "Everyone was glad. Mrs. Sharpe kissed me, and Mrs. Dales gave me a candy. Father Duffy said a prayer but Mrs. ——— just rolled her head like this—I knew she was sorry she has no little boy!"

The house had four bedrooms, all upstairs with but one register in the hall to supply the heat. Here the children dressed in winter, one at a time for peace sake. At least that was the rule, but rules are hard to keep, and nine o'clock comes soon. When the three were getting dressed at one time the sound effects would have done for a Mexican Revolution.

But we managed to get them fed and clothed and off to school, comfortably dressed in their "Red River" coats, red scarves tied around their waists, knitted toques and "cardigans" which were thick stockings with rubber feet and were pulled on over their boots; the most popular type of shoe was buttoned, and had bright plaid cloth tops, introduced into Manitou by George Sharpe, son of Senator Sharpe. This eye-catching bit of footgear became every child's ambition and the ordinary leather-topped shoe seemed a poor thing by comparison.

We got a set of Dickens when the children were small and read aloud to them in the evenings. *David Copperfield* was, I believe, the greatest favorite. I remember how terribly we all felt over that awful scene where David was whipped by his cruel stepfather. I could see it was cutting too deeply into their young hearts, and so "tempered the wind to the shorn lamb" by doing some improvising as I read. Soon after this, Wes had an attack of bronchitis, and Dr. MacCharles was in to see him when Jack came in from school. He didn't go out to play as usual and waited until the doctor had gone, and then came to me deeply agitated.

"Will Dad die?" he asked me. I quieted him as best I could. There was no danger, I told him. His Dad was young and strong, and bronchitis was not serious. "But could it kill him?" Jack persisted. "Did it ever kill anyone?"

I had to admit it had.

"Well then," he cried, "tell me this. If Dad died, would you get married again, ever?"

I was not prepared for this so I must have hesitated.

"You wouldn't, would you?" he said, shaking me, his eyes full of fear, "you surely wouldn't. You know what stepfathers are like, and I've had enough of them!"

Then I knew what was in his mind and I gave him my solemn promise there would be no Murdstones in our family. I took him downstairs with me and explained to him that his Dad had put on more insurance for each child and that we owned the house and the drug store, and besides I could earn money teaching, so we would always have a home—this home, and there would certainly be no stepfather. But the best of it all was that his dear Dad was not going to leave us. He would soon be well again.

And that, by the mercy of God, was the way it was.

I got a vision that day of a child's need for security and the depth of misery which comes to the child of a broken home. Surely if parents knew what trouble and anguish they bring to the tender hearts of their children they would not let their homes break up for any trivial cause.

I have known women and men too who have borne insult and cruelty to hold their home together, and in the ignorance of my untutored heart I have often looked with something like contempt at the people who endured too much, but now as I look back, I regret the blindness of my eyes. Belatedly I pay tribute to some of these heroic ones, who "in time of storm held the ridgepole up and spiked again the rafters of the house."

12

The First Move

I FIND IT HARD TO LEAVE the happy life we led in Manitou. I remember how often I heard my mother say that the happiest days a mother has are the years when her children are small and she knows where they are at night, when she makes her rounds and listens to their quiet breathing. I didn't believe it then, of course. Nobody does. It's hard to see the truth at close range.

But now, seen through the light of setting suns, I know that the quiet years in Manitou is the part of my life I would like to live over. They were abundant days, with plenty of everything. Plenty of work and play, laughter and joy; the great joy of seeing the children develop and grow, and acquire distinctive personalities. Then there were the small excitements of getting ready for company and planning a child's party, getting ready for Miss Govier, who came spring and fall to do the sewing, attendance at Friday afternoon entertainments at the school, and for me the occasional call to substitute for a teacher who was ill or going away.

We had major excitements, too. There was the time we entertained the Epworth League Convention, with delegates from all over the province, and attended by the veteran founder, Dr. Francis

E. Clark. I still remember how delighted I was when the *Free Press* of Winnipeg asked me to report the convention for them.

One of the real thrillers for the people of our community came when the oil well blew in, in the Pembina Valley eight miles away. For a year or so the Pembina Valley Oil and Gas Company had been drilling quietly and with fluctuating hopes. Mr. R. N. Lea, who first saw the prismatic color of oil seeping out of the bank of the river, never wavered in his belief that the precious fluid was there in abundance. A few chosen ones were allowed to contribute. Two hundred and fifty dollars was the price of one share, and secretly we all cherished hopes of future riches. The showings grew better and better and we loved to drive to the valley to see the progress of the well. It was a beautiful spot, which might well be the setting of something great and mysterious. The Pembina River, clear and cold, rippled over multicolored stones, and although the stream in its normal flow was small, it had made a wide valley of great beauty between softly molded hills, feathered with poplars. Scarlet lilies grew in the meadows. Silver willows gave evidence of the land's fertility, and in the season of their blossoming made the air heavy with their fragrance. It was the place for picnics and drives and neighborhood gatherings—a photographer's delight. The hills had a character all their own and seemed to follow a precise pattern, with their grassy sides dented by small gulleys where young poplars and birches ran down to the water. I have seen it at every season, at all hours of the day and in all weathers, but I always got from it a feeling of peace and plenty. The houses on the hills and on the river's banks with the smoke from their kitchens climbing through the trees, the sharply-gabled church, small but dignified and secure in its tradition of apostolic succession, these all combined to make the valley a place for dreams. I think I can safely say that that particular part of the Pembina Valley had charm. Any good thing might come out of it, and we were confident that this spirit of well-being was a promise of something that would cheer the farmer and lift his load. We believed that here was a pot of gold at the end of the rainbow, which would bring comfort for the cold of winter and lights for the darkest nights, a reward for the patient men and women who had labored long and often with meagre returns.

I remember the hot summer morning the news broke. We were having breakfast in the kitchen, and I was admonishing my daughter Florence on the general subject of being careless about her possessions, for she had left her sandals at the sand pile the night before. The sand pile was a common playground, near a new house which was being built. I was telling her that she must go and find them at once. Just at that moment, Alf Garrett, one of the shareholders, came running in at the side door of the kitchen, shouting:

"Wes! We've got it! The well has blown in! Oil and stones came cracking up over the derrick with a roar like thunder! We've struck oil, Wes! George Lea rode in on horseback to tell us! Come on, let's go! It's a fortune!"

We were all excited and the youngsters joined in the general jubilation. Then up spoke the adaptable Miss McClung, she of the lost sandals, and with great satisfaction in her voice announced:

"Now I won't need to hunt for my sandals. I'll just get a new pair, now we're rich."

People came from miles around to see the flowing well. They brought bottles and cans to carry away the heavy black substance, which rolled down the bank. The management said we must now have more scientific drilling; we could afford to hire an expert now—sure we could. Even the doubters now wanted shares. We would hire the best man we could find and no doubt many wells would be sunk, and we decided at once that this greatest of oil wells would be called "Lea" for the discoverer.

Lea, Manitoba, would be a shining place on the maps of the future. We liked the neatness of the name. The balance of the story is quickly told. We got the expert, who was highly recommended by a certain oil company. He had had great success in Texas. He would know what to do. Perhaps he did. Troubles began. Machinery broke, tools were lost. Every misfortune that could happen to a well, happened to ours. The expert was sympathetic and tried to temper our impatience by telling us that oil drilling has always been a heart-breaking business, and at last gave us his opinion reluctantly, that our showing of oil was just a freak of nature.

The valley is still there and still beautiful. Orange lilies still bloom for the twelfth of July, and the fringed blue gentian still comes in September; the river still carries patches of oil. Mr. R. N. Lea, who held his hopes to the last, has lain now for many years in the little churchyard beside the weather-beaten church, and not many of the first shareholders are left.

Once every decade or so there is a revival of interest in the Pembina Valley Oil project, and once, in a flurry of enthusiasm, a new company was formed and a well sunk, but in a different part of the valley, for some unknown reason. But all through these long years the first well, day and night, summer and winter burns its beacon of hope, a sturdy flame, standing straight when the air is still, or veering with the wind as it blows. The people who go to the valley now for picnics can boil their coffee on its flame. But in this year of war, 1943, there are few young people left in the valley.

There came a day when we suddenly made up our minds that we would make a change. The drug store was prosperous. Wes had built a new brick building across the street with a hall above where the Foresters and Masons met, and sometimes socials were held. We had not only a good drug business, but a good book business too. No, no sandwiches or coffee. Drug stores, in the early years of 1900, stuck to their own channels of commerce.

But the hours were long, and Wes had a primitive Methodist conscience, and had to be sure that every prescription was right. He had two good assistants, but he was the only licensed pharmacist, and he was always afraid that there might be a mistake.

There was a mistake once, in one of Dr. McGillivary's prescriptions—Dr. McGillivary was the veterinary surgeon. One of the boys put boiled oil into a horse drench instead of raw oil, and, of course, that would have been fatal.

There were no telephones then, no way of stopping the bottle from reaching its destination, only to overtake the farmer with a livery team. Wes did this, and all was well. But it left him more anxious than before.

He developed an over-cautiousness—such as getting up at night to go down to the store to see if the doors were locked, and I could see the responsibilities were getting too heavy for him. His usual good disposition began to cloud over. I kept telling the children about his many cares, and they did their best not to add to them.

One day when there was some unpleasantness about a misplaced hammer, Jack wrote a rhyming explanation of the episode which he left beside his father's plate at dinner. I remember the summary:

"Good old Wes would worry less
If he were free from the store's distress."

And that seemed to be the situation, and I could see something had to be done, even if we had to live on less. I could not stand by and see Wes drift into a state of nervous exhaustion, and his fresh complexion dull down to the drug-store bleach.

So we sold the store and bought two farms, both of which were rented. Wes built telephone lines, with his friend George Ullyot, for one season, and the years fell away from him, and the whole family was happy.

There was a great movement towards outdoor sleeping then, and we bought a large tent which was put up on the lawn, and here the McClungs slept until well into November, a hale and happy family.

But one day, an insurance man, hearing that Wes had sold his drug store, came out to offer him an agency, and Wes became an agent for the Manufacturers' Life Insurance Company.

In 1911 we moved to Winnipeg, bought a house on Chestnut Street, and the whole tide of life changed. I remember the day we left Manitou. I looked back from the window of the train as it made its labored way up the grade past Luke Armstrong's buildings and

Elijah Harmer's big barn. We had the whole family with us, except Jack, who stayed behind to write his examinations. It was a bright June day, full of greenness and beauty, the air full of the scent of pea vines and wolf willow blossom. The hush of noon-day lay on the fields for the workers had gone in for their mid-day meal. Peace and plenty lay over all and every building, grove of trees, every winding trail seemed like an old friend from whom we were parting. I knew one pleasant chapter of our lives was ending and a sudden fear gripped my heart—fear of the market place; fear of high places; fear of the strange country. If I could have gone back to the safety of the known ways at that moment, I would have gone. Tears rolled down my cheeks, which, fortunately, the children did not notice. They were too full of joy at the great adventure, and too full of plans for the beach, for we were going to spend two months at Lake Winnipeg where we had bought a cottage. I kept my face pressed to the window, trying to subdue this flood of emotion which was really downright homesickness, premature but nonetheless real. You can't go back, I kept saying to myself; no one ever gets the chance to try the other way.

"The moving finger writes, and having writ,
Moves on. Nor all your piety nor wit
   Shall lure it back to cancel half a line
Nor all your tears wash out a word of it."

13

A Gentleman of the Old School

THE BIG CITY gathered us in when the pleasant summer at the beach was over. Mark, our youngest child, was born on October of that year, and quickly became the idol of the family, with his blonde curls, blue eyes and quaint wisdom. The other children were all at school and Jack had started at Wesley College. Every day was full of interest. I enjoyed my association with the Canadian Women's Press Club, when we met once a week for tea in our own comfortable quarters. There great problems were discussed and the seed germ of the suffrage association was planted. It was not enough for us to meet and talk and eat chicken sandwiches and olives. We felt we should organize and create a public sentiment in favor of women's suffrage.

The visit of Mrs. Emmeline Pankhurst and of Miss Barbara Wiley, also one of the British Militant Suffragettes, created a profound impression. The immediate cause of our desire to organize was the plight of women workers in small factories. Some of our members had visited these and we were greatly stirred over the question of long hours, small wages and distressing working conditions.

Mrs. Claude Nash spoke one day on this subject at a Local Council meeting, and as a result of this meeting she and I were deputed to bring pressure to bear on the government for the appointment of a woman factory inspector. We decided to go to see Sir Rodmond Roblin, the Premier, and if possible, get him to come with us to see some of the factories. She knew him quite well and I had often listened to him in the Legislative Assembly from the visitors' gallery. He was a florid, rather good-looking man in his early sixties, somewhat pompous in manner but very popular with his party and firmly seated on the political throne by what was known as the "Machine." He believed in the patronage system and distributed governmental favors to the faithful in each riding. However, even in all the exposures which followed his defeat in 1914, there was no proof that he had ever enriched himself at the country's expense.

Mrs. Nash must have had some political standing, for I certainly had not, and we got an interview. We found Sir Rodmond in a very genial mood, and he expressed his delight at our coming. Mrs. Nash was a very handsome young woman, dressed that day in a gray lamb coat and crimson velvet hat. I wasn't looking so poorly myself for I, too, had youth on my side, and we could see that the old man was impressed favorably. I told him I had just come to live in the City from Manitou and I mentioned the name of W. H. Sharpe (afterwards Senator Sharpe) and I think that Sir Rodmond took it for granted that I, too, was a good Conservative, or, as he expressed it, was of the "household of faith." Sir Rodmond had once been a lay preacher in the Methodist Church, and scriptural references came natural to him. He balked a bit when we asked him if he would come with us to see some of the factories and tried to get us to be satisfied with one of his deputies, but Mrs. Nash and I held firm, and much to our surprise, he consented. He called his car and we set out. He looked very well in his beaver coat, and his car was the most pretentious I had ever ridden in. The cut-glass vase filled with real carnations impressed my country eyes.

On the way to the first factory, the Premier, who sat between us, with his plump hands resting on a gold-headed cane, gave us his views on women working in factories. He believed in work, especially for young women. There was too much idleness now, with electricity and short cuts in labor. As a boy he had worked from sunrise, and before, until the shadows of evening fell, and enjoyed it. Happiest days of his life . . . running barefoot under the apple trees. Perhaps we were over-sentimental about factory conditions . . . Women's hearts were often too kind . . . but he liked kind women— and hoped they would never change. And these young girls in the factories whom we thought were underpaid, no doubt they lived at home, and really worked because they wanted pin-money. Anyway, working wouldn't hurt them, it would keep them off the streets . . .

Knowing what we did, we let the monologue go on. He advised us not to allow our kind hearts to run away with us. Most of the women in the factories, he understood, were from foreign countries, where life was strenuous (that word was in the first flush of its popularity then). They did not expect to be carried to the skies on a flowery bed of ease! It doesn't do women any harm to learn how money comes. . . . Extravagant women are the curse of this age.

We conducted the Premier down dark, slippery stairs to an airless basement where light in mid-day came from gaunt light bulbs, hanging from smoky ceilings. The floor was littered with refuse of apple peelings and discarded clothing. There was no ventilation and no heat. The room was full of untidy women, operating sewing machines, and equally unattractive men cutting out garments on long tables. We urged Sir Rodmond to speak to some of the workers, but he was willing to call it a day at the first glance. He was shocked at the filth of the place, and asked one of the women if anybody ever swept the floor. He had to shout to drown the sound of the machines. The woman shook her head and kept on working. Then we reminded him that all these people were on piece work.

We led the Premier through a side door into the foul passage where a queue had formed before a door marked "Toilet." We could see that Sir Rodmond was deeply shocked that we should know about such things but Mrs. Nash led the way, and I pushed him along from behind. We drew his attention to the fact that there was no separate accommodation for the women, and we did not need to mention that the plumbing had evidently gone wrong. We knew that he was soon going to bolt away from us, so we didn't spare him anything.

"For God's sake, let me out of here," he cried at last. "I'm choking! I never knew such hell holes existed!"

"These people work from 8:30 to 6:00, Sir Rodmond. Six days a week," Mrs. Nash told him sweetly. "But no doubt they get used to it." I am afraid her sarcasm was lost on Sir Rodmond.

When we got him up on the street again, he remembered an important interview he had promised, but we coaxed him to come to one more factory where men's shirts were being made, and all the workers were young women, and by promising him that this would be the last one, he came with us. This workroom was in rather a better building and some daylight came in from the windows. We wanted him particularly to see these young girls who were being "kept off the streets." At one machine a girl worked with a bandaged hand, a badly hurt hand and a very dirty bandage. At another one a girl coughed almost continuously. I asked her how long she had had her cold and she said she had no cold, it was just a bit of bronchitis she had every winter, but she daren't stop work for there were plenty more to take her place, and someone had to earn some money in their family, as their father was out of work. She said she had been lucky to get the job. The manager came over to speak to us, anxious to show us the fine product they were turning out. Mrs. Nash asked him how often the factory inspector came around, but he didn't seem to know anything about factory inspectors. "In fact," he said, "we hardly need one. All the girls are glad of the work. I have no trouble with them."

"How about the girl who coughs so much?" I asked. "Couldn't she be given a few days off with pay to get built up a bit?"

The manager regarded me sternly.

"The company is not a charitable institution," he said, "and makes no provision for anything like that. If the girl is sick, she can always quit!" He threw out his hands expressively in a fine gesture of freedom.

Sir Rodmond was moving towards the door, and we followed. When we got back into the car we could see that the fine old gentleman of the old school was really shocked at what he had seen.

"Now, Sir Rodmond," we said, "do you still think that these women are pleasurably employed in this rich land of wide spaces and great opportunities?"

Sir Rodmond let down one of the windows of the car and said:

"I still can't see why two women like you should ferret out such utterly disgusting things."

"Your factory inspector knows about these places," we told him. "We mailed him a list of them and described them, but he has done nothing. He takes your attitude: Why should women interfere with what does not concern them? But we are not discouraged and have no intention of allowing these conditions to continue. We would like you to appoint a woman factory inspector, a real, trained social worker."

Sir Rodmond grew impatient at that. "I tell you it's no job for a woman. I have too much respect for women to give any of them a job like this. . . . But I don't mind admitting that I'm greatly disturbed over all this, greatly disturbed," he repeated. "I'll admit I didn't know that such places existed and I promise you that I will speak to Fletcher about it."

With this understanding we parted, thanking Sir Rodmond for giving us so much of his time.

Our investigations went on. We were only amateurs but we did find out a few things about how the "other half" lived. We made some other discoveries too. We found out that the Local Council of Women could not be our medium. There were too many women in it who were afraid to be associated with any controversial subject. Their husbands would not let them "go active." It might imperil their jobs. The long tentacles of the political octopus reached far. So one night at Jane Hample's house on Wolseley Avenue we organized the Political Equality League, with a membership of about fifteen. We believed that fifteen good women who were not afraid to challenge public opinion could lay the foundations better than a thousand. Some good work had been already done by the Icelandic women of the city, who had organized the first suffrage society many years before, and the W.C.T.U. women could always be counted on and the same was true of the Labor women.

We wanted to get first-hand information on the status of women in Manitoba, and, of course, the whole Dominion. Then it was our purpose to train public speakers and proceed to arouse public sentiment. We would be ready for the next election and hoped to make our influence felt. We had all the courage of youth and inexperience with a fine underpinning of simplicity that bordered on ignorance, but anything we lacked in knowledge we made up in enthusiasm.

On a sudden impulse one day I phoned to the Premier's office when the House was in session and asked for an interview with Sir Rodmond Roblin, and to my surprise I found myself speaking to the gentleman himself, who in his most gracious manner assured me he would be pleased to see me and I could come at once, which I did. There in his private office with its red plush hangings and heavy leather furniture, I told the head of the government what we were doing and what we hoped to do. He listened with amused tolerance, but I was grateful to him for listening.

"Sir Rodmond," I said, "the women of Manitoba are going to be given the vote, either by you or someone else, and as you are the present Premier, it can be your proud privilege to have this piece of progressive legislation to your credit. I know what you're thinking; you're not impressed with the importance of this matter but that's because you never thought of it and you really should begin to think about it. You can no longer afford to take this attitude of indifference, and that's why I came to see you."

He looked up at me then and said:

"What in the world do women want to vote for? Why do women want to mix in the hurly-burly of politics? My mother was the best woman in the world, and she certainly never wanted to vote! I respect women," he went on, "I honor and reverence women, I lift my hat when I meet a woman."

"That's all very nice to hear," I said, "but unfortunately that's not enough. The women of Manitoba believe that the time has come to make an effort to obtain political equality. The laws are very unfair to women. I would like to tell you about some of them, for I don't believe you know, and what I would really like to do this afternoon is to have a chance to talk to you and your cabinet. It wouldn't take me long; I think fifteen minutes would be enough, and if you and the cabinet could be convinced that it is the right thing to do, it would certainly be easier, more dignified and less disturbing than if we are compelled to make a fight for it. But that is what we are prepared to do, if that is the way you want it. I wish you would call them in, Sir Rodmond, there's plenty of room here in your office."

Sir Rodmond removed the dead cigar from his mouth and his eyes hardened.

"The cabinet wouldn't listen to you," he said.

"You'd be surprised," I answered. "I'm really not hard to listen to, and I don't believe the cabinet would mind at all. In fact," I said brazenly, "I think they'd like it. It would be a welcome change in the middle of a dull day."

He could scarcely find words to express his astonishment and disapproval.

"You surprise me," he said slowly. "Now who do you think you are?"

"At this moment," I said, "I'm one of the best advisers you ever had in all your life. I'm not asking you for a favor, I'm really offering you help."

"What if I tell you that I don't need your help?" he said severely. "And that I think you're rather a conceited young woman, who has perhaps had some success at Friday afternoon entertainments at country school houses, and so are laboring under the delusion that you have the gift of oratory. What would you say to that?"

"I wouldn't mind," I answered. "I wouldn't even resent it. But I wish to tell you again, Sir Rodmond, as clearly as I can make it, that we are going to create public sentiment in this province, which will work against you at the next election. Did you ever hear that quotation about there being a tide in the affairs of men, which taken at the flood leads on to fortune?"

We looked at each other across the wide space of his mahogany desk and the silence was eloquent. Then Sir Rodmond's mood changed. His self-confidence came back; for a moment a doubt had assailed him. But the absurdity of the situation gave him courage. After all, what had he to be afraid of? His party was firmly entrenched, having 29 of the 42 members. He grew jocular.

"It would never do to let you speak to the cabinet," he said in the tone that one uses to a naughty child. "Even if they listened to you, which I doubt, you would only upset them, and I don't want that to happen. They are good fellows—they do what they are told to do, now. Every government has to have a head, and I'm the head of this one; and I don't want dissension and arguments. I believe in leaving well enough alone. Take the Indians, for example, they were far happier eating muskrats and the bark of trees before the white man came with education and disturbing ideas. Now they've lost all their good old-fashioned ways. No, you can't come in here and make trouble with my boys, just when I have them trotting easy and eating out of my hand. Now you forget all this nonsense about women voting," he went on in his suavest tones. "You're a fine, smart young woman, I can see that. And take it from me, nice women don't want the vote."

His voice dripped fatness.

"By nice women," I said, "you probably mean selfish women who have no more thought for the underpaid, overworked women than a pussycat in a sunny window has for the starving kitten on the street. Now in that sense I am not a nice woman, for I do care. I care about those factory women, working in ill-smelling holes, and we intend to do something about it, and when I say 'we' I'm talking for a great many women, of whom you will hear more as the days go on."

I stood to go. Then he smiled good-humoredly at me and said:

"Now don't go away mad. You know you amuse me. Come any time, I'll always be glad to see you." My smile was just as good-natured as his when I said:

"I'll not be back, Sir Rodmond; not in your time. I hadn't much hope of doing any good by coming, but I thought it only fair to give you the chance. I'll not be back, but it's just possible that you will hear from me, not directly, but still you'll hear; and you may not like what you hear, either."

"Is this a threat?" he laughed.

"No," I said. "It's a prophecy."

14

"The Women's Parliament"

E VENTS MOVED QUICKLY after that. The Liberal opposition, led by that gracious, kindly gentleman, T. C.
Norris, invited us to attend their convention and present the case of Women Suffrage, which we did and received respectful attention. The government newspaper sneeringly commented
that the opposition would adopt any platform which would bring
them votes, but we had no reason, then or later, to doubt Mr. Norris's
good faith. He felt that the time was ripe for us to press our claim for
the next year would be election year.

We determined to inform ourselves on the whole broad question of women's position before the law. We would present our
arguments with logic and would be careful about our information.
Our society was growing in membership and we had many excellent
speakers. Most of the newspaper women of the city were with us,
so it was easy for us to get publicity. Sometimes it even slipped into
the *Telegram*, which was the government paper. Life was pleasantly
exciting for all of us. We were a close-knit organization, alert, and
keen, confident and unafraid.

As we studied the position of women in the eyes of the law, we were appalled at the inequalities. I remember one day when I was leaving for a ten-day lecture tour I bought an Accident Insurance Policy for five thousand dollars at the railway wicket, paying two dollars and a half for ten days' insurance. I had often done this before but had never really read the blue slip which I had received. But on this day I went over it carefully. It contained some excellent clauses, all beginning: "If the insured be a male." It told how much he would be paid in case of total disability, partial disability, the loss of a hand or a foot or an eye, but always the sentence began in that ominous way: "If the insured be a male." I wondered what the company had for me. On the other side of the slip I found it. In a little enclosure, fenced off in black, as if someone were already dead, appeared this inscription:

"Females are insured against death only."

When I went back to the office I sought out the man who had sold me the policy and laid the matter before him.

"Why is it," I asked, "that you take a woman's money and give her lower protection than you give men?"

He said he didn't know anything about it, but he would find somebody who might know. The next man assured me that he didn't know that women ever bought accident policies. He didn't know that they could buy them, but he would take me in to see Mr. Brown; Mr. Brown would know. Mr. Brown did know. Mr. Brown knew so well he was rather impatient with me for asking.

"Don't you know," said Mr. Brown severely, taking off his glasses, as if to let his brain cool, "that women are much more highly sensitized than men, and would be more easily hurt in an accident, they would be a victim of pure nerves, and many a woman, particularly not a wage-earning woman, would like nothing better than to lie in bed for a week or two, and draw her seven-fifty a week. They would think they were hurt when they really were not, and there would be no end of trouble."

"But, Mr. Brown," I said, "what about the clause relating to the loss of hand or foot? You would not be altogether dependent on the woman's testimony in that, would you? You could check them up—if they were pretending, could you not?"

Mr. Brown's face indicated that he couldn't be bothered answering any more foolish questions. He put on his glasses, and I knew I was being dismissed. I thanked Mr. Brown for his information and told him that I hoped to have an opportunity of bringing the matter before the next convention of insurance men.

Mr. Brown looked up then quickly.

"Have the insurance men invited you to speak to them?" he asked sharply.

"No," I answered truthfully. "They haven't. But they will."

We began to get invitations to send speakers to the small towns and so were confronted with the need for money and it was then that a brilliant plan unfolded. To Lillian Beynon Thomas belongs the honor of bringing in the idea, which really swept us into victory. She had been in Vancouver, and heard about a skit put on by the University Women's Club there, wherein women assumed the places held now by men and men were the voteless sex, dependent on the chivalry of women, and not liking it any too well. It had caused much merriment and discussion and when Mrs. Thomas told the committee about it, at once they saw its possibilities, and proceeded to work on it. In an incredibly short time they had their plans laid. I did not know anything about it, for I had been out of the city for two weeks, and when I returned every detail had been worked out.

The plan of campaign was as follows: We would send a delegation of women to the Legislative Assembly then in session, asking for the vote. Sir Rodmond Roblin, we felt sure, would refuse. He already sneered at the Liberals for putting a suffrage plank in their platform, saying it was supported only by "short-haired women and long-haired men."

The delegation would go on Tuesday afternoon, January 27th, 1914; then on Wednesday evening we would put on our play at the Walker Theatre. We called it "The Women's Parliament" and there on the stage we would present a replica of the Legislative Assembly of Manitoba, made up entirely of women, for in this land of fancy which we were presenting, only women voted and only women sat in Parliament. Our Madam Speaker, Mrs. Frances Graham, would be magnificent in a purple gown with high hat of gold laden with white plumes, and we had two little girl pages in correct costume, Ruth Walker and Florence McClung, who would carry glasses of water to the speakers, distribute bills and call the members to the telephone. I do not think one detail was forgotten. There would be a Government and an Opposition, bills would be introduced, members would read newspapers when the opposition members were speaking, and the heckling would be constant and clever. The climax of the session would come when a delegation of men would be received, men who humbly asked for the vote, pleading their cause with real eloquence, as they asked for joint guardianship of their children, and a right to their own earnings.

The committee had decided that I was to take the part of Sir Rodmond Roblin, so it would be my duty to receive the delegation and reply to them. I also had to make the closing appeal on the real sure-enough delegation, which would take place on Tuesday afternoon, so when I arrived in the city on Saturday, January 24th, I was told to come to the Walker Theatre for the rehearsal of the play, and I could see that there was a busy time ahead of me.

That day of fate, Tuesday, January 27th, brought a heavy snowstorm but the Legislative Assembly was packed to the roof to hear the women present their case to Sir Rodmond and his followers. They received us at three o'clock and the members were in "Committee of the Whole" with the Premier in the chair.

Those of us who were presenting the case were seated at a table in the middle of the room and when we spoke we arose and bowed to the chairman, and then to the members on both sides of the House. We had rehearsed our speeches carefully and covered the question very well, we thought, and when we were through, Sir Rodmond did us the honor of rising from his chair to answer us. I shall never forget the strain of that moment. What would be the fate of our play if Sir Rodmond were wise enough to give us a favorable reply? If he had only known it, he could have pricked our beautiful balloon, and taken the flavor out of every bit of our humor. I sat there in a nervous panic, but I need not have feared. The orator of the old school ran true. He was at his foamy best, and full of the eloquence which Anatole France once described as "that which glides but never penetrates." I wanted to make notes. I did not want to forget his exact phrases, but I knew I must not write a word, so I just sat with every fibre of my brain stretched to absorb his diction and the exact tones of his voice. He was making the speech that I would make in the play in less than thirty-six hours. O, the delight of that moment! He wasn't spoiling our play. He was making it!

He told us how he loved his mother, and for her sweet sake, reverenced all women. The present status of women was highly satisfactory. Noble characters had been produced. "Any civilization," he said, "which has produced the noble women I see before me is good enough for me. . . . Gentle woman, queen of the home . . . set apart, by her great function of motherhood. . . . And you say women are the equal of men." He paused here dramatically, blowing himself up like a balloon and shouted at us: "I tell you you are wrong. You do your sex an injustice which I shall not allow to pass unchallenged. Women are superior to men, now and always!"

He never had a closer listener in all his life. I observed every gesture, the attitude he struck when he caught his thumbs in the armholes of his coat, twiddling his little fingers and teetering on his heels. That denoted a jocular mood. When he wanted to be coldly reasonable though fair withal, he held his elbows close to his body with the palms of his hands outspread. I tried to absorb every tone of his voice, from the ingratiating friendly voice, calculated to set everyone at their ease, even though they were in the presence of a great man, to the loud masterful commanding voice which brooked no opposition.

I could hardly wait to get home and practice it all before a mirror. Every sentence was precious and lent itself to caricature. I had had two good observers in the audience, Wes and Jack, who was then seventeen, and so I tried my speech on them and received their contributions gladly. Before I slept that night I had Sir Rodmond's speech all written down, and the next day worked it over to meet our needs. I was well satisfied with the result, and if I ever had any feeling of irritation towards the Premier of the province, all was forgiven, for I knew he had given me a wonderful speech.

The play exceeded all our expectations. It was certainly a great community effort, and its phenomenal success was brought about by many factors. It was preceded on the program by a clever and witty sketch which put the audience in the mood to laugh, and the fact that the people of Winnipeg were keenly interested in the political situation at this time and well acquainted with Sir Rodmond's type of oratory made it easy for us to put over our burlesque. Many of the people in our audience had been at the delegation the day before, and those who were not, had read Sir Rodmond's speech which was reported at length in the government newspaper. So when I welcomed the delegation of men who came to us seeking the vote, in Sir Rodmond's own words slightly overdone, the audience began to laugh. I praised the delegation for their manly beauty, singling out the leader, Robert Skinner, as a type of manhood unexcelled, and said that any civilization which could produce such a perfect specimen of manhood was good enough for me, and then I grew stern and swept the audience with the beetling brow expression of Sir Rodmond and pompously added: "If it is good enough for me it is good enough for anybody." And then I drew myself up and by my attitude dared anyone to contradict me. It was interesting to notice how the laughs began running over the galleries, into the pit and back again, and we were well away.

Elsewhere I have written a full account of this evening. In 1921 I wrote *Purple Springs*, a novel, in which the struggle for the vote in Manitoba became the background for this, the third and last of my Pearlie Watson stories. It is a work of fiction, but the part relating to the Women's Parliament is substantially a matter of history, although the characters are imaginary, of course. We gave the play twice in Winnipeg and once in Brandon, and had crowded houses on all occasions. We made enough out of the play to finance our campaign in the province, and there is no doubt that it was a great factor in turning public sentiment in favor of the enfranchisement of women. It is still remembered in Manitoba as a great burlesque, and over and above its educational value, a great piece of entertainment. Because it was such a factor in the advancement of women and attracted notice all over Canada, I am going to include the two newspaper reports.

We were particularly pleased that the government paper, *The Winnipeg Telegram*, gave us such an enthusiastic report. The writer there refers to the "Premier's reply" to the delegation as "a piece of sarcasm," but "burlesque" would describe it more accurately. "Sarcasm" is an ugly word which means, literally, the tearing of flesh, and our play was not intended to tear anybody's flesh. We had one desire: to make the attitude of the government ridiculous and set the whole province laughing at the old conception of chivalry, when it takes the form of hat lifting, giving up seats in street cars, opening doors and picking up handkerchiefs, pretending that this can ever be a substitute for common, old-fashioned justice!

The Winnipeg Telegram, Thursday, January 29th, 1914

WOMAN SUFFRAGISTS GAMBOL
AT WALKER THEATRE

Judging from the aggregation of femininity at the Walker Theatre last night, Winnipeg homes must have been masculine manned for once in their existence during the evening. The big theatre was packed to the roof with all ages and types of "the female of the species," undoubtedly as a demonstration of sympathy with the women who sought in vain the other day for the extension of the franchise to women in Manitoba.

From the standpoint of an entertainment, it was excellent and few burlesques or light comedy productions have ever met with a heartier response than last night's burlesque on the system of government as it exists today. The performers may have been amateurs, but they were only amateur in name. As a matter of

fact they were the real thing so far as woman suffrage is concerned so they were naturally quite at home in their roles, even
if they were a wee bit nervous at first. But the spirit of the thing
seemed to catch them all and consequently the performance was
an entire success, from both the point of view of artists and the
audience. The women who portrayed the characters of politi-
cians both in and out of office appeared to take quite naturally to
their parts; in fact, it might be said that they actually revelled in
their pretence of holding office and that secret ambition they all
shared is undoubtedly accountable for the great success of the
entire program.

Highly Enjoyable

It was an evening on "Woman Suffrage," held under the auspices
of the Winnipeg Political Equality League, and if last night's
production is any indication and the campaign in future meets
with as much success, the cause of woman may not be so hope-
less after all and the vote may not be so far away as one might be
inclined to fear. It must have given the leaders encouragement,
that is, if they could pierce beyond that veil of burlesque that covered every move that was made and every word that was uttered.
From the standpoint of the anti-suffragist, the entertainment was
highly enjoyable, the satire and sarcasm of the whole business
being too good to miss.

This was especially the case in the burlesque entitled "A
Women's Parliament" in which the actual leaders in the local
suffrage organizations filled the leading roles in the skit, which
for sarcasm and satire of the deepest kind would be difficult to
beat. In it was given an idea of a Parliament run by women, with
men disfranchised, and an effort was made to picture what might
exist if women held the upper hand in affairs of state, and made
the laws. As nearly as possible the "rules of the House" were followed and the routine proceedings adhered to as much as could
be expected under the circumstances. Petitions were presented;
motions were offered; questions were asked and bills were read.

One was to confer dower rights on married men and was presented by Mrs. W. C. Perry, while Miss Kennethe Haig replied for the government. The bill was presented by Mrs. Perry in a brilliant speech which, if one might be permitted to remark under the circumstances, was meritorious for its common-sense. On the other hand, Miss Haig's reply in opposition to the bill was equally good for its absurdity.

Equal Rights for Fathers

Mrs. A. V. Thomas, also on the opposition, presented a measure to confer upon fathers equal guardianship rights with mothers, which was also supported and opposed by speeches bordering on the ridiculous yet productive of mirth of the greatest degree.

The feature of the session, however, was the delegation of men who waited upon the government with a bill for "Votes for Men." R. C. Skinner led this delegation and presented the case for the men, while the Premier, Mrs. Nellie McClung, replied. Mrs. McClung's reply was the choicest piece of sarcasm that has ever been heard locally and was purely and simply a burlesque of a recent speech made in reply to the bill of the women. It was somewhat overdone, perhaps, but for the purposes of the entertainment, was entirely suitable.

Mrs. Francis Graham acted the role of Speaker of the House and was attired in a handsome cloak of lavender hue trimmed heavily with ermine, while her hat was a stunning affair, also lavender and surmounted by a huge ostrich plume. It was also notable that in the Women's Parliament, the mace was decorated with yellow and purple ribbons and several bouquets of flowers.

Characters in Burlesque

The characters in the burlesque were:
Speaker: Mrs. Francis Graham.
Premier: Hon. Mrs. Nellie McClung.
Leader of the Opposition: Hon. Mrs. W. C. Perry.

Minister of Public Health and Education: Hon. Dr. Mary
  Crawford.
Minister of Economy and Agriculture: Hon. Mrs.
  Lipsett-Skinner.
Minister of Public Works: Hon. Mrs. C. P. Walker.
Whips: Miss Mildred Kelly and Miss Ducker.
Attorney-General: Miss Kennethe Haig.
Usher of the Black Rod: Mrs. Crossley Greenwood.
Clerk: Miss Alma Graham.
Pages: Miss Ruth Walker and Miss Florence McClung.

The first part of the evening was taken up with a satirical comedy in an act entitled "How the Vote Was Won," by Cicely Hamilton and Christopher St. John. The sketch gave an opportunity to various types of women to demonstrate their attitude and consisted for the most part of bold speeches about how they would make the men toe the mark. It dealt with a general strike called by the women, who threw themselves upon their nearest male relatives for support until the franchise was extended to women. It had many weaknesses and most absurd situations but it was wonderfully well acted, especially the roles filled by Frank Keall, Betty Cubitt, Mrs. Skinner and Miss Phyllis Cameron King. The sketch was directed by Mrs. C. P. Walker and Mr. Keall was stage manager.

A somewhat humorous touch was given the proceedings by the rendition of suffragette songs "specially typed" by the Assiniboine Quartette consisting of George Best, R. C. Skinner, Russell Hawes and Howard Richardson. H. E. Davey rendered two enjoyable violin solos.

During the evening, an opportunity was presented the audience to sign a petition calling upon the government to extend the franchise to women and pamphlets dealing with the various aspects of woman suffrage were sold.

Winnipeg Free Press, Thursday, January 29th, 1914

WOMEN SCORE IN DRAMA AND DEBATE

Clever Satire on Provincial Events in Mock Parliament— Bright Sketch Presented

A sold-out house at the Walker Theatre last night testified to the keen interest taken in the activities of the Political Equality League.

The Assiniboine Quartette opened the proceedings with some suffragette songs and then the curtain rose for "How They Won the Vote." Originally the locale was London but the names of streets and so forth were cleverly changed to Winnipeg. It only took about half an hour of determined action on the part of his women relatives to convert Horace Cole, a clerk, to rabid suffragist sentiments. By a concerted movement among the women, the thing was simple enough. They simply struck work. Each woman left her employment and went to live with her nearest male relative until such time as the state should recognize her rights. When Horace arrives home, he finds the maid has left and his wife is conjuring with the steak for supper. The worst is yet to come, however. Before he was able to appreciate the force of the first blow, his sister-in-law turned up and announced her intention of staying. Mollie, his niece, also arrives. Also Maudie Sparks, his first cousin, and Miss Wilkins, his aunt, and Madame Christine, a very distant relative. All were firm in the intention of staying until men foreswore that pious fraud about woman's place in the world. Under the circumstances, it was not surprising to find Horace ready to enlist among the "Votes for Women" band nor even to see him mounted on a chair full of enthusiasm for anything which would once again ensure him the peaceful enjoyment of his home.

Miss Betty Cubitt made a dandy wife and Frank Keall a very forceful husband. Mrs. Lipsett-Skinner played the part of the sister-in-law, Miss Phyllis Cameron King was amusing in a double role, first as a woe-begone slavey and then as the niece. Other parts were genially played by Misses Eileen Fallon, M. E. Corwin, Ethel Hayes and John Logan. Staged by Mrs. C. P. Walker, there was no danger of anything but efficient business. During the ensuing entertainment, H. E. Davey gave a couple of violin solos which were enthusiastically applauded.

The piece de resistance was, of course, the Mock Parliament. The Speaker, Mrs. Francis Graham, was gorgeous in purple and ermine. Miss Alma Graham made a charming Clerk, and Misses Ruth Walker and Florence McClung were natty little Pages. Mrs. McClung asked the audience to remember that the conditions for the next hour or so were to be reversed. The women enjoyed the suffrage and allied political rights. The men were entirely without them.

Facetious Papers

Petitions were first in order, and some facetious papers were read. One by the Society for the Prevention of Ugliness prayed that men wearing scarlet neckties, six-inch collars and squeaky shoes be not allowed to enter any public building whatsoever. Mrs. W. C. Perry, Leader of the Opposition, then read a bill to confer dower rights on married men. In a clear, sympathetic voice, she made a strong appeal for poor, downtrodden men. But the government was adamant. The Attorney-General, Miss Kennethe Haig, with a composure and elegance which might be envied by many a real statesman and with the necessary leaven of humor, said she was keen on men.

Miss Frances Beynon on the Opposition side asked when the perambulating university site was to become stationary. Dr. Mary Crawford said that only five sites had hitherto been used and a letter from the Real Estate Association was in her hands requesting that the site continue to perambulate until every real estate interest had benefitted.

Truancy Officers

Asked if she intended to introduce compulsory education in the Agricultural College, the Minister of Agriculture (Mrs. Skinner) said no, but she had something just as good. She proposed to change the label of the bottle and introduce the best system of truancy officers this country ever saw. The truancy officers would be appointed by the government and responsible only to the government. They would patrol the back lanes and the roads, she continued, "I venture to presume, my friends on the Opposition benches, that my truancy officers will capture every man in the Province of Manitoba who is over twenty years of age and put him in the Agricultural College in St. Vital for a course of two years in economics."

Mrs. A. V. Thomas, a speaker of well known earnestness and power, wanted for the second time a bill to confer upon fathers the rights of equal guardianship with mothers.

The climax of interest was reached when a delegation of men, headed by R. C. Skinner, arrived at the Legislature to petition for suffrage privileges for their sex. Their slogan was, "We have the brains. Why not let us vote?"

Plenty of Satire

The Premier, Mrs. McClung, compared the gentlemanly conduct of the members of the delegation with the rabid courses of suffragists overseas. If all men were as intelligent as the leader of the delegation, she would have no hesitation in according them the suffrage. But such was unfortunately not the case. Mr. Skinner, with the customary hotheadedness of the reformer, had not stopped to think of that. Down to the south where men had the vote, it had been shown that seven-eights of Police Court offenders were men and only one-third of church members were men. "Another trouble is that if men start to vote, they will vote too much. Politics unsettles men, and unsettled men mean unsettled bills—broken furniture, broken vows and—

divorce. . . . It has been charged that politics is corrupt. I do not know how this report got out but I do most emphatically deny it. I have been in politics for a long time and I never knew of any division of public money among the Members of the House, and you may be sure, if anything of that kind had been going on, I should have been in on it. Ladies and gentlemen, what I mean is that I would have known about it." At the end of her splendid address, Mrs. McClung was presented with a bouquet of red roses.

It is reported that two members of the Manitoba Opposition had deserted the civic dinner and secreted themselves among the audience.

15

The Campaign

WE KNEW that one success was not enough, so we continued our campaign with increasing enthusiasm. I wish I could remember all the good stories that were told about the suffrage meetings all over the country. We really had a great group of women and I have an uneasy feeling that I may be overlooking some of the best of our workers.

There were two sisters, tall, handsome businesswomen, Lynn and Winona Flett, who contributed largely to the success of our cause. A good story was told of Lynn's repartee at a meeting in northern Manitoba, where the Smart Aleck of the little town was her chief heckler. He was a big, hulking fellow who had fortified himself with a few drinks to give him courage. Lynn had answered his questions good humoredly at first, for as a matter of fact our speakers welcomed hecklers. They added to the enjoyment of the meeting. Then the big fellow, growing bolder, said:

"Miss Flett, you're all wrong about women. They're too scared to ever do anything by themselves. Why, my wife is afraid of a mouse."

Lynn stepped over to the edge of the platform and took a long look at him, while the whole room grew still.

"That's queer," she said, with wonder in her voice, "I would have thought that the woman who married you wouldn't be afraid of anything. Certainly not a mouse—or even a larger rodent!"

And that seemed to meet with the approval of the audience.

I had some exciting times of my own. I remember one night at Ninga, Manitoba, when in the course of my address I told the story of the well-off farmer, who had left his three sons his three farms in his will. To Martha, the eldest of the family, who had worked like a slave to give the boys a chance to go to school, and received very little education herself, he left a feather bed and a cow, and for the sixty-five-year-old mother who had worked harder than he to acquire the substantial estate, he made provision in his will that she would have her "keep" with the youngest son. Not a cent of money, just her keep. Just exactly what you would leave to a faithful old horse who had served you well.

It was a good example of the barbaric attitude of the law towards women's work, and I told the story well, if I do say so, and the people were moved. That night the story acquired an interesting footnote. When I threw the meeting open for questions, as I always did, a good-looking, well-dressed man arose and said, with some sarcasm:

"Mrs. McClung is undoubtedly a great weaver of tales, and she certainly knows how to stir people's emotions, but," he went on, "we must be on our guard against these sob stories and retain our sense of balance."

I asked him to go on and be specific. What story had I thrown out of balance? Then he explained.

"That story about the sixty-five-year-old woman," he replied. "You said she was left her keep with one of her sons; no doubt the one who inherited the old homestead. She would go on living in her familiar surroundings, happy and willing to help her son's wife and family. She would sit in her own rocking chair and look at her own flowers blooming in the window. Your big complaint was that she was not left any money. Now tell me what need has a sixty-five-year-old woman for money?"

He sat down then and I let a few seconds pass in silence just to let that last sentence "jell" in the minds of my audience. Then I said to him:

"I thank you, sir, more than I can tell you. You have completed the story better than I could ever have done it. What does a woman of sixty-five need of money? Say it over, all of you."

I picked out a group of elderly women who sat at my right hand, and I said to them:

"Do you ever feel the need of money? Do you ever want to subscribe to a magazine, or give a donation to the Missionary Society, or send presents at Christmas without asking anyone's permission?"

They answered me with a resounding affirmative.

"You wouldn't like to have to go to your own son and say: 'Please, Johnny, give me a dollar and a half. I want to buy Lucy's baby a present!'"

Then I addressed the gentleman:

"With your kind permission," I said, "when I speak at Boissevain tomorrow night, I will add your contribution, giving due credit of course. You are a better weaver of tales than I am, for I never would have dreamed that any person in their right mind would dare to say that a woman of sixty-five should be deprived of her financial independence."

Usually I travelled in the day coach when I was moving about the country because I would be sure to meet some of our local workers there, but on one particular day near the end of the campaign, I went into the chair car so I could have a sleep. I was coming into the city from Broadview, and I had a meeting in Winnipeg that night, so I settled down gladly in a comfortable plush chair with my face to the window, glad to have a few free hours ahead of me.

The campaign was going well and my heart was warm with the evidences of an awakened electorate. I was glad to be living and having a part in a great movement. Never had I seen such loyalty and such close communion of spirit. I was grateful, above all, for the loyalty of my own family, from Wes with his generous endorsement of all that I did, down to the fascinating sweetness of three-year-old

Mark; Jack and Florence, aged seventeen and fifteen, and Paul, thirteen, Horace, eight, were all at school, doing well, and interested in all my activities. The household ran smoothly under the capable guidance of two good Irish girls, Elizabeth Armitage and Maggie Galway.

Usually I telephoned home each night just before I went to the meeting, and often began my address by saying:

"Settle down now and don't worry about my children. They are all well and happy, clothed and fed. The baby is in bed and all is well." . . .

I knew, of course, that my family affairs were the subject of much discussion. I was vulnerable in five places and I tried to guard against any grounds for criticism. The children entered into the spirit of the adventure too, and I still have a picture of Horace leading home his young brother, much spattered with mud, and one stocking at half-mast, hurrying him along the lane and in through the secret entrance in the back fence, saying:

"Quick, now! It's a good thing I got you before the *Telegram* got a picture of you—Nellie McClung's neglected child!"—this with bitter scorn.

With all this background of loyalty, I was able to speak and write, catch trains at any hour, answer criticism, with a minimum of fatigue, for my mind was at ease and my heart was light, and I often quoted the words from the Psalmist:

"The lines have fallen to me in pleasant places!"

It was in this mood that I sought the comfort of the luxurious chair car that lovely June day, 1914. It was one of those green gold days in late June, when the wheat is in the shot blade, high enough to ripple in the wind, a day to remember, a day to warm your heart when the tides of life run low, the sort of day that Tennyson had in mind when he wrote:

"A light wind blew from the gates of the sun,
And waves of shadow went over the wheat."

When I wakened I heard my name mentioned, evidently I was the subject of discussion across the aisle, but that was nothing. People who express their opinions in print or from the platform must expect criticism, and these people behind me were just the usual run of critics . . . and I would get along with my sleep. We were just leaving Brandon.

A man's voice boomed out above the vibration of the rails.

"Oh, you're from the east," he said, "and you don't know her as well as we do in Manitoba. Nellie McClung is nothing but a joke here and I can tell you that the Government is not worrying about her or her meetings. T. C. Norris is the fellow who should worry. He is the leader of the Opposition, and believe me his candidates lose votes every time she speaks."

I couldn't hear what the woman said, but evidently she was asking for more details, and he proceeded to develop the theme.

"She's a big woman," he said, "badly dressed, with a high-pitched and strident voice, a regular rabble-rouser, the rough and tumble type. Irish, you know; Shanty Irish, with big hands and feet."

He nearly got me there! I thought of my dear old dad's pride in the "sparrow shins of the Mooneys" which all his girls had inherited, but I kept my feet on the foot stool and my head between the sheltering wings of the plush chair.

Another woman interrupted him at that point and said sharply:

"She must have something, all the same. Do you really know her? Have you actually heard her?"

"I certainly have not," he answered. "I wouldn't go across the road to hear her. I know all about that woman that I want to know. The way she treats her children is enough for me. She has a whole raft of them, seven or eight I should say, and she just lets them run wild! All the policemen know them, I can tell you that. My sister lives near her and she often takes them in, feeds and washes them, just sorry for the kids."

"What about her husband? What sort of a fellow is he?" the same woman asked.

"Quite a decent chap from all I hear," he said. "I think more of him since I heard he's getting a divorce. No one blames him either. I guess he got tired of being pointed out as 'Nellie McClung's husband.'"

"Well, of course, that wouldn't constitute grounds for a divorce," one of the women said rather dryly, and I could feel that she wasn't much impressed with the narration of my shortcomings. "But you certainly have me interested, and I'm going to stay over in Winnipeg just to hear her. She's speaking there tonight; I saw it in yesterday's paper; I think I have it right here, and there's a picture of her too."

I could feel that she shoved the picture in front of him.

"She looks very neat and tailored to me. I wonder if you're not a little bit prejudiced. There's nothing wrong with her clothes, or her face either."

My first impulse was to turn around and "down-face" the gabby one and call upon him to name the sister who fed and washed my neglected children, but something held me back. I had let the conversation go too far for that. After all he was only repeating the gossip which I knew many people hoped was true. I knew if I turned around the women would recognize me and the situation would be a bit painful for the narrator. So I slipped on a pair of colored glasses which would make a good disguise. I could take all the chatter he could produce about myself, my clothes and the "impending divorce." I could take all that and laugh at it. But the matter of my children I could not allow to pass. I would not let him get away with that. But I wouldn't embarrass him before the women.

When they went away to freshen up before we arrived in Winnipeg, I had a word with the gentleman across the aisle. I took off the dark glasses and swung my chair around. Then I recognized him. He was one of the civil servants from the Public Works Department, a party heeler, and he knew me too.

"You said your piece very well, Mr. M.," I said cheerfully. "But it's a poor piece!"

The color went from his face. "What are you going to do?" he stammered. He looked around helplessly wondering if anyone were listening. "My tongue ran away with me, and I certainly feel cheap."

"Don't worry," I said. He was a pathetic sight as he wiped his forehead. "Just tell me one thing. Who is your sister, this good samaritan who feeds my needy children?"

"I have no sister," he said miserably. "I heard a fellow say that, that's all. You sure have me over a barrel. You caught me red-handed."

"Oh, it's not serious," I said. "And I can afford to laugh at it. You know it's only the truth that hurts, and your conversation did not show a trace of truth. It didn't even impress the women you were talking to. You've got to do better than that if you're going to earn your expense money. I know you used to live at Alexander, and you have been sent out to oil the machine."

We sat in silence for a few minutes, and then he said:

"Are you going to tell this in one of your speeches? I know you can make me look like thirty cents."

"No," I said. "I'll give you my promise. I'll never tell it, though perhaps when I'm old and gray and have time to sit down and write my memoirs I may give it a place, for you know it has some good dramatic features, but by that time I'll be too old to remember your name. In fact I have forgotten it now. So cheer up and look out at the pleasant country we're travelling through, bright with sunshine. The Irish people say: 'It's a pity that a fine day could ever do any harm,' and that's the way I feel about you. You're like a smear on the window, so I've brushed you off. When it comes to fighting fair and honest, you could learn something from the Irish, even the Shanty Irish!"

I found out that hecklers at a political meeting are a real asset, and nothing pleased me more than to hear that I was going to have opposition at my meeting. I tried to make sure that the opposers would not weaken by announcing before I began my address that there would be time for questions and comment at the end of my address, and that I hoped there would be frank criticism. One night I noticed an infuriated little man in my audience, who kept on snapping the case of his watch, and squirming in his seat. I did not allow his impatience to divert my attention from what I was saying, but I felt that a storm was rising.

When the question period came, he was the first one on his feet, and delivered himself of a strong tirade against women who desert the sacred precincts of home. When the audience showed signs of disapproval, I asked them to give a respectful hearing. He had been invited to speak and must have every chance to state his opinions.

I knew there was a fight on in this town, led by the local women, to secure the use of the school grounds in the holidays for supervised play, and opposed by some members of the School Board, and it occurred to me that he was probably one of them. His pompous manner, his use of big words, and the usual stock phrases convinced me that he took great pride in his public speaking.

He ended his tirade by telling me that I would be better employed, at home, looking after my children, for after all that was a woman's highest duty. I was always careful to reply courteously, and pleasantly, and so I thanked him for his thought for my children and assured him they were all well, and had good care and were not deprived of the privileges of childhood, shelter, food and clothing and the right to be happy.

Then I walked close to the edge of the platform, and paused long enough to get the strained attention of the audience, and said:

"You're quite right in saying that our children are our greatest assets. You and I are in perfect agreement there, and while it is true that you cannot do anything for my children, there is something you can do for the children of this community. Help the women who are trying to make the School Board see the necessity of a safe playground for the little ones. I hear that some tight-fisted, short-sighted, mean-souled members of the board are holding out against it, saying there may be windows broken and to pay for supervision is a waste of money. Of course I know such sentiments are foreign to you—for you evidently are a lover of children, even taking thought for mine."

Then the audience broke loose. The little man was the leader of the opposition, and happened to be the Chairman of the School Board!

It was one of the lucky chances which come to speakers.

Lillian Thomas and I were the guests of the Board of Trade in a western city one night at a supper after a suffrage rally in the theatre. We sat around the table when the meal was over and the discussion was informal and friendly. But there was one discordant voice, the Secretary of the Board, a young man, a violent anti-suffragist. I kept wondering what was back of his bitterness. Sometimes it seemed he was merely drawing us out, but as the wordy battle proceeded, he became more and more vituperative, even insulting.

"Women voters would be too corrupt," he said, "too dishonest. They would sell their votes and then under cover of our secret ballot, double-cross the buyer. Men would, in the main, remain bought."

That, of course, brought a laugh and some of the other men joined in, partly to cover up for the irate young man, who happened to be one of our hosts.

But again he took the bit in his teeth, and launched into an attack on women, reminiscent of the avalanche of abuse which John Knox had poured on Mary Queen of Scots.

"When the devil plans a particularly evil fate for man," he said, "he sends a woman . . . the only place women are safe is in a harem."

I wondered what his wife was thinking. She was a sweet-faced little violet of a woman, in a sheath dress of silver cloth, as meek and mild as a spring day. Perhaps she understood him and did not mind. Certainly her face showed no emotion.

But we had no intention of allowing this glib-tongued dissenter to disrupt the discussion by turning it into a bit of vaudeville chatter and I was getting ready to strike him out when I noticed that Mrs. Thomas' face had a rising flush and I knew I could lean on my oars and relax. Lillian was about to take over. Lillian's voice was always soothing but now it had a therapeutic quality as she said:

"I don't believe this is a time for argument. Mr. ———— speaks out of a sombre background, and arguments will not avail. The heart knows its own bitterness. This case calls for a psychiatrist, and as this is not even a court of domestic relations, I think we will have to pass on."

There was a sudden silence and I knew Lillian had exploded a mine. I watched the face of the little violet but she was calm as the night and looked as innocent as the white carnations on the table.

Before we left on the train that night we heard the story. The Violet was not a violet at all except in appearance. She was a bit of poison ivy. She could faint, she could scream, she could dissolve in tears but she always got her own way and she could be beautiful through it all like the movie actresses who can suffer shipwreck, hurricane or tidal wave without the loss of a single curl. There was a tragic story back of the marriage which explained the young man's distrust of women. He was the son of a rich mother and had become engaged to his secretary, much to his mother's dismay, so the mother in haste invited the violet to come out for a visit to save her son from the wiles of the working class. Violet was the daughter of her dearest friend in Toronto and she arrived, with six trunks, and proceeded to break up the young man's romance and engagement, and married him in a blaze of glory. Then she settled down to spending the family fortune, with complete disregard for anyone, including her mother-in-law.

16

The War

THAT SUMMER of 1914 ran like a torrent. Each day was full of excitement—meetings, interviews, statements, contradictions, and through it all the consuming conviction that we were actually making history. I do not think that any of us ever felt either tired or discouraged. Every day felt like the day before Christmas.

Trying to reduce all this human emotion to cold words on a page fills my heart with both joy and sorrow. I knew life had reached a pinnacle and we were standing on a high place, a place easier to achieve than to maintain. We were in sight of the promised land, a land of richer sunshine and brighter fruitage, and our heads and hearts were light. Whatever else can be said about us, one fact remains: We were in deadly earnest and our one desire was to bring about a better world for everyone. We were not men-haters as our opponents loved to picture us. Some of our most faithful helpers were men. We were not like the angry woman who cleans her house and beats her carpets to work off her rage. Ours was not a rage, it was a passion.

We saw ahead of us a world of beauty and abundance, here in Canada, the country which had no enemies, no ancient grudges, no hymns of hate. We were not a nation by any act of aggression, but by Act of Parliament. The whole world was wishing us well. Surely we were meant to lead the way to a better pattern of life, for to whom much is given much is expected.

Each Saturday night the inner group met for a conference and these meetings had some great moments, when wonderful plans were laid for our country's welfare. We were young and vigorous and full of ambition. We would re-write our history. We would copy no other country. We would be ourselves, and proud of it. How we scorned the dull brown Primer from which we had learned Canadian history! Written as it was from the top down with no intimate glimpses of the people at all. British history was a fairy story in comparison. At least it had action and color and dramatic intensity, with its Magna Charta and the Spanish Armada. We could still recall how thrilled we were as we read of the beacon fires that burned along the coast to warn the people that the dreaded Spaniards were coming, and then how the winds of heaven blew upon our proud enemies and drove them from their course. That was surely great reading, full of readers' satisfaction, right down to the last sentence—"Sixty-seven battered hulks reached Spain." That was history well told.

We had something to write about too. Surely the fight against ignorance, isolation, loneliness and ugliness could be made more thrilling than quarrels between human beings. I had often thought of this as I travelled through the country and saw from the windows of trains the untidy little towns with their old cans and piles of discarded machinery, broken verandahs, crooked blinds and unkempt streets. Emancipated women could remedy all this. It was not caused by lack of time nor lack of money. Its root cause was the absence of an idea. Nobody cared. Nothing had been done to stir the civic pride of these people and the burden of making a living was ever present, heavy and constant. Work should not be a burden, and is not a burden when people learn to work together. God had made ample provision for everyone in this country. There was coal in the ground, electricity in the air and every turning windmill proclaimed the power in the wind. All these would some day lift the burdens from people's backs. We had not heard the word "chemurgy" but we were dreaming of it.

The election held on July 10th, which we had hoped to win for the Liberals, gave us an unpleasant surprise. Sir Rodmond's hold on the country was greatly lessened, but he did retain a small majority of the seats. Our discouragement quickly passed. We knew the powers of reaction had been dealt a mortal blow and would crumble under the pressure of public opinion, and in ten months this came to pass.

Our family had moved to the cottage at Matlock Beach on Lake Winnipeg, forty-five miles from the city, and there, in the pleasant environment of a long sunny verandah overlooking the dimpling waters of the lake, I rested body and brain and came as near to perfect contentment as I have ever been. This was the fourth year we had spent the summer at Matlock, and surely the Lord was good to us to let us have these long holidays, with all our children happily at play in this interesting place. The cottage which we called "Kee-am" was a roomy one with five bedrooms. We also had a smaller one for additional sleeping quarters, known as the "Royal Suite." Our relatives, Percy and Eleanor Anderson, were with us and their two boys with our children explored and fished, swam and hiked, sailed boats and built rafts, ate and argued and grew brown with the sun and the wind. My sister, Elizabeth Rae, and her two daughters, had a cottage near ours called "Raveloe." The girls were near Florence's age and they had happy times together.

Looking back at it now, I do not think we had a care in the world. In my old cook book, mentioned in an earlier chapter, I still have the "Work and Wages" program which was tacked on the wall, wherein each boy except Mark who was still under five, and therefore honorably exempt from manual labor, could find his chores for the day. I baked the bread and I think every woman enjoys bread making. We had a fine big black stove with a huge oven, which could turn out eight loaves at a time. I also made many individual loaves in baking powder tins for the enjoyment of the junior congregation. These were called "lighthouses."

On August 3rd the newspapers carried the flaming headlines: "England Declares War on Germany." Grandfather McClung was with us then, and to him we turned for information. He was our best authority on international affairs. "What did this mean? Could it be possible that we were going to war? Who was the Grand Duke Ferdinand? Was there any reason that we should go to war over a Grand Duke? Couldn't we let them fight out their own battles?" Even Grandfather McClung did not know. He did not know any more than did Mary, the Polish woman, who brought us vegetables and eggs three times a week. Poor Mary cried bitter tears that day as she counted out the eggs.

"It will be bad times for Poland," she wailed. "Always it comes to Poland, the wars, the bloody wars, and I'll never see my mother now. Saving my money I have been for three years to bring her out."

We tried to cheer Mary by telling her that this war must be some mistake; it would be cleared up. "People are too civilized to go to war now."

When the men came home on the 6:20 train that night they had no further news. They told of the crowds around the bulletin boards, and the threatened stock crash.

Strange days followed. The crowds at the dancing pavilion grew less and less. A shadow had fallen, even on the children, who now made forts in the sand and asked us questions we could not answer. Cottages were being closed every day. We closed ours on August 24th and on that day I wrote:

"All Nature conspires to make us feel sorry that we are leaving. A gentle breeze blows over the lake and rasps its surface into dancing ripples that glitter in the sun. Blueberry Island stands out clear and bold and beckoning. The more tender varieties of the trees show a trace of autumn coloring, just a hint and a promise of the ripened beauty of the fall."

Before the turn in the road hid it from sight we stopped and looked back at the "Kee-am Cottage." My last recollection of it is of the boarded windows, which gave it the blinded look of a dead thing, and of the ferns which grandma had brought from the big woods beyond the railway track and planted all round it, and which had grown so quickly and so rank that they seemed to fill in all the space under the cottage, and with their pale-green, feathery fringe, to be trying to lift it up into the sunshine above the trees. Instinctively we felt that we had come to the end of a very pleasant chapter in our life as a family; something had disturbed the peaceful quiet of our lives; somewhere a drum was beating and a fife was calling!

Not a word of this was spoken, but Jack suddenly put it all into words, for he turned to me as we walked together to the station and asked quickly, "Mother, when will I be eighteen?"

It was a fine warm day, but I still remember that the blood ran cold in my veins. Dear Jack!

17

Westward We Go!

T HE FALL of 1914 blurs in my memory like a troubled dream. The war dominated everything. Some of my friends were pacifists and resented Canada's participation in a war of which we knew so little. Why should we step into the age-old feuds of Europe? No one profited by wars except the munition makers. . . . British peers held stocks in the Krupp Works in Germany. . . . One of the first guns captured from the Germans and set up on a village green in England with appropriate ceremonies was found to have been made in England. Was this good enough to fight for? War was a game, a plot against humanity, and would go on as long as the common people could be depended on to do the fighting.

These bold utterances did not go unchallenged. Chief among the Empire's defenders among the women was Miss Cora Hind. Her views were clear cut and definite. We were British and must follow the tradition of our fathers. She would have gone herself if women were accepted. Miss Hind saw only one side of the question and there were times when I envied her, though I resented her denunciations of those who thought otherwise.

The old crowd began to break up, and our good times were over. Troop trains were leaving the stations every week. Bands played in the streets. The heart of the people was heavy and sad. I saw one man saying good-bye to his wife and eight children, a pitiable, shabby group on the platform. His wife watched him go through her tears and put her grief into words:

"'E's that pleased," she said, "you wouldn't believe it. It's all right for him, 'e loves a fight. 'Any war is better than no war,' he says, but I say there should be a lawr to stop a man from going who has eight children. But what can a woman do but just take what comes. 'E'll be a 'ero and I'll be a drudge with bunions on my feet."

I tried to comfort her. I told her I'd much rather have her job than his and that she and her family would not want for anything. The whole Canadian people were pledged to look after the soldiers' families.

She shook her head.

"It isn't that," she said brokenly. "I've always had the burden, but I did hope that Bill would settle down and behave himself. . . . I like to see him coming down the street, swingin' along as if someone had left him a fortune. Did you notice how fine he looks in his uniform? . . . And now he's gone, and he'll be in the front line, I can tell you, and I am proud of him in a way, but I know him, and I know he's glad to get away from us, and that's what hurts."

What could I say to that?

When the train passed and all the women were waving and throwing kisses to their men, Bill was not at the window. His liberty had begun.

Unemployment grew steadily. The government had foolishly shut down the Public Works, making more people jobless. Sir Rodmond and his followers could do a fairly good job in normal times, but in this emergency they seemed to be helpless. They were out of their depth.

Excitement, unrest, anxiety filled the bars and excessive drinking added to the ills which the people vainly sought to cure. Drinking gave them a brief respite, but it took its cruel toll as always.

We decided to ask the government to open the Public Works and stop the sale of intoxicants, substituting coffee, milk and soft drinks in the bars. Sir Rodmond agreed to receive a delegation and one morning at ten o'clock we arrived, about a hundred strong. Ralph Connor (Rev. C. W. Gordon) and I were to present the case, and we filed into the Legislative Assembly where all the members were gathered except Sir Rodmond. A strange hush hung over the Chamber and we wondered what was causing this long delay. Messengers came in, whispered to the Cabinet members and tip-toed out again. The Assembly room had the air of a hospital corridor when an operation is proceeding down the hall.

At last the spell was broken by the appearance of the Premier, somewhat flushed and disturbed. I had often watched the sessions from the gallery, and knew by his appearance that the First Minister was about to break forth into a denunciation of someone.

He did not even observe the formalities of the occasion, but bluntly announced to Mr. Norris, the leader of the Opposition:

"I'm not going to listen to these people, Norris. They can't tell me anything that I want to hear. I tell you they're here for no good. You can stay and listen to them, they're your friends, not ours. Come on," he shouted, waving to the Cabinet and members. "We'll leave Norris to entertain his friends."

The Cabinet and members rose as one man and followed him out of the room like a flock of sheep. One of them, as he passed me, jauntily threw me a kiss, saying:

"See you later."

I had an umbrella in my hand and I'll never know why I didn't break it over his head. I was glad I hadn't, for it was a pretty one, but it would have given me great satisfaction to wipe that insolence off his face. However, the next time I saw him, the insolence had gone. It was in the courtroom in less than a year when the Cabinet ministers were on trial for misappropriation of funds in connection with the Parliament Buildings.

In the fall of 1914 we moved to Edmonton. Wes had a chance to go to either Vancouver or Edmonton to manage the branch for his company, and we decided on Edmonton after much discussion. My brother Will and his family lived in Edmonton, and that was one reason for our decision. Besides that, we believed that Alberta, with its mines, prairies and mountains, its newness, its incoming settlers would suit us better than the seaport city. It was a wrench for me to leave Manitoba where the other members of my own family lived, and where I had spent all my life since I was six years old. My sister, Elizabeth Rae, had just moved to Winnipeg, Hannah had lived there for some years, and George and Jack lived on the old farms at Wawanesa. Paul had spent his holidays at his Uncle Jack's each year with Harry, his cousin, and had such a good time that it was hard to get him back to the city when school opened. More than once I had to go for him.

It seemed a pity to move away from all this pleasant association and from our comfortable home on Chestnut Street and yet there were some compensations. I would get a chance to go back to my writing in a new province, I thought. I would shed all my political alliances, and go back to the work I liked best. I knew, of course, that the Liberal party in Manitoba would soon be in power, and I knew too that the women would be given the vote and that I could be elected quite easily to the Legislative Assembly. There had been predictions that I would be invited into the Cabinet, and probably be made Minister of Education, all of which was very exciting, and in my moments of exaltation I had great dreams of what I could do for rural education, especially among the foreign born.

But when the McCurdy strain in my blood dominated I grew cautious because of my inexperience and the fear of high places held me down to earth. "I charge thee, Caesar, fling away ambition" I quoted to myself sternly. I knew I could make a good speech. I knew I could persuade people, and I knew I had a real hold on the people of Manitoba, especially the women, but I also knew that the whole situation was fraught with danger for if I, as the first woman to hold a Cabinet position, failed, it would be a blow to women everywhere. I could easily undo all I had done for I knew the world would be critical of women for a long time. If a woman succeeded, her success would belong to her as an individual. People would say she was an exceptional woman. She had a "masculine" mind. Her success belonged to her alone, but if she failed, she failed for all women everywhere. With this in mind, I hadn't the nerve to go on to the sixty-four-dollar question. I said nothing to anyone, but it reconciled me to the move. I felt I was being let down over the wall in a basket.

However on the night we left on the Grand Trunk Pacific all my high thinking deserted me. All I could see was that group of kindred souls, men and women, the people I loved and have always loved. I was leaving them and my heart was desolate. I said good-bye to each of them and told them not to wait until the train left, and then I walked away without looking back.

The children each had their own group to see them off, except three-year-old Mark whose social life was still limited. Alice Fitzsimmons, our Irish housekeeper, had taken him ahead to the baggage car to see where Philip the dog was lodged for the journey. When the last "All Aboard!" had sounded the children came in, with boxes of candy, flowers and games and jackknives, parting tokens from their young friends. Florence was the only sad one and her sadness was for Manitou and Irene McNamara, her friend, and Olive and Clara Rae, and Pearl Sweet, her cousins in Winnipeg. The others faced the future like seasoned travellers, full of the joy of adventure. Jack, who always seemed to read my mind, knew I was feeling low, so he sat with me at the end of the car while the berths were being made up.

"Cheer up, good wench," he said, laying his firm young hand on mine, "fair stands the wind for Edmonton. Who knows what fortune waits us there. Let us be merry as we travel. To travel hopefully is better than to arrive!"

He had been studying Shakespeare and Ivanhoe, and he and I often carried on our conversations in the fine old English phrases.

Two years afterwards when I wrote a book of short stories called *The Next of Kin* I ended it with a prayer which I hoped might comfort other people like myself whose hearts were torn with anxiety and fear. It ended with this verse:

"Or, if our faith is still so small—
   Our hearts so void of heavenly grace,
That we may still afrighted be
   In passing some dark place—
Then in Thy mercy let us run
   Blindfolded in the race."

I look back now and see that this prayer was abundantly answered in my case. Too well! In my next re-incarnation my prayers will all be for light!

18

We Take the Bitter
with the Sweet

I F I SEEM to the reader too introspective and disposed to spend too much time analyzing and examining and reporting on my own feelings and reactions, let my good friend Laura Goodman Salverson take the responsibility. When she wrote me, after reading *Clearing in the West*, she said I had not revealed myself in that book. I was too objective, too concerned with events, conditions and developments. Autobiography should have in it the mind and soul of the writer. "Be more personal in your new book," she said. "Break down and tell all! We want to see you and know how your mind was working."

So far as I can see the truth, and I do try to see it, there was a queer streak of cheerful imbecility in me up to a certain period in my life. I believed easily, I trusted people: I grew sophisticated at last, but it came the hard way. I used to say, when speaking of the ultra sensitive folk, who spend precious strength in the indulgence of hurt feelings, that if anyone wanted to hurt my feelings they would have to submit their case in writing. I would not take hints, I was always ready to believe no harm was intended. Naturally, I drew criticism. I broke new furrows, and attacked old prejudices. I was bound to step on

someone's toes, and so did not resent criticism. I tried to follow
Elbert Hubbard's wise slogan: "Get the thing done, and let them
howl."

Shortly after going to Edmonton, something I said gave offense
to the Editor of the *Vegreville Observer*, Mr. A. L. Horton, and he
made me the subject of a scathing editorial in his paper. A friend of
mine in Manville defended me and sent me the papers. Among other
things Mr. Horton had said: "People pay too much attention to Mrs.
McClung. In my opinion she is a much-over-estimated person . . ."

I wrote him a note, telling him I had often thought so, too. (I did
not add Bernard Shaw's rider: "But who are we among so many!")
Mr. Horton gave me another editorial, saying he liked my spirit,
and inviting me to use his columns any time I wished—and I often
did, but all my newspaper controversies did not end so happily.

I got my hardest blow from a group of women in an eastern city.
They taught me the bitter lesson that there are people who slap
you on the back apparently in great good fellowship, but in reality
they are looking for a soft place to drive in the knife. I had gone to
Ontario on their invitation to lecture in the fall of 1915 and had had
a very successful tour of many of the Ontario cities. Before I left for
home, the executive of this group approached me on the subject of
giving one more lecture, and they proposed the terms. We would
each pay half of the expenses, and take half the profits, if there were
profits. They would engage a large auditorium and work hard and
make it a great success. They were full of enthusiasm, and our meeting went off well. We had every seat full, and they all seemed to be
very pleased. I left the city the day after the meeting, feeling that my
eastern trip had been very pleasant and all was well.

Then a bit of trouble arose. The proceeds of the meeting had
been so good that one woman decided that she would make me take
a fee, about one-third of what my share would have been under the
terms of the original agreement. I knew nothing of this until I got
an unsigned letter telling me that some of the women felt that my
share was too much, and under the circumstances, seeing that the
project was a patriotic one, wouldn't I accept a fee?

I was not sure that this letter had the sanction of the executive, and considered it for a day or so before replying. Then I got an anonymous letter threatening me that if I did not accept the fee the society "will make your name stink in the nostrils of the Ontario people." It was hard to believe that such language as this could emanate from the kind friends who had flattered me more than I had ever been flattered before. But I remembered one woman in the group with whom I had had an argument one day; she had shown the white of her eye like a bronco about to kick. I felt pretty sure she was back of the trouble, and I should have taken warning, for though I did not know her, I knew broncos and their ways. However, I still thought I was dealing with honorable women, so I wrote back telling them that the success of the meeting was a poor reason for repudiating their own agreement.

Then the fat was in the fire. The bronco woman went to the newspapers and gave them an entirely false statement saying I had demanded more than my share. This statement came out in newspapers all across Canada. I wired the president asking her to make a statement, and she wrote a good letter to the papers, stating the facts clearly. But the letter was too long for the average reader, and the damage was done. Anonymous letters poured in on me, the liquor interests rejoiced and the newspapers they controlled revelled in what they called "The Suffrage Meeting Scandal." If I had robbed a collection plate, or rifled a baby's bank, they could not have said more. Most of the western papers ignored the whole affair. The *Calgary Albertan*, the *Winnipeg Free Press* defended me. Mr. E. S. Caswell of the Toronto Library wrote to the papers there appealing to their readers to look at the facts. The money was paid in full and I received many letters from members of the society, expressing their regret.

Trouble is a sieve to test our friends; the small ones fall through. I learned something from this thoroughly unpleasant experience, but the cost was heavy. I lost something, too. I was never quite so sure of people after that.

In spite of this regrettable interlude I enjoyed my visit to Ontario. I could understand better than ever how bleak and bare the western plains must have looked to my mother when I saw the rich fruitfulness of the Ontario countryside with its apple trees bending over and the glorious coloring of the copper beeches and the hard maples. I had looked forward to my trip to Owen Sound, the port from which we sailed in 1880, and especially Chatsworth on the Garafraxa Road, where I was born.

I had been away thirty-five years, but when we drove the ten miles to Chatsworth, I could recall some of the places. Inglis' Falls was there just as I remembered it. So were many of the old rail fences, making a border of fancy stitching around the fields. There were the stone fences, laboriously built in the fond but false hope that now the fields were cleared of stones forever; there was the old Hamilton house on the bank of a creek, and Chatsworth itself with its one long street.

It had been arranged that I should speak in the Methodist Church at three o'clock in the afternoon, but before that, I was to be taken to the home of the Hemstock family, old and dear friends of my parents. I remembered that before we left Chatsworth in 1880 I had been taken by my mother to say good-bye to the Hemstocks and had been given full permission to eat all the blue grapes I wanted. They grew on a stone fence beside the house and were sweet on my tongue. I had often thought of them in those first fruitless years on the prairie. I hoped they would be ripe now when I was returning to these green pastures and the kind friends who lived there.

On our way from Owen Sound our car broke down and so the time allotted for the visit was taken up with repairs and there was no way of letting the Hemstock family know for they had no telephone and it was with a feeling of real guilt that I pictured the family waiting. None of them would be at the church for the meeting for, according to the driver of the car, all of the family were hard of hearing. The meeting was a big one and I would have enjoyed it very much if it hadn't been for the disappointment I knew I had caused the Hemstocks. It was about five o'clock, two and a half hours behind schedule, when we went to the Hemstock home—a fine big old farmhouse, with a covered well in front of the kitchen door, the stone fence purple with grapes, crocheted curtains on the windows, tidiness prevailing inside and out and everything as I imagined it would be. The Hemstock farm and family had not been withered by the years.

First to greet me was Mary, the deaf mute and my mother's particular friend. I knew about Mary. I knew that Mary could mend what other people would throw away. She could take away headaches by her gentle massage, set broken bones, charm away warts, take motes out of eyes and cure eczema with her herbs and would have been a leader among women—another Helen Keller, if she had been educated. When I was a lonely child on the prairie I had often begged my mother to tell me about Mary Hemstock and her grapevine quilt of which she had made not only the quilt but the pattern, and her hair wreaths and seed wreaths, her skill in bringing children out of convulsions and how she saved the frightened young heifer that had "slipped her calf" and wouldn't let down her milk and would have had milk fever and died only for Mary, who was able to quiet her.

And now on this bright fall day in 1915 I was standing on the well-scoured doorstep of the Hemstock home and face to face with Mary. And strange as it sounds, Mary knew me. She could not have known I was coming. She could not read or hear, but Mary knew me, and her little withered face glowed with an inner light. She made me understand that she not only knew I was a Mooney but she knew I was the youngest Mooney by making a stairway in the air with her hand, and when she came to the lowest of the six steps, she beat the air again and again to show me that was where I came in the family group which was in her mind.

She told me too, I don't know how, that my mother was the best friend she ever had and that my mother always understood her, which I knew was true.

She told me about the war and that she knew my boy was in it and that she was praying for him night and morning. She pointed to the east and then to the west and lifted her work-worn hands to the sky and I knew what she was saying to me as surely as if she had used words.

Fanny, the other sister, told me that Mary sensed things without being told and could always tell what the weather was going to be and when one of the family was sick, even "as far away as the Soble" Mary knew it and sometimes they had to hitch up and take her to the ailing one for she could not bear to know that anyone was in pain.

Fanny apologized for her father who was not on hand to welcome me.

"He put on his blacks," said Fanny, "at two o'clock and kept them on till half past three and then we knew you couldn't come until after the meeting. He's down at the barn now feeding the pigs. He does all the chores, and you know what chores are like. Visitors or no visitors they have to be done."

Fanny shouted all this at me and I shouted back that I did know about chores and I roared out all the story about the broken car which had prevented me from coming at two o'clock as planned. Then I went down the path to find "Father." I knew he must be a very old man now. The Mr. Hemstock I remembered was a big man with side whiskers, the leading man of the neighborhood who pulled teeth with a real forceps and settled disputes. He had been a strong objector to our leaving the neighborhood thirty-five years ago. Mr. Hemstock had not believed Michael Lowery's enthusiastic reports of the Red River Country.

"Green fields are far away," Mr. Hemstock had said. "And the farther away the greener the fields." It had been hard for my mother to go against Mr. Hemstock's opinion.

And now here he was, a thin little man in overalls, no side whiskers, just a little sliver of a man, but smart as a boy with a face like a wrinkled yellow Newton apple, but with bright eyes that almost twinkled.

With Fanny's shouts ringing in my ears, I roared at the old man and apologized for my failure to appear and told him how tenderly all my family remembered him.

The old man regarded me quizzically and I thought he was searching my face to find some likeness to my parents. He had put down the two pails and leaned against the fence surrounding the pigpen. We had shaken hands but he had not spoken a word.

"No doubt he hasn't heard a word I've said," I thought. So I redoubled my efforts and lifted my voice to a new high. I used sign language and gesticulated. Then in a final vocal effort I roared:

"Can you hear me, Mr. Hemstock?" To which the little man in the overalls replied quietly:

"My hearing is perfect." And at that I leaned against the fence too, and wondered if I would ever learn anything. When I looked up the old man was laughing heartily.

"I am accustomed to being shouted at," he said. "And I would have let you go on only I think perhaps you had better save your voice."

19

New Places and People

WE WENT TO ALBERTA in December, 1914. The first winter seemed too beautiful to be true, blue-eyed skies with soft white clouds, no wind, clear sunshine, children sleigh riding and tobogganing on the steep Saskatchewan banks, hockey games on vacant lots. I did not wear my fur coat once that winter. I was greatly interested to know that cattle and horses ran out all winter, finding their living in the straw stacks or pawing the snow to reach the prairie grass.

In my enthusiasm for the wonders of this mild climate I wrote to Miss E. Cora Hind, Agricultural Editor of the *Free Press*, and was soundly reprimanded by her for daring to think that Alberta had a better winter climate than Manitoba. Manitoba cattle and horses could do the same, Miss Hind wrote, but it was not humane or economically sound to let them run wild all winter. Manitoba farmers made provision for their stock, being wiser and more provident than the people of Alberta, and Miss Hind reminded me it was not well to judge any climate by one winter.

But I still think "Wintering Hills" has a pleasant sound, and I have seen cattle and horses coming in from the range in the spring looking hearty and well, their coats thick as plush. Old-timers assured me that the only thing that bothers the stock in running out is fences. They like to know they are free.

Edmonton to us in 1914 was a city of glamor. To the north lay the great white world of mystery, the land of dog teams, northern lights and undiscovered treasures. I met a woman that winter who had come from the north with her sixteen-year-old daughter, who had not seen a street car nor worn shoes and who was now homesick for the quiet of her northern home.

"There are too many people here," she said sorrowfully. "How can you know them all?"

I liked to linger in the hardware departments of the stores and see the prospectors buying their supplies; stately Indians in moccasins and beaded coats walked the streets. Prospectors were panning gold along the river. Farmers backed their wagons up to the banks of the Saskatchewan and dug coal without money and without price. One part of the old Saskatchewan Trail was paved with tar sands from Fort Norman. Surely we had come to an abundant land! The people of Edmonton interested me, too. "Janey Canuck," Mrs. Arthur Murphy, one of the best known of Canadian writers, was one of my first callers. Robert Service, the poet, had once worked in an Edmonton bank and his mother and brother Stanley were still living here; it was also the home of many missionaries, voyageurs and trappers and the whole atmosphere of the city was young, hopeful and full of surprises; expectancy was in the air. It may have been the high altitude which stimulated me, but I never felt better or more keenly alive. I could work all day and all night, and in addition to the duties of a home and a family of five I wrote the book called *In Times Like These* and several short stories that first winter.

Still, below the surface of my thoughts and forever dulling the pleasure of my many activities lay the blight of war and the dread of Jack's enlistment. The call was sounding; every day it drew nearer. I will not dwell on it here. In my book called *The Next of Kin* I have told about that fateful day when the boys left for Montreal, the 5th Company of the Princess Pats. Young and beautiful they were, boyish and yet serious; Freeman Kelly, Reginald Boyce, Clyde Smith,

Victor Horner. We knew they were leaving their childhood and youth behind them and that even if they did come back they would be changed, so it was more than good-bye we were saying to our boys. It was good-bye—forever!

In my diary I wrote that day, December 4th, 1915:

"This morning we said good-bye to our dear son Jack at the C.N.R. station where new snow lay fresh and white on the roofs and on the streets, white, and soft, and pure as a young heart. When we came home I felt strangely tired and old though I am only forty-two. But I know that my youth has departed from me. It has gone with Jack, our beloved, our first born, the pride of our hearts. Strange fate surely for a boy who never has had a gun in his hands, whose ways are gentle, and full of peace; who loves his fellow men, pities their sorrows, and would gladly help them to solve their problems. What have I done to you, in letting you go into this inferno of war? And how could I hold you back without breaking your heart?"

So I wrote that snowy morning when we came back from the station. Through the windows in the den of the Victoria Avenue house, I could see the wind whipping up the snow as it fell in the street, into ragged ribbons, opaquely white and beautiful; with the chill beauty of white crepe!

During that first year in Edmonton it was my privilege to move around and meet many of the people in the province. The Red Cross was in need of speakers and I gladly volunteered to do all I could. I liked this work, this going out among the people. The city people have too much done for them; they have too many choices and opportunities, but the rural people are often left to their own devices. No one knows this as deeply as those of us who have felt the shades of evening come down heavily and the long darkness of winter close around us like the walls of a prison. There were no radios then to pierce the veil of isolation. I was writing for the *Edmonton Bulletin* at that time and for some of the women's magazines in the east and from these I have refreshed my memory.

There were four of us in the party which toured the country north of Edmonton: Miss Isobel Sutherland, the owner of the Dodge car in which we travelled, Rev. R. N. Matheson of Namao, who drove the car, Pte. James Stockman, invalided home from France with a bad heart, and myself. We had a list of places where meetings had been arranged and with a map of the country and a tankful of gas we went out on faith. None of us knew where we were going but it was a bright September day and we were full of hope and enthusiasm.

We were hopelessly lost one day in the Pine Creek area, and were glad to see a man, an Indian, approaching. He was a plain, overalled, blue-smocked fellow with piercing black eyes and high cheekbones and when he turned to answer our inquiry as to the road we saw that the dark color on his face was not all due to ancestry. He spoke with a hesitant manner of a man who is not accustomed to answering questions, and he told us he couldn't very well tell us where to go but he would show us, as he was going out to the "Trail" himself. Here we had evidently a new sort of guide; hitherto we had not met anyone who admitted there was the slightest difficulty in finding the road.

"You can't miss it," they all had told us, but we showed them up, for we certainly missed it nearly every time. We gladly accepted our brown friend's kind offer to show us how to get to the trail for the autumn evening was closing in and we were due at the Mission at eight o'clock.

He stood on the running board of the car and directed operations. As we bumped over the beaver-meadow road, he told us many things, with his soft Indian accent slightly tinged with Aberdeen.

"I am going a matter of seven miles," he said, "and I am glad of this lift, for it is the first time I ever was in an automobile. I've seen them—but I never rode in one—till now. I am going to get my bread—I am no good at the bread-making whatever, and I have had none in my house for a week. It is lonesome to be without bread."

"Are you alone?" we asked, although we knew he must be. Surely no man could be so neglected, if he had people living with him.

"I am alone since—awhile," he said. "My woman died a year ago—and then my boy enlisted."

"You have a boy—over there?" we exclaimed.

"Yes, ma'am, since a year—he has gone—he is all we have—and he never said a word while his mother was sick, but I knew he was thinking, for we got the papers every week, and he read it to his mother and me—he had more learning than we had—and I could see, and so could his mother. The last night she said: 'It won't be long now, Steve, and you waited well.'

"She always was thinking about me, for she knew I wasn't smart to cook or wash, and she sent word to this woman, would she bake for me. She got Steve to go—he told me, after she had gone. . . . And the last thing she said was 'We've had a long time together, Ed, you and me and Steve, and now we're scattering out a bit, but we'll all come back together sometime—when the war is over. It's lonesome, just here, where the trail splits up into three, but it's all right— they all come together again, Ed, like the trails around the marsh.' She was a good woman and learned lots at the Mission, and she passed out like that . . . cheerful. . . . Then Steve, when we had buried her, got the minister from the Mission to tell me he wanted to enlist, and I said it was all right. . . . He came back in his uniform to see me before he went, and we fenced her grave, and Steve writes back often. . . . He's a good boy—like his mother."

Then suddenly it occurred to the whole four of us that the running board of a car was not the place where this man should be riding. We stopped the car, and we found room for him in the back seat by putting one big valise on the front. He was no longer a plain Indian with torn clothes and a dirty face. He was one of us—and one who had made a big contribution. We were all citizens of the British Empire; we were all of the great family of the Next-of-Kin, and, after all, what is a dirty face and a torn coat?

When we came to the place where he was going to leave us, we couldn't think of letting him strike out on the three-mile walk for his bread, when we could take him so quickly. So, in spite of his protests, we turned off the trail, and brought him to the house of bread, where a great barking of dogs and scurrying of children indicated that a car was a real surprise.

It did not seem so important that we should reach our next appointment in time to change our clothes, as that we should show a kindness to Steve's father and the husband of the woman who had gone fearlessly out on the lonely trail, strong in the faith that all trails meet again—somewhere beyond the marsh!

I'll never forget the sudden warming of my heart as the new tide of friendliness swept over me. I saw this Indian man for the first time and I knew that our changed attitude contained something precious and vital, the one thing that can take away the sin of the world, which is selfishness and pride and complacency. I saw the heroism of his lonely life, and blessed the Mission for the hope it had given to a dying woman and the two men she loved.

These moments of illumination do not last. Perhaps we could not bear their radiance if they did. We lost ours when we made our next stop and found a bitter feud going on between the people who lived on the two sides of the creek. They could not agree where the meeting should be held. So we had two small meetings instead of one big one.

The people "across the crik" were a bad lot and that was firmly believed on both sides. The stories were almost identical. Mrs. —— was too bossy, she ran everything, she wouldn't take anyone's advice. We met the two leaders and saw the conflict; it was not religious or racial; it was just plain human nature. Miss Sutherland, who had lived long in country places, believed these quarrels were undertaken as a substitute for entertainment. Mr. Matheson quoted from the classics to prove that a natural barrier breeds discord:

> "Lands intercepted by a narrow strait, abhor each other. Mountains, interposed, make enemies of men."

But I refused to believe that the gently flowing Pine Creek could be blamed for the trouble. Hardly stirring the rushes that lined its low banks and with scarcely a ripple on its surface, this placid stream that obligingly twisted around every obstacle could bring only thoughts of peace. Jimmy Stockman, the twenty-year-old veteran, with his tragic memories of the war could only shake his head and say:

"They don't know they're alive. I wish they could see some of the villages in Belgium."

Before we returned to the city, we had widened our own horizons, whether we did anything for our audiences or not. We did raise money for the Prisoners of War Fund, and the Red Cross, and we hoped we had strengthened the ties of Empire, which is a fine elastic phrase, meaning much or little.

At one meeting, when we appealed on behalf of the prisoners of war, urging the adoption of a prisoner by individuals, the first "taker" was an Indian farmer in the Andrew district, who walked up, laying his seven dollars and fifty cents on the table. Five white men followed his example. When we made the same appeal at Pakan, one of the adopters was a little Scotch girl who worked at the hospital, receiving twenty dollars a month. She said she could manage very well on what was left.

Pakan is one of the oldest settlements in northern Alberta and it was here that that intrepid man of God, Rev. George Macdougall, lived for several years, and it is here that two of his daughters, Mary and Georgina, lie buried; small white stones bearing their names and ages, and the dates of their deaths, stand on the river bank, leaning a little, as if the weight of the long years has been too much for them. It is forty-seven years since the earth was fresh on these graves.

Owned by the Methodist Church, the Pakan Hospital was financed in its beginnings by the Campbellford and Brighton districts in Ontario. It performed a great service for the people of a wide district and many tired feet went over its welcoming threshold. Christianity took on a new meaning, interpreted by the skilful hands of Dr. Lawford, the Superintendent, and his able assistant, Miss Ellen Berry.

The houses around Pakan, and there were many good houses even then, were plastered with mud and then white-washed. The earliest settlers were almost all Bukowinians and Galicians. The work of white-washing seemed to be done by the women. We saw one woman at work on a house near the road and we waved to her as we did to all the people we passed, but she did not respond. She was too busy to be picking up with strangers. She had put laths on her house first and was plastering in between the laths and doing it with such skill and speed that we forgave her for her lack of cordiality. Great artists can afford to be temperamental.

Into one of these mud-plastered, white-washed houses we were taken by Dr. Lawford. There was a splendid garden of cabbage, red and green, neatly fenced by twisted willows, and a well-kept farm-yard, where ducks and turkeys swaggered about as if they had read the market page and knew what aristocrats they were.

Mrs. Natchsan was sewing a very modern-looking article on a Singer machine when we went in, and although she could not speak much English she gave us a graceful welcome. She had been very sick, she told us, by gestures, and now her general feeling she described as "No Dobra!" But Annie, her daughter, sixteen years old, could talk well, and after a hurried conversation with her mother told us we could come in and see "The Room." She seemed to know we would like to see her mother's beautiful tapestries. The room was hung with the most gorgeously colored rugs, such brilliant blues and greens and purples, in strikingly beautiful and bold designs. There were more too, in a trunk, which was opened, and they were shown to us. Some old-country tapestries Annie said they were. We praised their beauty, but Mrs. Natchsan shook her head sadly. The no-dobra feeling was on her. What were all these trappings to one who had not her health? Mrs. Natchsan had pitched too many sheaves and raised too many children to enjoy life.

Pakan has a picturesque situation, on the high bank of the Saskatchewan, which in the fall of the year flows clear and zinc-coloured, but swift as ever. The last of the golden leaves were on the trees and made bright spots on the sombre grayness of the valley. Below the hospital and close to the water stands a gristmill, where the wheat is ground into flour, and this gave a welcome air of activity to this remote little outpost.

I was glad to have an opportunity to visit the Ukrainians in their own homes. Because the Government had not yet provided sufficient schools for the people of the district, the Methodist Church had three boarding schools in this area, and it was not long until the education given by the missionaries had an effect on living conditions. The boys and girls learned about fresh air, and tooth brushes, board floors and more windows and improvements came naturally.

The people belonged to the Greek Orthodox Church, and had their own bulbous-towered churches scattered over the wide areas, but the relations between the Methodist missionaries and the priests was one of neighborliness. The mission schools were careful not to interfere with any child's religious life, and the priests found that Dr. Lawford was a friend in need.

The Ukrainians had come to Canada to find freedom and a chance for their children, and they were appreciative of what the boarding schools were doing. The church was fortunate in its choice of missionaries, teachers and nurses, men and women more concerned with human welfare than with creeds.

One day in winter, Dr. Lawford was passing one of the churches where a number of men were standing at the door. They hailed him to stop and he, thinking someone was in need of medical aid, came in with his satchel, but their needs were not physical. For some reason their priest had not been able to come and so they had decided to press the Doctor into service. Would the Doctor say a few words, read a bit out of the New Testament and say a prayer, maybe? It would be too bad to go home without even a word of prayer. The Doctor was only too glad to comply.

Another time when Dr. Lawford was ordering a supply of Testaments from The Book Room in Toronto one of the priests ordered one for each of his families. Under the stress of pioneer conditions there is no room for the petty differences which loom so large when people become more comfortable.

One of the nurses in the hospital told me a beautiful story concerning a poor woman who had been fatally injured in a runaway, and had been brought in to the hospital in great pain. She was made as comfortable as was possible and a merciful drug was administered to wear off the sharp edges of her agony, but as the night wore on she grew more and more restless and distressed in her mind. It was a bitterly stormy night and it was not possible to get the priest but Dr. Lawford knew enough of her language to read the prayers for the dying. The only candles in the hospital were red Christmas candles but a row of these were lighted and placed at the head and foot of her bed and poor Mary Ragowsky grew calm and comforted when the darkness around her was lighted by their flickering gleams and she heard the strong words which had comforted her mother and her grandmother in the far away Ukraine, when they too were embarking on their long journey.

The missionary workers had their discouragements, of course. Children were sometimes taken out of school as soon as they were able to work and it was especially hard to persuade the fathers that education was a good thing for a girl. Early marriages were the rule of the community and were planned almost entirely by the parents. Many a promising pupil had her education cut short when some grizzled old widower thought a good strong red-cheeked young girl would be right handy around the house and it would be cheaper to marry her than to have to pay her wages. The father of the girl could usually be persuaded by a few loads of hay, or in extreme cases, a yoke of oxen. Women and children did not count for much in the grim battle for existence.

One of our missionaries told me of having to make a survey for the Missionary Board to ascertain the infant mortality rate. At one house, where only the father could speak English, he asked him how many children he had and found that there was some confusion in the father's mind.

"We only got seven now," he said. "But we sure have lost plenty. I don't exactly know how many. Seems for a while we lost them all. Pretty hard on a man to have all the time sickness in his house. Years now she cannot do much outside to help. And bygosh, even the kids get sick!"

"Have you ever had a doctor?" the investigator asked.

"Oh, no," the father answered. "We've had a lot of sickness one way and another, but thank goodness we've never needed a doctor."

That was the condition before the coming of the schools and the hospitals. But the Ukrainian and the Russian people as a rule were keen to give their children a chance and many a man and woman who went into that north country in their sheepskin coats to drain the marshes and subdue the wilderness lived to see the day that their children graduated from the University of Alberta, and I am happy to think and proud to record that the missionaries, teachers and doctors sent to them by the Christian churches were the great factor in helping these sturdy people to a better way of life.

I remember once, at a neighborhood meeting in the Kolakreeka School, hearing one of the Ukrainian young men make a prayer at the opening of the meeting. As a young lad he had been hired by Dr. Lawford to drive him on his rounds, and had caught the spirit of this pioneer Christian as he saw his labors of love, and surprised the Doctor one day by telling him that he was going to go to Edmonton, to work his way through college, and would be a minister of the church some day, and that is exactly what happened. He is now and has been for many years an ordained man in the United Church.

But when I heard his prayer he was a boy of perhaps eighteen, a fine square-faced lad with broad shoulders and keen gray eyes, and this was the burden of his prayer:

"Lord, send us more Christians, real Christians to let my people see the right way to live and have a good time, too. The teachers are good and the ministers, and the doctors. They're always good to us, not soft, but good. But Lord, send us Christian storekeepers and machine agents and government men. The missionaries and the doctors can't do it all."

I wished then that that prayer could have been heard all over Canada. I still wish it, for it touches the need of today just as it did then. More Christians, "not soft, but good" are the need of the world. People who let their lights so shine that others, seeing their good works, will catch their spirit. I like that phrase, "seeing their good works," there is nothing like actually seeing to bring conviction.

The hospital at Lamont, Alberta, which was part of the missionary effort of the Methodist Church, gave many a demonstration of
Christian brotherhood and far-sightedness. One of these I recall
with pride.

There were two Chinese girls of Victoria, who applied for admission in the coast hospitals for training as nurses and were refused.
They tried in Calgary and in Edmonton, but with the same result.
But they were gladly accepted at the Lamont Hospital. Dr. Archer,
who was, and still is, the Superintendent, had no race prejudice and
the two girls were received and in due time graduated with honors
and became valued members of the nursing profession.

Since 1925 the Lamont Hospital has had at least one Oriental
girl in training each year and their work has been uniformly of high
standard. This is what Dr. Archer has to say regarding the Oriental
question:

"We have never had any reason to regret the policy which was
initiated years ago. The sooner we in Canada can come to the point
where we speak and think of all as Canadian citizens and Canadians,
disregarding or minimizing racial origin, the better it will be for
Canada. Our American friends have done better than we have in this
respect. In my mind, it is partly because they magnify the American
citizenship. I do not know what the outcome would be, and I would
be among the last to minimize the importance of our British conventions, but it would appear to me to be very useful, if when people
become naturalized that they become full Canadian citizens, and by
virtue of that Canadian citizenship, British subjects. I think that all
the diverse elements which come to make up Canada are enthusiastic about Canada. Can we not make it a point to get closer together,
instead of tending to form the Nationalistic groups, somewhat separated by their origin and its culture?"

I thought of these two girls the other day when a young proba-
tioner at the Jubilee Hospital here in Victoria told me that she had
drawn a Chinese girl for her room-mate.

"I think I'm lucky," she said. "I feel I'll learn a lot and if I'd had
my choice of all the girls in the room I certainly would have chosen

her. She is so bright and intelligent looking. I think we're going to be great friends."

And so it seems Tennyson was right when he said:

"The thoughts of men are widened by the process of the suns."

The leaven of kindness has never lost its power and all through that vast north country it was working, in ever-widening waves of influence. The vibration even penetrated to an overworked, unhappy little girl, twelve-year-old Susie, whose widowed mother had unfortunately married a hard old curmudgeon. Susie's life became unbearable and her mother was unable to help her. There was no use sending Susie to one of the mission schools for her step-father would bring her back. The neighbours were powerless to help for they were frightened of old Mike's rages, but Susie and her mother had heard that there was a place in Edmonton where a little girl would be made welcome and have a chance to go to school and be well-dressed and well-fed. But neither Susie nor her mother knew just where Edmonton was. They only knew it was far away and it was a great city, for someone had told them that the bright lights could be seen for a long distance, shining in the sky. They did know the direction. It was over there!

There was no one they could ask, for Mike had forbidden his womenfolk to talk with the neighbors and Mike had evil ways of enforcing obedience. Susie and her mother decided that Susie would run away. A pitiful little bundle of clothes, a tin pail full of cracked wheat bread and a tin cup made up her luggage, and Susie departed one night when old Mike was sound asleep, so she had many hours' start before he missed her. It was in harvest time anyway, and he was too busy to hunt for her. The poor mother was afraid to tell him she had encouraged Susie in her flight and with good psychology begged him to go and look for Susie. Mike prophesied cheerfully that the wolves would eat her. But he was wrong.

Hiding in the straw stacks by day and travelling by night, milking a friendly cow into her tin cup and digging a turnip out of a farmer's field, and above all, avoiding being seen by anyone likely to send her back, Susie made her way without misfortune. Susie did her best to keep her hands and face clean by washing at creeks and in the cow troughs in the pastures and once she made bold to go to the back door of a farmhouse and was given not only a good meal but clean clothes by a kind woman. Susie was afraid to tell her she had run away, but being a child of some imagination, she made up a good story about being on her way to her Aunt's. The woman persuaded her to go to bed and have a good sleep and that was the only time that Susie slept in a bed. Susie was never quite sure of how many days she spent on her trip. Twice she got a ride, but the last time the man asked her so many questions that she got frightened. However, there came in the sky one night that warm glow of light which gave her courage to go on.

She was dirty, tired and ragged, but undaunted. In the gray light of morning she crept cautiously into the city. She came in on Namao Avenue glad to find the streets deserted, for little Susie was not afraid of anything but human beings. The smell of bacon frying brought her to a stop and her feet led her through an open door, and so it happened that Susie had her first meal, in a Chinese restaurant. Sam Lung was preparing to go off for the night when this queer little apparition appeared at his elbow. Sam took one look at her and then produced a slice of bread with a fried egg on it, hot from the pan. He took her out to the kitchen and put her in the rocking chair and said:

"Kid, you're lost."

But Susie shook her head and went on eating. Sam was accustomed to feeding all kinds of waifs and strays at his back door; this was the first time that a child had come in; Sam's pensioners had been cats and dogs. So he looked at her with another wrinkle in his already wrinkled forehead. He was wondering what to do with her. Susie herself solved that problem. For she suddenly felt that here was a man she could trust, so she told him that she was looking for the home where kind ladies took care of little girls and let them go to school.

That afternoon with a new dress, new shoes and stockings, a clean face and a neat head of bobbed hair, a little girl accompanied by a kind friend, a Chinese gentleman in his best clothes, arrived at the front door of the Ruthenian Home on Third Street and a new name was added to the roll of the pupils. This story has a happy ending, for Susie proved to be an outstanding pupil, and the hard life that she had led seemed to fall away from her. Word was sent to her mother through one of the schools. The last I heard of Susie was that she had obtained a teacher's certificate, had gone to the Normal School, and was teaching in a Ruthenian School.

20

Alberta Politics

THE WAR dragged out its dreary length. War maps hung on kitchen walls and were dotted with black-headed pins as we followed the course of battle. We raised money for the Red Cross and the Patriotic Fund in every conceivable way from autographed quilts at ten cents a name to personal subscriptions which sometimes ran into high figures. The newspapers printed many extras, and hardly a night went by without one at least. The boys sold them all over the city. When the first cry of "Extra! Extra!" punctured the night, lights appeared in upstairs windows, and front doors were hastily opened as we rushed out for copies. We were avid for news! We get it more easily now by turning a dial, but the news is the same—dark testimony to man's failure to live at peace with his neighbor!

Women worked then as now, but not in the well-paid jobs. In the absence of price control, the cost of living soared beyond all reason. We have only to look back at 1917 and '18 to see how thankful we should be for the measure of government control we have now. Farmers were urged to produce more and more, and with the mounting prices, they certainly responded. Sloughs were drained, pastures were broken up, groves of trees were cut down and every bit of land that could be put under cultivation was plowed and harrowed.

Nobody warned the farmers that they were lowering the water levels and destroying the natural protection of their land from drought, and so, unwittingly, the way was prepared for the soil erosion and crop failures which came all too soon.

But during the war years the rainfall was abundant and the farmers' dream of $2.00 wheat was reached. So at last the farmer could be patriotic and prosperous at the same time.

There were a few warning voices in the wind. I remember letters to the paper by someone whose nom-de-plume was "Economist," and these letters warned the farmers that "the high color of prosperity on the cheek of agriculture, was not the glow of health, but the flush of fever." I remember that sentence because of the aptness of its phrases, but no one listened to a croaker like that when the crops were abundant and prices rising.

Then came the end of the war, the 1918 epidemic of 'flu, 1921— trade barriers with the United States caused by the expiration of the ten years of reciprocity, which began in 1911, and the dark clouds of depression settled firmly down on western Canada.

Wiser people than I have written about this heart-breaking period and its causes and to them I will leave its economic aspects. None of us who lived through it will ever forget the tired rebellious faces of the bewildered farm boys who drifted from place to place, not wanted anywhere. Their hands were full of strength, they were willing to do anything, but it seemed there was no place for them; no wonder they grew hard and bitter.

Kind-hearted people did all they could, in supplying meals and bed tickets and clean socks, but that long depression and its destruction of youth was a sadder experience than the war.

We know now that there could have been great projects of housing, road building, reforestation, the making of parks and the conservation of water supply which would have taken up the slack of our manpower and enriched and beautified our country, but to all our entreaties that this should be undertaken we were met with the cry:

"We haven't the money!"

Professor Morgan of Toronto University has just written a star-tling little book called *The Morgan Plan for Perpetual War* in which he advocates that a nice quiet little war, played according to all the rules, would bring a remedy for the spectres of hunger and unem-ployment which stalked the country during these tragic years of peace. It is a satire, of course, but a clever one, with so much truth in it, it cannot be laughed off!

In 1921 I was elected to the Legislative Assembly of Alberta on the Liberal ticket, and in my support my brother, Will, cast his first Liberal vote. I was surprised when he told me he was going to vote for me and I took advantage of Will's lapse from his old loyalty and told him he might as well vote for the whole five Liberals, to which my dear brother replied sadly:

"I know I shouldn't—but no doubt I will. When a man begins to go downhill all nature is greased for the occasion!"

The five Liberals were elected in Edmonton but the party was defeated by the United Farmers of Alberta. The opposition num-bered thirteen, out of the total number of sixty-two.

I was not a good party woman, and I'm sure there were times when I was looked upon with disfavor. I could not vote against some of the government measures, which seemed to me to be right and proper, and I tried to persuade my fellow members that this was the right course to pursue. I believed that we were the executive of the people and should bring our best judgment to bear on every question, irrespective of party ties. The Hon. John R. Boyle was the leader of the Opposition and I grew to have a great respect for Mr. Boyle's judgment and political foresight.

It was a matter of deep regret to me that Mrs. Louise McKinney was not re-elected. I had hoped to have her companionship in the House. Mrs. McKinney was elected in 1917 and thereby became the first woman member of any Legislative Assembly in the British Empire. A portrait of Mrs. McKinney by J. W. L. Forster of Toronto now hangs in the main corridor of the provincial buildings in Edmonton.

Mr. Forster's fee for painting a portrait was $2,000, but because Mrs. McKinney's portrait was to be presented to the Province by the women of the Province, Mr. Forster generously agreed to do it for half this amount. The money was raised by the societies all over the Province and I like to remember how quickly the response was made. We had a refusal from only one society and the excuse that they gave was rather an interesting one. The president wrote that in view of Mrs. McKinney's temperance activities, a society which was made up of all shades of opinion could not ask their members to make a contribution. I was the chairman of the Portrait Committee, so I called the president on the telephone and reminded her that no matter what they thought of Mrs. McKinney's temperance activities, as first woman member in the British Empire she was entitled to this honor, but that under the circumstances I was glad they had not made a contribution, for we were determined that every cent paid into the Portrait Fund should be freely and gladly given. The society decided later they would make a contribution but the judgment of our Committee was that we would return it—with thanks.

The Portrait Project was begun in 1932 and while in Toronto, Mrs. McKinney had two sittings. She expected to return in the fall, and Mr. Forster hoped to finish the portrait while she was there. The weather was very hot that summer and when she came home after a speaking tour she was worn out with the heat and the constant strain of travelling and lecturing. The day after her return she was taken ill and was dead in a week, leaving the forces of progress bereft and sorrowful, for Louise McKinney was a great woman and a great leader. She bound her followers to her by her strong sincerity, her unselfish love, her utter devotion to truth. She certainly never flattered anyone, but her love for all of us was deep enough for her to tell us the truth, even if the truth was unpleasant.

I remember once I had prepared a reply to a group of some obstreperous women who were giving us trouble during the war, and I showed it to Louise, fully expecting that she would be pleased with it. I thought I had done a neat piece of business. She read it through carefully and said:

"You've certainly demolished their arguments, but you have made them ridiculous and there is no need to do this. These women are sincere, though mistaken. It is never wise to kill your enemy, even if you can do it and get away with it. It's better to kill his enmity, and then you have acquired a friend."

I knew in a flash she was right. Louise had a way of being right and I did not forget her gentle rebuke.

Mr. Forster finished the picture from photographs, Mrs. W. T. Ash, formerly of Edmonton and then living in Toronto, gave him her assistance. She was one of Mrs. McKinney's intimate friends. When the picture was finished Mr. Forster returned $800 of his reduced fee to be used for Temperance work in Alberta. This was his graceful and generous tribute to Mrs. McKinney's work. Visitors to the Parliament Buildings in Edmonton will look long at the face of Louise Crummy McKinney with her lustrous brown eyes and strong, sweet face and we who knew her well and loved her, venture to hope that her sweet influence is still felt and will ever be felt in the life of that great Province.

I enjoyed the five years I served as a member of the Legislative Assembly, but looking back at it now I cannot see that much remains of all our strivings. Mrs. Irene Parlby, of Alix, was a member of the Cabinet and I was in the Opposition, but we united our forces when questions relating to women were under discussion. One member in the House was determined to have all married women dismissed from their positions to make way for the single, unemployed women, but Mrs. Parlby and I were able to head off this piece of sex-prejudice. We contended that whether or not a woman was married was her own business, and that no woman should be penalized because of marriage.

Dr. J. S. State, who sat for a small constituency in the north, was my left-hand neighbor in the seating arrangement. He was one of the oldest members in the House and had served the scattered population of his constituency for many years. He was not a believer in having women in public offices, and I found out that he was very angry at having been placed beside me; to have to sit beside a woman was something he thought he would never be called upon to do, so he had gone to the Assistant Clerk of the House demanding that his seat be changed. Mr. Andison persuaded him to try it out for a day or two; someone had to sit beside me, and I might not be so bad. Then the tactful Mr. Andison told me many things about the old Doctor, his devotion to his people, and mentioned casually that he was a masterhand at puzzles. I did not know anything about his objections to sitting beside me, but I wondered why Mr. Andison spent so much time building him up. I acted upon the suggestion regarding the puzzles and the old man and I became friends over a problem of making squares with matches. When he found out that I was interested in puzzles the whole problem was solved, and I was careful not to work the puzzles too quickly for I knew he would like me better if I were slightly dumb, and honesty compels me to add that I did not need to do much pretending for the old man had some tough ones.

Another gentleman of the old school, who feared women's entry into public life, had a rougher passage than my good old Doctor. This one lived in one of the small towns east of Edmonton and had been on the School Board for years. After the women were given the vote in 1917, a woman trustee was elected, much to this gentleman's disgust. He declared he would not remain on the Board with a woman member, and at the first meeting arose with dignity and in a carefully prepared speech said that he believed that he could now retire honorably for he felt he was no longer needed now that women were prepared to take over the duties of men.

He expected, of course, that the whole Board would coax him to stay and something of this sort might have happened, but the new member was also prepared and she asked leave of the Chairman to speak. She was full of praise for the excellent work that the retiring member had done and gave a summary of his achievements—somewhat colored by a bright imagination—and moved that his resignation be accepted with regret but complete understanding and it was carried forthwith. The old trustee went out so surprised he did not even slam the door; he had never been praised so much in his life and was halfway home before he realized what had happened to him, and then it was too late.

I have spoken elsewhere of the Hon. George Hoadley and his excellent work for human welfare in the province of Alberta. He had been a member of the Legislative Assembly for many years and had been a Conservative. But seeing the tide of opinion flowing towards a farmers' government in 1921, he quickly changed his political label and was elected as usual, and in the new government was made minister of Agriculture and Health. He was perhaps the ablest man in the new government next to the Premier, John E. Brownlee, and in matters of strategy Mr. Hoadley was second to none. He always managed to get the business of his Department off to a good start. His reports were the first to be received and accepted.

Thanks to the foresight and courage of Mr. Hoadley, Alberta had the first Act authorizing the sterilization of the unfit in the British Empire.

Mental deficiency in the schools had increased from one to three per cent, and this seemed to be one measure of prevention. There was fanatical opposition from certain religious bodies, but, I am glad to say that our Opposition Party gave it our support. I saw the working out of this measure soon after it became law, when a poor distracted mother from southern Alberta came to see me, bringing her eighteen-year-old daughter who was not quite normal. She was, unfortunately for herself, rather an attractive girl and eager for life at all costs. She had never been able to get past Grade Three in school, but she was strong as a horse and as good as a man in the harvest field. Her mother was naturally fearful for her safety. In the neighborhood where they lived the young people had played cruel tricks, taking advantage of her credulity, and someone had written her a letter, purporting to be from a young man, asking her to come out for a sleigh ride, naming the place of meeting, some distance from her home. She made her escape from the house wearing the best clothes she had—her summer clothes as it happened—and when she had reached the place there was no one there and she had spent the night in the barn afraid of her father's rage. From this adventure she had caught cold and nearly died of pneumonia.

"I could manage her when she was younger," the mother said. "But now she goes into great rages and I'm afraid of what will happen to her. Her father has no patience with her and still thinks he can beat sense into her, but I know that she is torn by feelings and desires that she cannot control. And now there is another complication. There is a man ten years older than Katie, and he's not quite right either and he has been hanging around, and my husband seems to think it would be all right to let Katie marry him, but I know it would be awful, and I will never consent. I would rather see her dead. I think Katie has the mind of a six-year-old child, but no more, and surely she deserves our protection. Things can't go on this way. She's on my mind night and day and sometimes I'm afraid I'll go crazy."

I got in touch with one of the Doctors in the Department of Health and a meeting was arranged the next day. We got the father there, too. The mother was quite willing to have the operation performed and Katie given institutional care until she had fully recovered, but the father, a powerfully-built Scandinavian, resented the whole matter and was angry at his wife for going outside the family to find help. It touched his pride and he declared that he was well able to look after his own child. We reasoned with him and pointed out that the mother's health was suffering and the whole atmosphere of the home was one of tension and anxiety. The mother had told me about the unmerciful beatings that the poor girl had received from her father, but I had not mentioned this to the Doctor. The father seemed to have preserved just enough of the religion of his forefathers to believe that everyone had a right to propagate their kind, no matter how debased or marred the offspring might be.

"And besides," he said, "I cannot bear to think of Katie being hurt."

I wanted to break in there, but I was afraid he would take it out on the defenseless and distracted mother so I held my peace. The

Doctor assured him that Katie would be given the best medical care and would feel no pain.

"But it's against Nature," Katie's father protested.

Katie was not in the room during this discussion. She and the mother had gone out while the Doctor and I were working on the father, but at this place in the conversation, Katie came in quietly. Her father had his back to the door so he didn't know that she had entered. I saw her unfastening her blouse, then she pulled one arm out, exposing her shoulder. She moved across the room and stood in front of the Doctor. Across her shoulder lay an angry welt like a burn.

Her father stared at her with eyes full of guilt and shame and for some time no one spoke. The Doctor looked from the daughter to the father and his eyes were full of pity for both of them.

"I think this settles it," he said slowly.

Then he laid a paper on the table and handed the father his fountain pen.

"Sign here," he said. "Your wife has already signed."

Then he reached out his hand and shook hands with Katie's father.

"I give you my word," he said, "we will not hurt Katie."

I saw Katie and her mother a year later. The mother looked younger and happier. Katie was well and neatly dressed. Her mother told me that she was taking full charge of the chickens now, and in the evenings was doing Norwegian knitting which had a ready sale in the neighborhood. The home was happy again.

21

Singing Up the Hill

I T IS NOT MY INTENTION to weight these pages with political happenings. Nothing is duller to the average reader than a blow by blow description of other people's battles. Even the battle for women's emancipation, with its delegations, petitions, amendments, conventions. These have taken years of my life and other women's lives but the centre of gravity has shifted since then, and while I will not give way to regret that I spent so many years working for the equality of women, I cannot refrain from saying that the sight of women lined up in front of the Government Liquor Stores fills me with a withering sense of disappointment.

Of course I know women have as much right to drink as men. But I wish they wouldn't! It is not in keeping with their character. Children may get along with a father who drinks but when both parents are given to periods of indulgence it makes tough going for the children.

Almost every day the newspapers reveal the tragedies which result from this equality of indulgence: the little two-year-old found dead from a head injury after a party in his home, neither parent knowing anything about it; the nineteen-year-old girl who came to this city to visit her fiancé spent the evening in the beer parlor and ended the night and her life by falling through a hotel window; the carload of people who drove into the harbor after a night of celebration and the innumerable accidents, quarrels and broken homes and broken hearts—how can any person be calm and unconcerned who has any love for humanity?

Women could have sobered this country if they had willed it so; that is a sore and withering thought. Why do we hold life so lightly? We, the women who pay for it with sweat, blood and tears? How can we be indifferent to the evils which mar our creation?

But these bitter observations had no part in our thoughts while we were waging the battle for what we called the emancipation of women. We were so sure that better home conditions, the extension of education and equality of opportunity would develop a happy race of people who would not be dependent on spurious pleasures.

"These things shall be, a nobler race
Than e'er the world has seen shall rise,
With flame of freedom in their hearts
And light of battle in their eyes."

We believed that with all our hearts as we went singing up the hill.

The rural women of Alberta were the white hope of the progressive movement in that province. The Women's Institutes and United Farm Women were not afraid to tackle social problems and their reading courses and discussions showed serious purpose. The women of the cities were more likely to be entangled in social affairs and in danger of wasting their time in matters of constitution and procedure, such as "Who should sit at the head table at their annual banquet?" but there was real stuff in the countrywomen. I can see them yet, coming across the fields to the meeting, to the bare school house, carrying their sandwiches in one hand and a plant in bloom in the other; and it was not long until the school houses ceased to be bare, for the children were encouraged to raise flowers and shrubs by contests and prizes, and in many of the schools, too, the women put in equipment so that hot lunches could be served in the winter time.

Alberta led all the provinces, too, in the matter of public health. The first four health nurses were appointed in 1917. Alberta also had the first municipal hospitals and free dental and medical care for school children.

A new province, such as Alberta was then, naturally attracted the adventurous people of the older parts of Canada. People who were not afraid to go out like Abraham, not knowing whither. The critics of this province had described Alberta as the laboratory guinea pig on which social experiments had been tried for the whole continent. But in these experiments great ideas have come to life.

William Aberhart, one of Calgary's high school principals (and one of the best in the province), while marking examination papers in Edmonton, asked one of his fellow examiners to give him a book to read one night as they parted. The book happened to be one on Social Credit by Maurice Colborne, the actor. Mr. Aberhart was a radio commentator, and naturally was looking for interesting material for his listening audience. As he explained Social Credit to them he convinced himself.

The eager-minded Albertans took to the plan, and the promise of $25.00 a month for everyone sounded like the golden promise of a fairy godmother. It just couldn't be! But, after all, who knows? There might be something in it. Social Credit associations were formed all over the province, and put a candidate in every field. A good story was told during this election—not however good enough to stem the Social Credit flood. A prospector once approached the heavenly kingdom, footsore and weary, but was refused admittance. St. Peter said they were simply swamped with prospectors and simply could not admit any more for at least an eon. The old prospector was naturally disappointed but he was not the sort of man who would give up easily and he knew the mentality of prospectors. So he asked permission to put up a sign on the celestial wall—a small, insignificant sign, which read: "Great Gold Strike on Nehanni River."

That was all. Then he sat down outside by the gate and waited. The news spread like wildfire and soon there came pouring out of the gate a stream of prospectors, complete with tools, earthward bound.

St. Peter beckoned to the old man and told him the glad news. He could go in. But the old man hesitated, he seemed somewhat uneasy as he looked after the disappearing line of prospectors. He suddenly picked up his pick and set off in haste to join the exodus. As he passed down the airway he was heard to murmur: "You never know—there may be something in this."

Always in Alberta there is a fresh wind blowing. It began to blow when the farmers organized during the First War and swept away the Liberal government in 1921. They were an eager, earnest group of people, that first farmers' government, burning with zeal to banish forever the taint of party politics. They had convinced each other there was no health in either of the old parties. They knew there must be dark scandals to be uncovered in the Big House under the hill. So their first act was to conduct an audit of the books at a cost of $40,000, only to find that all was in order. It was a blow to the young crusaders but they settled down to give much the same service as their predecessors had given.

The women of Alberta have always been tireless in their pursuit of knowledge and human betterment. One of the newspaper women, Mrs. McCorqudale of High River, in the *Calgary Herald*, once wrote that she would be able to tell the Alberta women when she goes to Heaven; they will be there in little groups with pencil and note-books, by the side of the river of life giving the finishing touches to resolution B.72894 urging that more rural children be taken into the Heavenly Choirs.

To the province of Alberta belongs the credit for clearing up the vexed question of whether or not women are persons, according to the laws of the British Empire.

The legal gentleman who started the agitation of whether or not women are persons must not be blamed for his part in it. He had not intended to further the cause of women. Not at all. He was convinced that women had already gone too far. He was a very angry young man who had lost a case in the Women's Court in Edmonton, and in his indignation had denounced the Magistrate, the first woman Magistrate in Canada, by telling her that her appointment was illegal, for women are not persons in the eyes of the law, and never have been.

Magistrate Emily Murphy took this without blinking an eye but was too wise a woman to make the mistake of underestimating an opponent's argument. So she looked into the matter carefully, and sure enough there it was in the common law of England, enacted in 1876 and not yet rescinded.

That is how it all began. The displacement of a small stone on the side of a mountain can start an avalanche. The enactment of 1876 had come about by the action of one person, too. A woman, in England this time. She knew that certain women once had the privilege of voting, but it had been taken away from them when they weren't looking, so she decided that she would vote and would see what would happen. She went out on election day, beguiled the poll clerk into giving her a ballot, and voted!

She was arrested for this misdemeanor and tried, and out of this case—Charlton vs. Ling—came a ruling on the matter in dispute, and this is the ruling: "Women are persons in matters of pains and penalties, but are not persons in matters of rights and privileges."

There was no doubt that this law was still valid though public opinion had rendered it obsolete. Mrs. Murphy, as well as others of us, had interviewed honorable gentlemen at Ottawa from time to time on the matter of appointing women to the Senate, and we had received the same reply. The gentlemen would like nothing better than to have women in the Senate but the British North America Act made no provision for women and the members feared that women could not be appointed to the Senate until this great foundation of our liberties was amended and that would take time and careful thought.

On one occasion Madame Marchand and I went to see the Hon. Arthur Meighan and when he brought out this same answer the witty Frenchwoman flashed at him:

"And for what are we paying you, and the other gentlemen, if it is not to keep our laws up-to-date?"

But still time went on and nothing happened. One day, near the end of August in 1927, Mrs. Murphy called in four of us: Mrs. Irene Parlby, a member of the Alberta Cabinet; Mrs. Louise McKinney, ex-M.L.A.; Mrs. Henrietta Edwards, author of a book entitled *Laws Relating to Women*; and myself. We gathered at Mrs. Murphy's home in South Edmonton. It was a perfect day in harvest time. Blue haze lay on the horizon, and the air was filled with the smell of ripening grain. Bees droned in the delphiniums and roses in her garden as we sat on the verandah and discussed many things.

Mrs. Murphy had a plan to lay before us. She told us that any five people, British subjects, can ask for an interpretation of any Act, and she had decided that we would petition Parliament to give us their interpretation of the clause in the B.N.A. Act which deals with Senate appointments, reading, "From time to time properly qualified persons may be summoned to the Senate." We put our names to the petition and it was sent to Ottawa.

I wish I had a copy of the letter which accompanied the petition, for Mrs. Murphy was a master craftsman in the handling of a pen. She had no difficulty in finding the apt word.

The Prime Minister to whom the petition was sent referred it to the Minister of Justice, and his Department referred the matter to the Supreme Court of Canada, and time went on. The Supreme Court of Canada did not render a decision until April 24th, 1928, and then in the newspaper we read that in the opinion of the Supreme Court of Canada, women are not persons.

Four out of the five judges based their judgment on the Common Law Disability of Women to hold public office. The other one believed the word "person" in the B.N.A. Act meant male person because the framers of the Act had only men in mind when the clause was written.

We met again and contemplated our defeat. Mrs. Murphy was still undaunted. We would appeal from the Supreme Court's decision. We would send our petition to the Privy Council. We asked what we would use for money for we knew that lawyer's fees, particularly when they take a case to the Supreme Court, are staggering. When a lawyer is writing his fee for a service of this kind, his hand often slips. Mrs. Murphy said she would write to the Prime Minister, and perhaps he could devise a way. This was every woman's concern and she believed that Mr. King would be glad to have it settled. The letter was written and we had a prompt reply.

Newton Wesley Rowell was going before the Privy Council in October and he would be glad to take our petition. The petition should have been in Mrs. Murphy's name, but it seems that names are arranged alphabetically, so our petition appears on the record in the name of "Edwards and others."

On the morning of October 18th, 1929, newspapers all over the British Empire carried black headlines: "Privy Council Declares That Women Are Persons!" It came as a surprise to many women in Canada at least who had not known that they were not persons until they heard it stated that they were.

The Lord Chancellor had given a decision and it was so simple and so plain that we wondered now why we didn't think of it ourselves. Lord Sankey, after listening to the case for and against (our petition was opposed by two lawyers from the Province of Quebec), found the solution in the British North America Act itself. There are clauses where the word "person" is used which would lead one to believe that where the word "person" is used it must mean "male and female person," and in addition to this there is one clause where the word "person" must mean "male and female." In Clause 153, provision is made that either the French or the English language may be used by any person in any Court established under this Act. The word "person" must include women for it is inconceivable that this privilege is intended for men only.

When we read this in its clear simplicity, we thought about the Judges of the Supreme Court of Canada, and wondered if their faces were red!

It was a matter of regret for all of us that Mrs. Murphy was not appointed the First Senator, and that is no reflection on the excellent appointment that was made in the person of the Hon. Cairine Wilson, and later the appointment of the Hon. Iva Fallis.

The circle was completed when the Business and Professional Women of Canada placed a memorial plaque in the lobby of the Senate, House of Parliament, Ottawa, to celebrate the victory. It was a memorable occasion when the plaque was unveiled, June 11th, 1933, but tinged with sadness too, for of the original five signers, there were only two of us left, Mrs. Parlby and myself. Mrs. Murphy had died in 1933, but all the women of Canada, and of the British Empire too, will ever be indebted to her for this definite victory, which has clarified the position of women for all time.

22

The Glad Day

THE YEAR 1919 broke in gladness over our family. The Armistice was signed. Demobilization was under way, and Jack was coming home, a Lieutenant now, having won his commission on the field.

For the joyous homecoming, the house on 123rd Street was getting a going-over that it would remember, if houses have memories. It was a good, big, square, honest house, built for a big family, with a fine attic the full size of the house, and a basement to match, so there was room for everyone's possessions—sleighs, skates, hockey sticks, one toboggan, numerous baseball bats, though I am not saying they were always to be found in their rightful places. Having been built in the time when sleeping porches were in fashion, we had one at the back of the house and one at the front, where fresh-air seekers could fill their lungs with northern ozone.

Jack had not seen this house, so we felt we must present it in its best light. There is something about hard physical labor that satisfies the heart when emotion is running high and even at this distance I can recapture the joy of that season of house-cleaning and curtain making. My sister-in-law Eleanor Anderson, from Winnipeg, came to visit us, and together we manicured that house, lifted her face and made a lady of her, with scraped floors and new stairs carpet and new chintz for the living room.

Listening to a radio speaker today I hear that in the art of sculpture only the principal lines must be shown, so that a sculptured figure will have the detachment which only simplicity can bring. All minor folds and wrinkles must be smoothed out. Perhaps this applies to literature also, but who is able to choose and say: "This is a primary fold and therefore must be left in, but this is a secondary wrinkle and therefore we will rub it out"? What I am writing now may well be a minor fold in Life's drapery, but it came flooding in upon me, sweet as the perfume of an old bouquet, the other day, when I found a piece of the living room chintz in an old scrap bag. When I saw what it was I ironed it out for old times' sake, and loved every blossom of the blue delphiniums, with their background of pale pink daisies. Anything that can bring back the feeling of that happy time will never get a low rating from me.

The great morning came at last, a misty, beautiful morning in March, when we drove to the C.P.R. station to meet the troop train. Just as we were about to leave the house, the youngest member of the family suddenly decided he did not want to go. He said he would rather watch at the window and see us driving in. Then we found out the cause of this sudden gloom.

"I won't see anything," he said, "but the backs of legs. You big ones will all be seeing Jack before I do. He'll never see me, so I won't go."

We knew he wanted to go, with all the love of his loyal little heart, so his Dad came to the rescue by telling him he would carry him high on his shoulder and no doubt he would be the first to see Jack coming down the steps.

Happiness was thus restored and the reception committee made its joyous way to the station, down Jasper Avenue, under the subway, around to the parking place and then to the platform, which was packed with people.

We saw the train crossing the long bridge, then it disappeared as it came through the cutaway, but its silvery plume of smoke rose straight into the bright air, and the big black engine pulled panting into the station as car after car passed us. The doors opened and uniformed men began to come quickly down the steps.

"I see him!" Mark called in a voice as shrill as a siren. "It's Jack!"

The days that followed are confused in my mind like a happy dream. Jack was so glad to be back, so pleased with everything and took the greatest interest in getting back into civilian clothes. His tin hat was presented to Mark, who wore it all day and had to be forcibly separated from it at night. We thought his craze for wearing it would wear out in a day or two, for it was a heavy weight on his young head, but he declared he couldn't feel its weight at all. When we insisted that it was too heavy for him, he carried it on his arm like a shield.

We felt that life had dealt bountifully with us, in letting us have our boy back from the inferno of war. From December 1915 to March 1919 he had been away from us, spending three birthdays in the trenches, and now he was back and had come through without a day's illness or even a scratch.

He had changed, of course, grown taller and filled out, and in many ways he seemed older than either of us.

Another incident of which the blue delphiniums reminded me was that the mother of Jack's friend, Freeman Kelley sent me roses for Jack's homecoming. Her beloved Freeman, her only boy, the gentle, dark-eyed Freeman, was not coming back. He had come through the war safely until November the 11th and then in the last minutes of the last hour had been shot down.

And yet his mother, with her own heart breaking, could think of flowers for me and mine in our hour of rejoicing! I have received flowers many times and on many occasions, joyous and sorrowful, but never flowers like these!

Jack was anxious to get back to the University, and settled down to his work, gallantly fighting back the restlessness which engulfed some of the other boys. He was soon established in the activities of his class. We had many happy gatherings of the students during this period and we still laugh over their clever impersonations and debates and *Gateway* editorials. They were a gay and happy company. Jim Nicol, Bobby Cameron, Marjorie Bradford, Helen Kerby, Victor Homer, Clyde Smith, Helen Armstrong, George Ferguson. . . .

Jack never spoke of his war experiences. He gave me his war diaries and told me he never wanted to see them again. The other boys could tell us incidents of their experiences in the trenches and happenings on their brief leaves, but Jack, the best story-teller of them all, had nothing to say. He sat silent, with a strange tension in his young face.

He had times of depression, too, when he was sharp and irritable with Paul and Horace. Their exuberance and lack of discipline irritated him. He thought I was too easy with them. Behind his back they called him the "Iron Duke," but they were ever ready to please him if they could, and never wavered in their devotion to him and their admiration. With the little fellow and with Florence he was always the adored Big Brother.

We had a big gray cat called the "Jeopard" (so called because, when a kitten, he was found in a place of jeopardy on the street car tracks), and he attached himself to Jack at once, slept on the foot of his bed, and followed him around like a dog.

One day, when Jack had come with me to a Board of Trade luncheon, the speaker, a typical solid businessman, full of bubbling optimism, greeted Jack with a resounding slap on the back and asked:

"Well, young fellow, how does it feel to win a war?"

"I did not know that wars were ever won," Jack said quietly. "Certainly not by the people who do the fighting." His voice cut like a sharp paper edge and his face had gone suddenly old. Word had come that day of the death of one of his friends in an English hospital.

Looking back now I can see our whole way of life bothered him. We were too complacent, too much concerned with trifles. He had seen the negation of everything he had been taught, and now here we were going ahead, almost as if nothing had happened.

Alfred Noyes, in his great poem "The Victory Dance," interpreted the spirit of the returned men more faithfully than anyone of that time, but his poem was too sad for our spirit of jubilation, and we were not wise enough to heed its warning. He pictured the spirits of young soldiers coming back after the Armistice to find the whole population celebrating victory in a wild exaltation of mad joy. The spirits stood on the sidelines watching the revels, amazed, shocked, saddened. One of the spirits pleaded with his companions not to judge the dancers too harshly.

"They are young you see." "Aye," said the dead man,
   "so were we."
"What did you think we would find?" asked a shade.
"When the last shot was fired and the last peace made?"
"Christ!" said the fleshless jaws of his friend,
"I thought they'd be looking for worlds to mend."

Jack tried hard to adapt himself. He worked long hours and made a name for himself as a student. There were times when he wanted to leave the University and get a job, but we coaxed him to stay and get his degree in Law, and this he did with distinction. He was honored by his fellow students in many ways, and won a scholarship which took him to Oxford.

But I knew there was a wound in his heart—a sore place. That hurt look in his clear blue eyes tore at my heart strings and I did not know what to do. When a boy who has never had a gun in his hands, never desired anything but the good of his fellow men, is sent out to kill other boys like himself, even at the call of his country, something snaps in him, something which may not mend.

A wound in a young heart is like a wound in a young tree. It does not grow out. It grows in.

The boys who came back from this war have a better chance. Wise men and women are giving deep thought to their problems, and in every way possible are showing the soldier's family how to cushion the shock of his return. I wish we had known more, but all I could see then was the miracle of Jack's safe return, and to us he was a glorified being, clothed in the shining raiment of one who has come back from the dead.

Soon after his return from Oxford he was appointed to the position of Prosecuting Attorney in the City Police Court, and his success there led to his appointment as one of the lawyers in the Attorney-General's office. No trouble was too great for him to take to ascertain all the truth in every case he handled, for there was always a fear in his heart that some innocent person might suffer if he were negligent. I remember once there was a case pending which had to do with the guardianship of a family whose parents had separated. The case looked favorable for the father, who told a plausible story in court, and had made a better impression than the mother. But Jack was not satisfied, and decided to go himself to see the children, who were on a farm in the Peace River country, left in the charge of the eldest boy, who was only fifteen years of age. It was winter weather, bitterly cold, a few days before Christmas. I remember this case because I helped him to fill a valise with things for the children. He borrowed his Dad's coon coat and gauntlets and made the trip, the last thirty miles from the station with a livery team. But he found out what he wanted to know and the children not only had a Christmas tree, with presents for everybody, but soon had their mother restored to them. The fifteen-year-old boy gave the deciding vote. He told Jack that his mother had always been good to them and if they could only get her back they could do fine without the father.

I wonder if that boy still remembers.

When he was in the City Police Court a case came up one day of a man who had killed a dog on a street crossing and did not even stop. He was quite arrogant about it when summoned into court, and said the dog had no right to be crossing the street, and if people didn't want their dogs hurt they had better keep them in their own yards. But when the proceedings were over he was chastened in spirit and had his knowledge enlarged, and the Humane Society were delighted with Jack's handling of the case. He brought the fact to light that a dog properly licensed, as this one was, has the same right to cross the street as any other pedestrian.

When he was appointed Prosecutor in the Supreme Court of Alberta he wrote me about it. He was pleased with the promotion but used this sentence: "I enjoy this battling of wits and could be happy if I could forget its grim significance."

One of the judges whom I knew well often spoke of Jack's ability to get the truth from the witnesses. "He has something which makes people want to tell the truth," Thomas Tweedie said. "Some way he gets the idea over that the truth must be told, and strangely enough even the people who receive sentences respect him and like him. He builds up their self-respect by his understanding and never in his life did he deliberately try to confuse a witness. He is always kind, patient and human."

23

The Prairie Pilgrim

WHEN THE MOONEY FAMILY made the journey from Winnipeg to the Souris River in 1880, the journey took two weeks, and my mother walked all the way. It was a rough road, with pitch holes and rivers to cross, but her heart was light and strong. She was looking ahead to the great new land for her sons. There they could all farm together and help each other on the rich prairie, free from stones, from weeds, and from insects. Surely no effort was too great to achieve such a family triumph.

Mother walked to lighten the load, and besides, it was best for her to be where she could keep her eye on the caravan, which consisted of two ox-wagons, one pony cart in formation, and one cow, two small children, one small dog, on the loose!

It was a long two weeks, no doubt, for the adults, but to me, aged six going on seven, it was a time of great adventure. We were on our way to a new country and a new life and we were all together, all except George, eighteen-year-old George, who stayed behind on the homestead near Millford to look after the stuff.

Forty years later, in 1920, again the Mooney family made that same journey and again we were all together, except one, and this time it was my father, who had left us twenty-seven years before.

The distance was the same but this time it required only four hours in the train. My mother was not walking this time, but she was with us—dominating every thought, as we sat there hushed and silent—her three sons and three daughters, all in sober dark clothes just as she would want us to be, for she loved decorum. It was strange for us to be silent for we were a family of talkers.

We did not talk because we were too busy remembering, as we looked out on the familiar landscape, shivering that day in a blustering March wind. Cattle were huddled in straw stacks and smoke was veering from well-stoked furnaces and stoves. Forty years had marched over all of us, but her death had rolled them back, and that day we were all her children again. She had been the tie that bound us all together and now we were like a broken string of beads, in danger of becoming separated.

I was thinking of the bannocks that she made on that first journey, in the mouth of the flour sack. The process was simple, but there was art in it too. Lard was mixed with the flour into which baking powder had been added with salt, and then this was made into a soft dough with milk, and pressed down into a sizzling hot pan where bacon had been fried. The pan was covered to keep off the ashes, the bannock turned just once and cooked through and then eaten hot with "Golden Drop" syrup poured over it. Nothing can ever taste like that. My mother had the gift of making simple food romantic.

The Minister, Rev. S. E. Caldwell, who had conducted the funeral service at Hannah's home in Winnipeg, had spoken about the light in the window which mother had always burned on stormy winter nights to guide the traveller on his way if there should happen to be one abroad. It was an invitation, too. It said, "Here is shelter and food!" The light was a ritual with her, and symbolic of her life. Coal oil might be running low and the source of supply far away, but that lamp burned without fail, even if we had to carry on with tallow candles.

I wonder if every family has regrets when the day comes to bury their mother. Do we all fail and come short of our filial duty? I do not think Lizzie or Hannah could have had regrets, they had done much more for her than I had and had been more patient. She had lived the last three years of her life with Hannah in Winnipeg and before that had lived a year with Lizzie in Holland, and both had spent their days and nights at her command.

A year before her death she had suffered a fractured thigh bone by a fall one dark morning. She had sprung out of bed without turning on the light, under the delusion that the thrashers were driving into the yard and there was nothing to eat in the house! The habits of years are hard to break. All her active life she had been concerned with the feeding of hungry men coming in off the land, and so even in the days of her retirement, when the task of feeding the hungry men had been taken over by younger hands, her mind went on planning for their needs.

I went to see her as soon as I heard about the fall, wondering how she would take it. It had always been her greatest fear that she might become a care to her children.

"Anything but that!" she often said. "Surely God won't leave me to wither away, as I've seen some old people do, tiring out their family. People should be like bank notes, called in by the bank when they become worn and faded. . . . I can stand pain as well as anybody, but I don't believe I could be patient and resigned to a long period of waiting."

It shook my faith, too, that this could happen to her. She had asked so little for herself. Surely God could have answered that one prayer. . . . After all she had done. . . . I thought of how unselfish she had been. Bought all our clothes, before she even thought of herself—and then would say, "I do not need as much as the others; I will not be going out, and you youngsters must go." On the trip from Winnipeg . . . sleeping out at night . . . making camp in the rain . . . her problem was to keep father from catching cold . . . for once he had had a serious attack of bronchitis . . . his stockings had to be kept dry, and that was not easy . . . I thought of these things and many more, and rebelled at the thought that this valiant soul would be fettered in a broken body, perhaps for years. I thought of how she kindled to those lines from the Rubaiyat:

"Why, if the soul can fling the Dust aside,
And naked on the Air of Heaven ride,
　　Were't not a shame—were't not a shame for him
In this clay carcase crippled to abide?"

I had bought her a copy once, not knowing how she would like it, but she read it.

"It's a heathenish thing, Nellie," she said. "But there's truth in it."

She was too old to have her leg set, so the doctor put her in a cast to ease the pain as well as he could. When I went to see her I got a surprise and a rebuke for my lack of faith. Her God had answered her prayer. Not as she expected, but nevertheless she was spared what she dreaded, for during the year that she was confined to bed, she did not know that she was bedfast, nor did she suffer. By a merciful delusion her mind went pleasantly back to the years of her strength. She was back in Ontario with her sister Ellen and Mrs. Edward Lowery. She was getting ready to move to Manitoba, weaving blankets and getting clothes made for the children, or it was harvest time in Manitoba and she was walking out with my father to look at the wheat. It was the best crop we had ever had, and there would be money enough to buy all the supplies this year; it was time for the children to be coming home from school and she wondered what was keeping them; the cows were coming up to the bars and she would have to get out and get the milking done before supper.

Her mind had become a sun dial which recorded only the sunny hours. She slept for long periods and enjoyed her meals. Sometimes in the morning she would waken up in a panic, loudly demanding her clothes and to know where she was, and where everyone else was, and why no one had called her. She knew it was late by the sun on the wall, but she had not heard the clock strike, and couldn't understand that for she had never forgotten to wind the clock!

That mood quickly passed as the kindly curtain fell again between her and reality and her spirit wandered in the green pastures and beside the still waters. The doctor thought it wonderful that she was free from discomfort and pain.

But now her eighty-five years were accomplished, and we were on our way to the Millford cemetery.

We stayed overnight at the Prince Arthur Hotel in Brandon. Many of the old friends came to see us there. They all had something to tell of her goodness and her overflowing hospitality. They told us death was just as much a part of life as birth and that Heaven lies at the end of a well-spent life, and I knew it was all true, but even that could not make me forget that something had gone out of the world forever, something dependable and satisfying. I had lost my sense of being young, for the only person to whom I was young, had gone.

We left for Wawanesa on the morning train, called the "Cannon Ball," and mother was buried from the Union Church by the Methodist minister, and although the day was cold and stormy the old friends were there from near and far, many of whom I had not seen for years. A weather-beaten company the older ones were, for they had faced many a cold wind, and had endured the vicissitudes of hail and frost. But their spirits had never faltered. They were a gallant company. The minister's wife had chosen the hymns and sang a solo which was one of my mother's favorites: "The City Four Square." One hymn seemed to me to be exactly the right word, and when I hear it sung now it takes me back to that little church where again I see that company of old friends and feel the fellowship of their presence, lightening our bereavement as the sunshine struggled through the frosted windows.

> "I've wrestled on towards heaven,
>   'Gainst storm and wind and tide,
> Now like a weary traveller
>   That leaneth on his guide.
> I'll bless the hand that guided,
>   I'll bless the heart that planned,
> And glory, glory dwelleth
>   In Emmanuel's land!"

We laid her away on the high field overlooking the Souris Valley, that cold March day, while the horses under their blankets stamped impatiently, blowing out their frosty breath in clouds, and there they lie, John Mooney and Letitia McCurdy Mooney, two people who played their part well, standing up to life while life lasted, two members in good standing of that innumerable host which no man can number called the People, the Common People, who carry on from day to day, without benefit of applause, unconsciously keeping alive the best traditions of humanity.

We stayed that day and night in Wawanesa and many of the old friends came in to my brother Jack's house. George lives three miles out in the country, and we had a family reunion there too before we separated. We had a feeling that we might not all be together again and we were anxious to see our nieces and nephews. I was glad to know that there were still Mooney children attending Northfield School.

In the first volume of this autobiography, *Clearing in the West*, I mentioned the name of Fred Vigfuson, who worked for our family for many years, working in the summer and travelling in the winter, believing that money was made for spending, not saving. Fred travelled with us to Brandon and to Wawanesa, and he was one of the pallbearers with Will, George and Jack. Fred had been on one of his trips when he heard of my mother's death, but managed to arrive in Winnipeg in time for the funeral. He brought with him a huge wreath of flowers made of glass, much like those I saw afterwards in Normandy.

The real flowers were frozen, of course, before they reached the grave, but Fred's offering gleamed bright and indestructible, defying the elements. I agreed to write to all the people who had sent flowers, but we all thanked Fred for his. I remember saying to him that his wreath was a symbol of something enduring and everlasting, the very thing she carried in her own heart.

"If she were here," I said to Fred, "—and maybe she is—she would tell you she liked it."

We were sitting around the table at my brother George's and suddenly, to all our surprise, Fred covered his face with his hands.

"She was the only mother I ever knew," he said when he could speak. "She was the only person who ever thought enough of me to scold me like a mother . . . One day at the table in the kitchen in the old house, I was mad about something. I guess you all remember that I was often mad, and I swore. No one ever swore before the Old Lady, because she wouldn't stand for it. This day it just slipped out, and I said that something or somebody was as slow as the second coming of Christ, and she reached out her hand and stopped me, as you would stop a child who was getting too close to a hot stove and she said—

"'Fred, don't speak like that of the Best Friend any of us ever had. The Man who died for us all. I don't know whether He will come again out of the clouds as He went away—I hope He will. But I know He does come to us when we are in sore need. He came to me, when my little boy died, and I knew the doctor could have saved him, only he was too drunk to see how sick the child was, and told me I was making a fuss about a simple colic . . . When the little boy died I cursed that doctor. Fred, I could have choked him with my own hands, but Some One came to me with hands soft and comforting and said, "Your little boy is safe with me, safe forever. He will never know sorrow or pain or temptation. Don't tear your heart in sorrow and anger. Death is not the thing you fear . . . I have overcome death." He wasn't slow that time in coming and He is never slow when we call . . . Many a time I've called on Him in sore need and He has never been slow.

"'So don't say it, Fred—I cannot bear to hear my best Friend criticized. My Friend and yours and everybody's . . . who came to show us how to live.'

"And I walked out like a chump, and never even thanked her or apologized to her. That's what seems so terrible now, I never even said I was sorry!"

We comforted Fred as well as we could, telling him we all had been chumps at one time or another and taken all her goodness for granted. We sat late that night, remembering, and I hope she was listening. My brother, Will, remarked that it is too bad people have to die to have their good deeds remembered, and he spoke of how he had found out something that mother did on the two weeks' journey which we should not have allowed her to do, admitting at the same time that he wouldn't have known how he would have stopped her for Mother was not easily turned aside from her purpose. He said that one of her big problems on the trip was to be sure that Father had dry stockings, for since he had had the long bout with bronchitis she feared a recurrence of the trouble, so when there was any doubt of having a pair of thoroughly dry stockings for the morning, she put a pair on her own feet at night to make sure, and when Will had remonstrated with her and wanted to take over this duty, she would have none of it and told him to never mention it. She was always sure that nothing could happen to her.

Long after midnight we sat talking and then Lizzie spoke up and said:

"I know what's the matter with the Mooney family. There's no one now to tell us to go to bed."

I lay awake a long time that night, listening to the snow that lisped against the windows—a soft spring snow that deadened every sound. It comforted me to think of its falling on that jagged wound on the high benchland above the Souris River, turning it into a soft white mound. She loved the snow and it was right that it should wrap her grave in a white mantle on this first night.

24

Family Matters

THE NEXT DAY we separated. Lizzie and Hannah returned to their homes in Winnipeg. George and Jack settled back into their routine on the farms and Will and I went back to Edmonton.

In our generation the line which separated men and women was sharply marked, even in families. As families go, we got along very well, the six of us. There was always a strong family loyalty and no doubt we would have gone gladly to each other's help if help had been needed, but as individuals we lived our lives behind invisible mountains in which there were deep ravines where no path of communication ran. It always seemed easier to keep our deepest thoughts to ourselves, but on that train journey Will and I seemed to draw closer together. I always had a deep affection for my brother Will, and a great respect for his judgment.

"We are the older generation now, Nellie," he said, "and pretty soon we'll be the old folks. The wheel of life has made a complete revolution for us!"

"We are the old folks now," I said. "I got the first cold blast of it a couple of weeks ago when Jack and Florence were having a party. Refreshments had been served. Twelve o'clock had come and gone and it really was time that the guests were going home. I had always been able before to draw attention to the flight of time without actually saying a word, but this time I suddenly felt I was nothing but a spoil-fun. I remembered being at a party at "Bosky Dell," the home of the Turnbull family in Millford, many years before, and just when we were having a wonderful time Mr. Turnbull appeared pacing up and down, wrinkling his forehead, until the top of his bald head ran into billows. I wanted him to go away, anywhere, to fall down stairs, break a leg, anything just so he would leave us alone. I know now how he felt, but I know, too, how the youngsters felt and so I just couldn't break up the party. I went meekly to bed and knew I had lost control."

"It is strange about family ties," Will said after awhile. "When you are young they simply choke you. Parents are really an impediment and quite often an embarrassment to children. When I left the County of Grey at the age of nineteen, I wanted to shake the dust of home off my feet, not that I had anything against either my father or mother. It was just the natural urge of youth to break a new path, but as we grow older we long for the old pattern of life and grow misty-eyed and tender when we think of it. You and I are the rovers of the family, Nellie, and perhaps we are more sentimental about the old home than any of the others for we have been farther away from it. To us its hard outlines are softened by distance. . . . When I heard the old clock strike in Jack's house, it fairly twisted my heart. I could just see mother standing on a chair winding it up at night. I hated that clock as a kid for its iron voice meant I had to get up in the cold dark winter mornings. But now it opened every pore in my heart. I had forgotten how it cleared its throat before it struck and then bustled into the new hour faster than ever as if it had to make up for lost time. It's good for another lifetime and will go on, measuring off the time impartially, while the people it served will wear out and die."

"It's strange about time," I said. "We all get our quota, the same number of hours, while they last and at the same rate, we pay for them whether we use them or not."

"You certainly make a queer use of some of your hours," said my brother, suddenly coming out of the misty past into the present.

Then I knew I was in for it, but I was always ready to take Will's criticism. There was thirteen years between us in age and I always knew there was a kindly import in anything he said.

"The world isn't ready to accept advice from women," he said. "Men naturally resent women's interference in public matters . . . I know the liberation of women will come, but it's bound to be hard on the advance guard, and there are so many other things for you to do, Nellie. You have a good home, Wes is one of the finest men I have ever known. You have five lovely children. Can't you pipe down and live like other people? I get tired telling people that you and Wes get on well, and you have no personal reasons for raising such a dust about the liquor traffic and the burdens of women. The world has gone on for a long time, Nellie, and you can't change it!"

"That's the old Conservative doctrine coming out in you, Will," I said. "'Leave things alone.' If you're all right yourself, why bother?— Sir Rodmond Roblin talked like that, but don't you see that the fact that I have a good man and a good family lays a responsibility on me. The broken-hearted, embittered woman cannot do anything to help anyone else. You need not worry about Wes either. His mother, God bless her, educated him. She was interested in exactly the same things that I am and so Wes is not the sort of a man who thinks his wife should always be standing behind his chair ready to spring to attention. Don't ever forget that I married carefully. I was only sixteen when I got my eye on Wes, but I knew what I was doing."

We were travelling through Manitoba, west of Brandon, and the small farmhouses looked gray and lonely in the gloom of that March day. Cattle foraged in the straw stacks. Children were on the roads going home from school, and cheerful columns of smoke rose from the chimneys of the little houses.

"Look at these little houses, Will," I said. "Where any recent building has been done you'll notice, it's a new barn. A small house and a big barn mean that the man of the family has had his way. These little houses are places where people have the minimum of comfort. They go in and out, eat and sleep, but everything's done the hard way. The women are tired and overworked and sometimes very cross. They battle against hard water and chapped hands, and chapped hands would lower the morale of an arch-angel. The houses are cold, the floors full of splinters. Some of these houses have not one book, except Eaton's catalogue. When there is a good crop the men buy more land or more machinery for themselves. I'm not begrudging them their machines, but the women could do with some help, too, and in addition to all their hard work and their strivings to keep clean and make a decent living for themselves and their families the women have still to bear the additional burden of childbearing. No one can blame them if they do not welcome the coming of another child under these conditions. It isn't good enough to say that things have always been this way and always will. This is a rich country, and there should be enough to go around of the good things of life. I want to see these people have some pleasure in their work.

"The first part of life here, the pioneer period, is closing, and a new era is about to break. Some day, before long, there will be electric light in all these houses and new machines to lift the burden of drudgery. Co-operative movements are coming too, but to bring all this about the people must develop a new mentality. The people of Mother's generation were great people in their own way. They took great pride in their endurance. You remember the old man in our neighborhood who took great pride in the fact that he never owned a pair of mittens in his life, and I knew a woman at Manitou who had the distinction of having never lain in bed for more than twenty-four hours after her children were born. But these feats of endurance sound foolish now, for the angle of life is changing. Machines have come and just ordinary animal strength has had its day."

"That's all very true," Will said. "And no one is gladder than I am to see machines lifting the burden from human beings, but I still don't see why you should appoint yourself a sort of an unofficial guardian and defender of women's rights."

"I know these people, Will," I said, "and they listen to me when I talk to them. I've had meetings in nearly every one of these little towns and in some of the school houses, too. The women bring their babies to the meetings, Will, and that means they are determined to come. Women themselves are largely to blame for conditions. They are too much inclined to suffer in silence. They will not speak up on their own behalf and develop a martyr complex which is hard to break, but I can get closer to them than a stranger, for they know that I know what I'm talking about for I, too, have travelled the cold road and had my hair frozen to the bed clothes at night. I have warmed my bare feet in the place where a cow has been lying on a sharp October morning, and when I tell them these things I see their faces brighten and their eyes glisten, and they accept me. I have opened doors in their imaginations, I have made them see that life need not be all trials and tribulations. Canada is destined to be one of the great nations of the world and Canadian women must be ready for citizenship. No nation ever rises higher than its women and that's why I must go on."

"I know they like to hear you," Will said. "I like to hear you, too. But I can see that you are in a fair way of being hurt, and I don't like it, and I don't like the way some people talk about you. Why can't you let some of these bright maiden ladies carry the Fiery Cross over the country?"

"Well, I suppose I could settle down into a state of apathy," I said, "and have teas for other idle women and listen to their chatter about their dressmakers and their maids. This could be called 'making social contacts for my husband's business,' but really, Will, my husband doesn't need any such help. Wes is a successful insurance manager on his own merits. People like to do business with him because he's honest and fair-minded and knows his work, and that is a better foundation for business than having a wife who can throw a good party. It's more enduring and more dignified. Wes can run his own department very well indeed. He needs no bolstering from me. When I hear people say they're insured in "Wes McClung's company" I feel proud of him. He is pulling his own weight and certainly I do not want to pull through life like a thread that has no knot. I want to leave something behind when I go; some small legacy of truth, some word that will shine in a dark place. I never could believe that minding one's own business was much of a virtue; but it's a fine excuse for doing nothing. You remember old Scrooge made a great point of minding his own business."

"You will certainly never get into the hall of fame because you minded your own business," Will said rather severely.

"I'm not worried about the hall of fame," I said, "but I do want to see some of the old prejudices which have bound women fall like the leaves in autumn when a wind shakes them down and blows them into fence corners. And I want to do more than that, too! I want to see our people get something to take the place of the old prejudices, because they did give people something to talk about and be proud of.

"There's a woman living near Alexander who has not spoken to her son and his wife for twenty years and she's proud of it. It is the high spot in her drab life, and has brought her through several attacks of gallstones. She just wouldn't die for fear her son's wife would get her fur coat, but you can't say that that's a healthy frame of mind. All that determination could be put to a better use."

"What burns me up," Will said after a pause, "is that women are harder on you than men. How do you account for that?"

"Oh, that's easy," I said, "and it is exactly in keeping with what I've been saying. Women have but few interests and live on a narrow canvas. I do not resent their criticism. It's just talk and not so malicious as it sounds. I do not mind."

"Well I do," Will said, "and I wish you'd get out of the uplifting business."

"I'm sorry to cause you embarrassment, Will," I said, "but don't forget that I have some good friends, even among the women."

Then I told him what happened one night in a little town on the Goose Lake line, when I drove in during a bad winter storm and went into the one hotel. I was expecting to leave on a train which went through early in the morning but was anxious to get a few hours' sleep and asked for a room.

The night clerk took one look at the name on my suitcase and told me he had no room for me.

I knew they had, but for a moment did not grasp the significance of his refusal.

"How does it happen you have no room?" I asked. "This is a big hotel, in a very small town."

"We have no room," the little man intoned like a curate. Then I knew what he meant.

"You can't refuse to give me a room," I said. "This is a public house."

"We just don't like you," said the little man, bristling like a badger, "and we don't want you. Better go and stay with some of your pious friends around town—the Nosey Parkers who want to take the bread out of honest men's mouths!"

"I am going to stay here," I said, "and you can't do anything about it! It's a bad night and it's nearly midnight, too late to disturb anyone. So whether you like it or not I am staying until train time tomorrow morning and I want a room! Where is the proprietor?"

"That need not concern you," he growled. "I'm in charge here, and we do not want you."

I noticed a bell on his desk and I knew I could rouse the house. But I did not want to do that.

Just then someone came down the stairs, a big woman in a red satin dressing-gown.

"What goes on here?" she demanded brusquely.

The little man sat low in his chair.

"This lady wants a room," he said meekly.

"Well, what's the delay? We have plenty of rooms," she said. "Take her bags to Number Three."

Then she turned and put out her hand.

"I'm glad to see you again, Mrs. McClung. When I attended the Normal School in Edmonton, I often heard you speak . . . I knew your voice, too. I hadn't been asleep yet and could hear the voices down here at the desk and wondered if Harry might be a bit difficult. It's the wrong time of the moon for Harry."

Harry was disappearing up the stairs with my bags, looking like a little bow-legged gnome.

"The moon must have changed just when you appeared," I said. "I was beginning to think all the signs were against me, too."

"Harry's just recovering from a protracted spree," she said later as she filled the water-pitcher and brought me towels, "and is ready to fight with his own shadow. He knows what you stand for, and in his present state of mind he thinks of you as a mortal enemy, but believe me I'll be glad when we get rid of the bar. I've seen too much misery come from it, and it has certainly left its mark on our family.

"My mother ran a boarding house right here in this little town, and made enough to educate us all, but when my brother grew up he wanted a hotel with a bar—a boarding house was beneath his dignity . . . and sometime when you want to write a modern 'Ten Nights In a Bar Room', come back and I'll give you the dope on it. But now you need sleep; don't worry about the train, it will probably be hours late. I'll get you up in time."

The train was a day late, and not only did I get the story, but found a real friend. She is still there, running a good hotel, without a bar.

"What would you have done if she had not come down?" Will asked. "Would you have had to sit in a chair all night?"

"No," I said. "I'd have gone upstairs and found a room—I've done that, too. The first unlocked door, then cautious investigation with a flash light. It's easy—I might have to try two or three before I found an empty one. Often there is a couch in the hall. I can sleep any place."

"I still cannot understand why you do it," Will said. But I did not believe him and I said so.

"You, too, went ahead when you were only nineteen, because you saw something better than the things you were leaving behind and you were not thinking of yourself only. Were you ever sorry? Wouldn't you do it again, even if you knew that it meant fatigue and frostbites and hours of doubt and distress. No one wants a fiddling job . . . when Frank Kinley carried on the Sunday School at Northfield School long ago someone asked him why he stuck to it, in the heat of summer and the cold of winter, pointing out that the parents of the children were indifferent, and the youngsters themselves often trying, noisy and inattentive. Frank made a reply which I have never forgotten. He said: 'I knew what the Sunday School has done for me, as boy and man. I know, and I want other people to have it. I cannot eat my bread alone.' With that phrase 'I cannot eat my bread alone,' I joined Frank Kinley's lodge. You called me an uplifter a few minutes ago, which is, of course, a term of disdain. But that's what I am and I'm not ashamed of it. And don't forget that I'm having a good time at it. No one need feel sorry for me. It is the greatest adventure in the world, and I would not change places with anyone. You see I understand why people sneer at uplifters. It's a form of defense mechanism. It's a cover for selfishness but no one need ever envy a selfish person, for no selfish person is happy."

There was a long silence between us then, as we watched the flying landscape. Then Will spoke:

"You'll never change," he said. "And you will have a good time, as you say. You'll have plenty of friends and many enemies. You'll probably make mistakes and know both joy and sorrow, but at least you'll have the satisfaction of having lived . . . and you know how I feel about you."

I knew.

We lived in the same city until our family moved to Calgary in 1923, but that was the last serious conversation we had, although we often saw each other.

In 1926, I remember spending a very pleasant time with him and my sister-in-law in their home on 100th Avenue, which had been remodelled and decorated and was complete in every last detail. I spoke of this as we sat before a cheerful fire in his den. "You're very comfortable now, Will," I said, "and I hope you'll have long and happy years here."

There was a quizzical smile on his face as he answered.

"Not likely. No one stays long when everything is exactly right. Nothing to complain of? It cannot last!"

We laughed about it then, but he was speaking truly.

He died the next year.

25

Up to London

WHEN IN MAY, 1920, I read in a brief news item that a General Council of the Methodist Church of Canada had appointed me as one of their twelve delegates to the Ecumenical Conference to be held in London, England the following year, my first desire was to know what this imposing word meant. I found it meant "world wide in extent," and I felt that a great honor had been given to me; in fact I was somewhat frightened at the prospect, for the news report said it was the first time the Canadian Council had appointed a woman to this gathering which took place every ten years. I did not know until two years later how my name came to be placed on the list. Mr. T. W. Duggan, manager of the Dale Greenhouses in Brampton, Ontario, had ventured to suggest in the Council that a woman should be appointed, and in the silence that followed that remark he ventured to say that he knew a woman who would at least bring back a good report, and bless his kind heart, he was thinking of me. And so it came to pass that I went to London in 1921.

My housekeeper, Mrs. Fuller, was concerned for my social success in London and did her best to prepare me for this, my first visit. She was very tactful about it, but I discovered that she was somewhat fearful of my table manners. I did not always hold my fork correctly, and my way of breaking an egg in a glass egg-cup was just not done. She found me willing and anxious for guidance, and so I learned not only about how to eat an egg, but to eat a peach with a spoon and fork delicately held and I learned too that the eating of peanuts constitutes a social error into which I must not fall, remembering that in the eyes of the British they are "monkey nuts" and have no place on a lady's menu. I learned, too, that I must have a case for my night-gown—preferably one with a monogram, and the night garment should be of linen at least. Mrs. Fuller said that accessories were significant. Fortunately another English friend of mine was like-minded and presented me with a fine linen night-dress and case, embroidered and monogrammed, and Mrs. Fuller felt that my star of social success might be about to rise.

It was just as well she did not know what happened in Troon, where I had gone after the Council meeting was over, to speak for the "Women's Guild of Empire." Mrs. Flora Drummond and I were travelling companions and at Troon we were entertained in a beautiful mansion. I slept in a high, four-poster bed with curtains, and a bell rope as thick as a ferry cable.

When we arrived and were received by her Ladyship, she said to me when the greetings were over:

"Wilkins will unpack for you." I wanted to tell her that I was travelling light and would much prefer to do my own unpacking, but remembering what Mrs. Fuller had told me I tried to look as if I had never unpacked a valise in my life and so watched my modest black bag disappearing up the crimson stairway in Wilkins' firm grip, without a flicker! It contained by way of clothing, one afternoon dress, one evening dress, and two blouses, and I know they would look pitifully inadequate when hung in the long high wardrobe. But the thought of the nightdress case with its beautiful and yet unworn garment sustained me. Wilkins would see, I hoped, that I was a lady of quality. At the very bottom of my bag was the garment I really wore, a good, honest, long-sleeved "L" sized white flannelette gown from the second floor of the T. Eaton Company in Winnipeg, and

very glad I was to have a supply of these for the draughty spare rooms
I had occupied.

I felt quite secure and at my ease all evening, but when I ascended
the stairs and reached the spacious room allotted to me I found I was
discovered! Wilkins had probed deep into my slender belongings
and laid out not only the embroidered garment in its well-pressed
folds, but beside it the other one, the long-sleeved flannelette. Never
had its pale blue machine-made embroidery looked so crude and I
shrivelled under her gaze.

"Which garment, madam, do you prefer?" she asked me coldly.

I wanted to talk to Wilkins. If there had been the slightest twinkle
in her eye, we might have become good friends then and there, but
her face was as unpersonal as the marble-topped washstand, and Mrs.
Fuller had warned me I must not show any interest in the servants.
They would not understand and might resent it.

The meetings of the Council were full of surprises, some pleasant and others depressing. At the opening banquet in the Cecil
Hotel, I saw the great Methodist Church in evening clothes and I
wrote in my diary that night: "The brightest spot of the evening was
Lady Pearkes' diamonds." To Sir Robert Pearkes was given the honor
of moving an address to the President of the United States from
which I remember one sentence. The President was reminded by
Sir Robert that it had been the policy of the church from the day of
Wesley not to be a mere platonic preacher of philosophic sophistries
or idealistic nostrums, but to translate the plain truths of the Christian faith into the activities of everyday life! In other words Wesley
had sought to translate Methodism into "Christianity in earnest."
I find I made a note of this, on my program, with the addition:

"Sir R. knows some crackling big words."

I also have notes of another happening at this dinner. We had
among the delegates many colored people—Bishop Carey, Dr. Phil-
lips, Bishop Caldwell of the African Methodist Church and many
others. Mr. Oscar Adams was one of the Secretaries of the Conference, and I was intensely interested in these people, and glad to hear

their resonant voices. But at the dinner some of the southern delegates objected to sitting with them. We all drew our table partners by
chance; and my partner was a man from Witchita, Kansas. We were
seated near the malcontents, and quickly changed seats with them,
wondering if they would carry their race prejudices to Heaven, if
and when. It was a sore shock to me to find that Christian people
could be so cruel and ill-mannered. The colored people conducted
themselves with great dignity, but my soul was scorched with shame
for my race.

When the President of the Conference lit his cigar as soon as the
toast to the King was concluded, my partner was ready to go back to
Wichita on the first boat. I tried to tell him this was the custom of
the country and I reminded him that the Americans and the Canadians have some habits which are objectionable to the British people—
gum chewing, for example.

"But we do not chew gum at a church banquet!" he said indig-
nantly. "These people are followers of John Wesley. They have a
tradition of self-denial and should avoid the very appearance of evil."

I didn't like it any more than he did, but I was still so shocked at
the display of race prejudice that smoking seemed insignificant. The
next day we ran into another rough place and the offender this time
was one of the American bishops. He was telling us somewhat boast-
fully of the significance of the stars and stripes in civilization's forward march and of the great part the Methodist Church had played
in the war and then he made this astonishing statement:

"In this last great conflict the Methodist Church has sent more
soldiers to the front, more nurses to camps and hospitals and more
prayers to Heaven than any other Christian community." That was
too much for at least one of his compatriots, who mildly rebuked his
brother for making statistics a basis for spiritual pride.

"Let not the Methodist Episcopal Church degenerate into the
Methodist Statistical," he said.

The first few sessions left me cold and disappointed. The speakers were eloquent, easy to listen to, polished and prepared. The
programs rolled off the assembly line according to plan. It was a

great gathering, well-planned and executed, but my heart was not warmed.

Then came the Sunday morning service in Wesley's Chapel on the City Road. From where I sat I could see the gallery and its row after row of widows, not merry widows, but not sad ones either. I would say proud widows, wearing their white-edged bonnets, as old soldiers wear their medals. And the hymn which opened a door in my mind, and sent a warming flood through my veins was one I had sung many times:

> "The Church's one foundation
>   Is Jesus Christ her Lord:
> She is His new creation
>   By water and the word:
> From Heaven He came and sought her
>   To be His holy bride;
> With His own blood He bought her,
>   And for her life He died."

I was looking at the faces of the widows in the gallery as we sang the last verse and it was from the glow in their eyes that I received the greatest sense of triumph. They knew what it meant to carry the banner of love and sacrifice. They knew that the promises were not given in vain and that in spite of human frailties and human mistakes the great work of regeneration goes on. It is always hard to express a spiritual experience in words but it seemed to me that in a flash I saw the history of the church revealed. Past, present and future met here and were blended. Outside in the churchyard John Wesley had been laid to rest and here in this place, this very place, his words had vibrated the ether and now after all these years people from all over the world had gathered here for one purpose, one thought, one desire, and I was privileged to see it and feel it and be a part of it. Even now, so many years after, as I write these words the glory of it comes back to me and fuses my soul again in its burning heat.

"Yet she on earth hath union
　　With God the Three in One,
And mystic sweet communion
　　With those whose rest is won.
O happy ones and holy!
　　Lord, give us grace that we,
Like them, the meek and lowly,
　　On high may dwell with Thee."

That night we walked back to Bedford Place and that is a pleasant memory. I had for my companion Miss Riley, who had been a missionary to the Indians at Norway House, and her Indian protégé, Frances Nikawa.

"Don't worry about the bewildering London streets," Miss Riley had said, when we were discussing whether or not we would take a bus. "Frances will find the way. Civilization has not dimmed that blessed native instinct." And so Frances brought us safely back without having to enquire from any person and there was something about that which comforted me as the unerring instinct of the wild fowl confirmed the poet's faith in God's overruling providence. I mentioned this to Frances and as we walked along through the crowded streets she recited the poem to us in her deep voice:

"Wither, midst falling dew,
While glow the heavens with the last steps of day,
Far, through their rosy depths, dost thou pursue
　　Thy solitary way?

. . .

"All day their wings have fanned
At that far height, the cold, thin atmosphere,
Yet stoop not, weary, to the welcome land,
　　Though the dark night is near.

"And soon that toil shall end;
Soon shalt thou find a summer home, and rest,
And scream among thy fellows; reeds shall bend,
    Soon, o'er thy sheltered nest.

"Thou'rt gone, the abyss of heaven
Hath swallowed up thy form; yet, on my heart
Deeply hath sunk the lesson thou hast given,
    And shall not soon depart."

When I read these words over now I can hear the soft voice of the Indian girl, mingling with the London traffic, sweet as the chiming of bells.

The high spot of the Conference speeches came the day that the Right Honourable Walter Runciman addressed us, for he, of all the speakers, seemed to have the clearest grasp of world conditions. He was the first speaker who impressed me as being an internationalist.

"The brotherhood of man," he said, "is a reality whether we like it or not. The law of the jungle must give way to the law of the family. We are all one, whether we are white or black, brown or yellow. No country can self-contain its sin. Opium grown in China slays young women in London flats. Alcohol distilled in Scotland curses West Africa, and decimates tribe after tribe. The misfortunes of the low-wage Japanese have an influence on wages paid in Britain and America.

"The old standards fall. The heart of man must be fired with a new affection. The New Testament must supersede the Old."

When the Conference was over I stayed another month, enjoying the sights, sounds and smells of this greatest city in the world. I loved to see the great flood of humanity pouring down the gray canyons of its narrow streets. I saw the good-natured queues waiting to buy theatre tickets, sitting on their camp stools and happily eating hot chestnuts, reading the *News of the World*, or knitting, or watching the street artists bring sunsets, or cataracts to their canvasses.

I read the *News of the World,* too. It was the first periodical to welcome me to London. (Mrs. Fuller told me afterwards I had better not mention that.) At that time it seemed to specialize on the finding of skeletons in attics and under park benches. The Londoners certainly did leave their skeletons in strange places.

I went to see the Guard change at Buckingham Palace. I visited the Editor of the Children's Newspaper, the energetic and charming Arthur Mee. I was even allowed to sit in the Distinguished Strangers' Gallery in the House of Lords, and looked down at the nineteen noble Lords and the many empty seats. Lord Lonsdale was speaking on the rehabilitation of Germany, but no one listened—none of the Lords, I mean. The reporters took it down, and I read it in *The Times* the next day. Lord Lonsdale was advocating a fairly sound principle too, when he said—"we cannot be prosperous in a bankrupt world, so let us try to put Germany back on her economic legs."

Some of my happiest hours in London were spent with Mabel Durham, whom I had known when she edited the "Women's Page" in the *Vancouver Daily Province*; in 1921 she was working for the Canadian National Railway, and from her I learned much, not only about London, but about rural England, for Mabel has a sharp eye and the gift of imparting information. Each Sunday evening we went to the Guild Hall Fellowship to hear Maude Royden, who in our opinion was one of London's best preachers. She had been denied ordination in her own church, the Anglican, and so carried on independently and very successfully. We had to go early to get a seat.

Miss Royden was a scholarly speaker, but in her aftermeetings when she left the pulpit and answered questions ranging from British foreign policy to advice to the lovelorn, she captivated her audience with her radiant good humor. She was very impressive, too, in her blue gown and blue cap, but when I met her once at a luncheon and had the honor of sitting beside her we had hardly a word to say to each other. All her lights seemed to have gone out or perhaps the fault was in me.

I could write much about the hospitality of the British. Two Scots-women contributed greatly to my happiness, Miss Jean C. Watt of Glasgow and the beloved Jenny Morris of 34 Bedford Place. They were friends of our son, Jack, and received me with generous affection. Many a lonely soldier in the last war and in this one, too, was cheered and cared for by these two noble women.

There came a day in London when I decided that I must have a warmer room. The little plaintive fireplace with its tiny wigwam of sticks was ineffectual in its efforts to lift the damp chill of the London climate, so I approached the manageress. She was a fluttering little thing full of apologies for her country and her establishment.

"But surely you do not feel the cold," she said in mild reproof. "You have such terrible temperatures in Canada. I never dreamed you would be cold. I thought this would seem like summer weather to you."

I tried to explain about outside and inside temperatures and what good facilities we had in our houses for keeping warm.

"It is all very puzzling," said Miss Crowe. "I never will understand the colonials."

I had with me a delightful young Englishwoman whom I had met on the boat. She had lived in Saskatchewan, but was going back to England to stay with her family, her husband having been killed in France at the end of the war. She and I had stayed together at Miss Crowe's establishment, and when we decided to make a change she found very good accommodation at one of the Carleton Mansions, where we could share a large room which had a good old-fashioned coal stove and by paying extra for the service we could have a fire all the time. Many theatrical people were staying in the same house and we learned much of life behind the footlights from them. They were a queer, temperamental, good-hearted, improvident lot who would do the kindest and yet the meanest things to each other.

At the end of September we went to France, all arrangements having been made for us by one of the Travel Agencies. Mrs. Leonard, the young war widow, wanted to visit her husband's grave in the cemetery of Louez, and so we went by train from Boulogne to Arras. According to my diary we were in Arras on September 26th, staying at the Hotel de la Univers, arriving there in the early evening. A dance was going on in the courtyard below our window, which we were able to watch, and soon discovered it was a wedding. The cobblestones in the courtyard must have been hard on the feet, but no person seemed to mind that. One lovely girl in a pink dress had a graceful black cape over her shoulders, which swung gracefully as she danced. The men of the party wore white gloves and many of the people taking part were quite old. At one end of the courtyard the cab drivers sat on the floor of their cabs as soundly asleep as their horses who stood with hanging heads. A priest walked up and down in deep thought and a quiet group of children played hopscotch. Three violinists supplied the music and they played "The Flowers of the Forest." There was no hilarity about it and yet no sadness.

Less than three years ago Arras lay in ruins, with one thousand of her people dead in the debris and her soldiers facing the German guns. The Hotel de la Univers had all been rebuilt, but her people now, young and old, could still dance at a wedding, howbeit a little more gently than they would have done before the war. I was very thrilled to be actually in Arras to see the labyrinth of narrow alleys, the bridge across the Crinchon River and the Court House where Father Madelein proclaimed to the world that he was Jean Valjean the convict. Then I remembered that the Court House was under repairs that year, according to the story, and it was in the great hall of the Bishop's Palace that the trial was held.

We went out early the next morning and we found the Court House, and again it was under repairs, for a German bomb had taken off the roof and the same fate had befallen the Hotel de la Poste, where Father Madelein had arrived that night a hundred years ago. The whole place was familiar to me for I had read the story again and again and each time was gripped with its magnificence and splendor.

Not even the attrition of the years could wear away one atom of its power. The story of Jean Valjean is more than a story—it's a life in which we live, we breathe and feel. I found myself thinking of the story in Victor Hugo's own words, not my own. My friend, Mrs. Leonard, was as keen about it as I was and together as we stood outside the Bishop's Palace we recalled it bit by bit. We remembered how the brass knob of the door of the court room gleamed like a horrible star, as Father Madelein waited without, struggling with the great decision.

He could so easily have gone back to his beloved people at M sur M. Surely he owed something to them, but at last he turned the knob of the door and walked in and saw himself in the tragic figure of the poor wretch on trial and heard him tell his story.

It was a sad story of cold, hunger and disappointment. Surely life meant nothing to him; he had never known any happiness. He might as well go to the galleys. Father Madelein saw his old companions from the galleys who had been brought as witnesses and each of them declared this wretched man to be Jean Valjean. All Father Madelein needed to do was to do nothing.

Then suddenly the court room rang with the cry so lamentable that all who heard it were chilled to the heart. Father Madelein, who sat among the privileged spectators, had risen to his feet and stood in the middle of the hall. He held his hat in his hand. His hair, which had been touched with gray when he arrived in Arras that night, had turned snow white in the hour he had sat there fighting his great battle.

He was so calm, so composed, no one thought the terrible cry they had heard had come from his lips.

"Gentlemen of the Jury," he said, and his voice was sweet and gentle, "order the prisoner released and have me arrested. I am Jean Valjean."

Consternation sat upon the faces of the Judges. Father Madelein, the beloved mayor of M sur M, was known to all of them. He had gone mad, surely.

"Is there a physician in the audience?" cried the Judge. Then followed the great words that can still restore one's faltering faith in the nobility of humanity.

"God, who is on high," said he, "sees what I am doing and that suffices. I have done my best. I concealed myself under another name and tried to re-enter the ranks of the honest, but it seems it can't be done. A man who has been so greatly humbled as I have has no remonstrances to make with Providence and no advice to society. Before going to the galleys I was a poor peasant, stupid, perhaps; they made me vicious. I was a block of wood; I became a firebrand. Later on kindness saved me as cruelty had destroyed me, but you would not understand. Now take me. Here I am, and let that man go free."

And no man there dared to arrest him for in that chamber there were no longer judges, accusers, gendarmes, nothing but staring eyes and sympathizing hearts. No one could have told how he felt. All were inwardly dazzled. They had witnessed the magnificent act of a man who freely delivered himself up that another man might go free.

I think it was the France of Victor Hugo I had come to see.

That year, 1921, brought many of the next-of-kin to see where their dead were buried and the French women made wreaths for the graves of great variety and beauty. The forget-me-nots made with blue beads could hardly be told from the real flowers. Mrs. Leonard bought a big cross of violets at a little flower shop, and a spray of beautiful roses, real ones, and then we went back to the Hotel to wait for the car to take us to the cemetery, two or three miles from Arras. The town looked battered and grim in the bright light of morning. Soap-sudsy water was running over the cobblestones as if many housekeepers had already finished their washing and turned the suds loose in the open drains.

When the car came we started with Mr. Morrell, our driver and guide, on the way to the cemetery. It lies on a northern slope facing red-roofed farm buildings in the lowlands across the road and on this day it was bathed in the hazy amber sunshine. An edge of young oaks ran around it inside the fence and on the hill above, outlined against the sky were beautiful trees of uniform height standing close together, so even, so symmetrical, and dark against the sky, they looked like an elaborate mourning border for the field of crosses below.

At the east of the field were the French graves where Michel, Jean, Peter, Paul and Francois lie. Then come the Scottish and English heroes. At the west were the Canadians, many of them C.M.R.'s.

The grass was growing green on their graves, and yellow and white poppies were blooming as well as snapdragons and sweet clover. Many of them had fresh wreaths of flowers, showing that their friends had lovingly remembered them.

Mrs. Leonard had no trouble in finding the grave she was looking for. Its number and row was stamped on her mind. She tied on the beautiful cross of violets and lovingly laid the roses below. We did not speak and walked away, leaving her alone with her dead, though I think she knew our hearts were mourning with her.

Many of the French graves had not even grass growing on them. Only the pale, yellow lumpy clay, and nothing on the cross but the tin rosettes bearing the tricolor for France, faded now by the wind and rain, loosened too and rattling as the wind passed over them, making a weird singing in this quiet street of the dead.

I had not known that there were acres and acres and acres of these white crosses and as I looked at them my heart was swept with a feeling of desolation and horror at the enormity of war. Surely it was not for this that these brave young fellows were born. I tried to think of them as lying at peace in the land they fought to save; I tried to pray that it might lie lightly to their bones and that God's richest treasures in heaven might be their inheritance, but I knew it was all wrong and my heart was hot with rebellion.

We climbed Vimy Ridge one day and there were many like us who had come to see this tragic place. Great rolls of rusting barbed wire, wheels, shafts and other bits of wreckage of what once had been machines of death littered the grass. Below us, and not far away, men in blue smocks plowed their fields, one man leading the horse and another man guiding the plow. Farther away we could see cattle grazing. Below our feet small yellow and pink flowers bloomed in calm assurance that Nature still has a way of hiding her scars.

There was something about all this placidity and composure which seemed wrong. I don't know what I expected to find, but certainly it seemed that we had forgotten too soon the wanton destruction of human life. How cheaply blood had flowed into this unheeding soil!

Once I stooped and dug into the soil with my hand, wondering what I might find. A button met my touch; a button attached to a piece of gray cloth. I put it back hastily for I was not hunting for souvenirs.

When we reached the top of Vimy Ridge a beautiful panorama met our eyes; the land fell away in a gentle slope for miles and miles and it seemed as if we were looking into the very heart of the enemy country. To our right lay the village of Lens, and we remembered how often this name has appeared in the news. It was a desolate sight, shelled and broken.

26

On the Writing of Books

T HE MATTER OF CHURCH UNION came before the Legislative Assembly in 1925, in all its fury and bitterness. We who were Methodists or Congregationalists knew very little of the trials our Presbyterian friends were enduring. As a matter of history, the subject of the union of the three churches was first thought of by the Presbyterians. Many years before. So no matter what happened afterwards, to the Presbyterians belongs the honor of instituting the first move.

The Methodists and Congregationalists went into union without a dissenting voice, but in many places the Presbyterians suffered all the heart scaldings of a family quarrel.

To some of the older people the Act of Union tore at their hearts like the burning of the peasants' cottages when the landlords in the Highlands of Scotland wanted room for their hunting. If they had been asked to burn their Bibles and deny their Lord they could not have been more fiercely rebellious.

I did not know this until a delegation came before the Legislative Assembly to present the case against Union. We all knew, of course, that some of the Presbyterians thought the prestige of their church would suffer if they united with the Methodists. One dear old lady said it was "just as if the son of a nobleman forgot his station and married the servant girl." But after we listened to one of the speakers of the delegation we knew that it was not only from the aged that the bitterness emanated. The last speaker on the delegation was a minister from Central Alberta, a man I knew very well and respected highly. He was an able fellow, pastor of a missionary church, known for his wise leadership in social problems and a fine brotherly spirit of co-operation with all the other churches in his town. I had heard he was opposed to Union but found it hard to believe. Surely, I thought, he cannot be blind to the advantages of Union, especially here in this new part of Canada, where the little towns have three and four churches and many wide areas have no preaching service at all.

I will never forget that man's appeal to us. It lacked all sense of balance, but its sincerity was shattering. I knew it came from his heart. He pleaded with us not to do this iniquitous thing. His eyes flashed like lightning in a dark night, and his face was white with rage. He ended with a declaration of undying defiance: "Give my roof to the flame, and my flesh to the eagles." Then he walked out with the proud bearing of a man of God on his way to the stake.

No, it was not melodramatic. It was something far worse. It was an exhibition of spiritual strabismus, the like of which I had never seen before. There was something terrible in it.

I had been born and bred in the tradition of the Covenanters and had thrilled to their brave words of defiance and the courage of the people who gathered in caves to sing their psalms and worship God as freemen in their own way, unhampered by a proscribed form of worship. But that day I saw another side of this whole matter of religious tradition, and what a deadly thing it can be when divorced from the saving grace of common sense. No wonder Christ warned his followers to "try the spirits and see whether they be of God."

I spent many pleasant hours in the Library of Parliament Buildings in Edmonton, during the five sessions I served as a member there. The House sat from three to six Monday to Friday, and this allowed us ample time for other activities. In one corner of the reading room I often saw a reserved little man in a gray lustre coat, poring over reports and records. I knew he was Sir Cecil Denny, who was writing the history of the Royal Northwest Mounted Police. I tried to talk to Sir Cecil but I did not get far. He was not to be beguiled into conversation. It may have been because he was intent on his writing, just as I should be intent on mine now, knowing the days are evil. He certainly had the "work-for-the-night-is-coming" look upon his face.

Sir Cecil Denny died in 1928, with his work uncompleted, but he made provision in his will for its revision and publication and this was faithfully done by W. B. Cameron, author of a valuable book called *When Fur Was King*. Sir Cecil also provided that 350 copies should be given free to the schools of Alberta.

I wanted to know Sir Cecil because I had heard about him from his friend and mine, E. N. Higinbotham, who had homesteaded beside him on Willow Creek, near Lethbridge, in 1885.

I know him now through his book, *The Law Marches West*, a copy of which I have on my desk, a gift from our mutual friend. It is an authentic and carefully written account of the "Riders of the Plains" in their earliest years, a real contribution to our history and a fitting tribute to the brave men who brought law and order to the great unknown land which lay west of the Red River. The Royal Northwest Mounted Police came into being the year I was born, and, like all other Western Canadians, I was brought up on that great and proud tradition of incorruptible men who knew no fear, a "terror to evildoers and a praise to them that do well." Many novelists have written about them, Sir Gilbert Parker, James Oliver Curwood, Agnes Laut, to mention only a few, but no one had a greater first-hand knowledge of their early struggles and strivings and triumphs than the dignified little man in the gray lustre coat poring over yellowing manuscripts and letters in the Provincial Library at Edmonton, insulated from the world by the urgency of his task.

It may have been Sir Cecil's industry which drove me to do some serious reading while I had the Provincial Library at my elbow. For years I had wanted to write an immigration story in the form of a novel. I wanted to portray the struggles of a young girl who found

herself in Canada dependent upon her own resources, with everything to learn, including the language.

I thought first of taking a Ukrainian girl as my heroine for it
was easy to get books on the Ukrainian background, but I had
been greatly attracted to Finland because of its advanced attitude
to women. Finnish women received the vote and sat in parliament
long before any other women, and I wondered about this and what
quality of mind had brought it about. I knew, too, about the Continuation Schools in Finland, where boys and girls whose education
had been neglected were sent after working hours at their employer's
expense, with the result that illiteracy in Finland was being entirely
overcome.

I had a Finnish girl in my kitchen at this time, a fine-looking
blonde with reddish hair, high cheekbones, even white teeth and a
passion for cleanliness, dating back to a long line of steam-bathing
ancestors. I knew about their soft-soap scourings and beatings of
birch branches followed by rollings in the snow if the time happened
to be in winter, and there is a long winter in Finland, and I reasoned
that people who take their bodily cleanliness so seriously must be a
great people, and I still think so.

One day my Finnish maid had a visitor, a man of perhaps forty
years of age, with a rugged, weather-beaten face and the dress of a
lumberman come to town who has just had a shave and a haircut
and is a bit uncomfortable in a starched collar. I thought, of course,
that he was one of Hanna's admirers, for she had many, but he told
me that he had come to see what sort of people we were and to find
out how his countrywoman was faring at our hands.

I was somewhat doubtful of this fine-looking gentleman in the
blue suit. I knew from past experiences that foreign girls have often
been bitterly deceived by their own countrymen in Canada who
shamelessly take advantage of the girls' ignorance of our laws. I knew
one girl who believed she was legally married because her countryman had shown her a "paper" and told her that was all that was
needed in Canada. The paper turned out to be an overdue tax notice.
So I scrutinized Mr. Emil Milander carefully and I wished that the

head of the house were at home for his judgment of men was much better than mine.

But I need not have doubted. Mr. Milander was all that he appeared. He had been in Canada for five years; had a farm on the Athabaska, lived alone, and gave himself a holiday each winter in the city, visiting his Finnish friends. He told me that he was older than many of the Finns who had come to Alberta and he tried to give them good advice, which was much needed, for, he said, there are black sheep Finns, too, many of them, who in this new country often forget the good religious training they had from their fathers and mothers.

I asked him to come back again for I wanted him to meet the whole family, and we enjoyed many visits with him. His English was picturesque but adequate and he carried a dictionary to be used in case of a deadlock.

He gave me the first book on Finland that I had seen, "Through Finland in Carts," by Mrs. Alec Tweedie, and from it I got a fascinating picture of the Finns with their songs and sports and their heroic struggle for existence as a nation. The book was written in 1913 and it is still interesting reading. I wonder if the countrywomen still wash their clothes in the streams and if they still think it queer to see people eat jam with their bread.

In Mrs. Tweedie's book I got my first taste of their epic poem, the "Kalevala," which was published in 1835 but was centuries in the making. I scoured the libraries for further information on it and found it had been gathered up bit by bit by a Doctor Lonnrat as he went on his rounds picking up bits of folklore, and it became a great factor in preserving their native language against the inroads of Swedish. For the native authors had discovered that the well-to-do people, the intelligentsia who could afford to buy books, spoke Swedish, and their books would have more buyers if written in the more genteel language, and for that reason the native tongue was neglected by native writers.

The "Kalevala," unlike many other antique epics, is characteristically gentle and domestic, delighting in situations of moral beauty.

Dr. Lonnrat was successful in collecting twelve thousand lines. These he arranged into thirty-two runes. A more complete text was published in 1887 by A. V. Forsman and the importance of this poem was at once recognized in Europe, and translations were made. It was translated into English by J. M. Crawford in 1888. An idea of its style may be obtained from Longfellow's "Hiawatha," which was written in imitation of the Finnish poem. I cannot refrain from quoting a few lines to show its beauty and also the interesting bit of information that in those days when the trees were burned down to clear the land, the ashes were used as a fertilizer:

"On the mountains grew the berries,
Golden flowers in the meadows,
And the herbs of many colours,
Many kinds of vegetation;
But the barley is not growing.

"Osma's barley will not flourish,
Not the barley of Wainola,
If the soil be not made ready,
If the forest be not levelled,
And the branches burned to ashes.

"Only left the birch-tree standing,
For the birds a place of resting,
Where might sing the sweet-voiced cuckoo,
Sacred bird in sacred branches."

I read many books about Finland, some sent to me by Erick Korte, the Finnish consul at Port Arthur, and I began to get the feeling of the country, their intense nationalism, their delight in communal singing. Music and verse filled their very souls and kept their spirits alive during the long dreary winter nights as they sat in their small houses, prisoners of darkness.

No wonder the coming of the spring intoxicates them with happiness and sends them singing with delight, dancing through the woods, released at last from the spell of the ghosts and goblins that dominated their souls in the long black hours.

I tried to put myself into the character of Helmi, who came from Finland to her Aunt in St. Paul, Minnesota, only to find that her Aunt had been stricken with a fatal disease. Her Aunt implored the little girl to return to the safe shelter of her homeland, but Helmi had a mind of her own and had no intention of retracing her steps. She was in the land of freedom, romance and easy money and here she would stay. I called her Helmi Milander in compliment to Emil Milander, who had really introduced me to his country and countrymen.

Painted Fires was the name I chose for the book, lifting these words from the fragment of a poem which stuck in my mind; I do not know from what source:

"We cannot draw from empty wells,
Nor warm ourselves at painted fires."

I called the book by this name for I wanted to lay down a hard foundation of truth as to conditions in Canada. As a Canadian I blush with shame when I think of the false flattery which has been given to our country by immigration agencies in Europe, anxious to bring out settlers for the profit of steamship and railway companies. It's all fantastic now and seems long ago and far away, but there was dark tragedy in it for the deceived ones and Canada got a black eye, which in the minds of some people has lasted even until this time.

Painted Fires was published in 1925 and has gone through many editions, been serialized many times and is still in print. The year after its publication in Canada it was translated into Finnish and published in Helsinki and I think all the Finnish papers on this continent ran it as a serial.

It brought me into pleasant contact with many Finnish people and I was particularly pleased to receive letters written in Finnish, telling me that although I had not a Finnish name, they felt sure that I must have Finnish blood to be able to enter into their spirit. Could any author ask for more than that?

In addition to the help and encouragement I received from Erick Korte of Port Arthur, I am also indebted to other Finnish editors and writers: John E. Rantamaki of Hancox, Michigan, Rev. W. Rautarien of Warren, Ohio, J. T. Ruolsslainen, editor of the Canadian Finnish paper at Port Arthur, and Consul Carl H. Salminen, Duluth, Michigan, all of whom wrote reviews, and in many ways brought the book to the attention of their countrymen.

From Finland I had a long and delightful correspondence from the publisher, Dr. Eino Railo, and as a result of the publication I took payment of royalties in two oil paintings by one of their artists, Arthur Heickell, and these beautiful pictures are among my treasures. I have not, during my earthly pilgrimage, gathered about me much impedimenta. I have endeavored to travel light. But I do treasure these two beautiful paintings and my file of Finnish letters, as well as a book about Finland published by the Government and sent to me "with the best wishes of all Helmi's countrymen." I count it a great privilege to have had this pleasant contact with the indomitable Finns.

Speaking of travelling light through life, I recall a story of Bob Edwards, the founder and editor of the Calgary *Eye-Opener*. He was telling about a boy who had gone from Alberta to make his fortune in New York and came back with "fifty-two pieces of matched luggage," which, however, turned out to be a deck of cards.

27

The Middle Years

THE MIDDLE YEARS OF LIFE come on like thunder. In 1923 we moved to Calgary. And Wes had a long and painful illness. Paul had gone to Texas the year before and Florence was married and now lived in Regina. Jack was at Queen's College, Oxford. So the family had scattered.

But we knew the inevitability of change and rejoiced to know they were all well and happy, following their own ambitions and desires.

While the House was in session I spent five days each week in Edmonton, with only Saturdays and Sundays at home, two crowded days, but happy ones, too, beginning with the black dog's welcome. Pal, our black retriever, sat on the top step watching for me as I walked the short distance from the street car. He sat with his head between his paws like a dog of stone, giving no sign of recognition. This was our game. Before I stepped off the sidewalk to our own walk I stopped and said:

"Good morning, Pal." Still he made no sign, but when I stepped down to our own walk he came bounding to me, a huge black weight, full of gladness. Each Saturday morning we went through this ritual and I believe he looked forward to it all week. One Saturday I did not come until the afternoon train and Pal sat all day on the step.

I must not, in these days of paper shortage, indulge in the blessed memories of this clever and devoted dog, who not only understood human speech, but was actually a mind reader.

I was defeated in the Provincial Election of 1926, but that was a minor matter compared with the loss of our dog the same year, who was struck by an automobile whose driver did not even stop.

While we lived in Edmonton I enjoyed my membership in the Legislative Assembly, but after we went to Calgary to live it took me away from home too much, so my defeat had many compensations, and I know my feelings were not much hurt because the next week I wrote an article entitled: "How It Feels to be a Defeated Candidate," and I know from experience that the grief that can be turned into words soon heals.

Two days before the election an official of the Hotelkeepers' Association had come to see me and asked me if I couldn't put the soft pedal on my antagonism to the liquor business.

"Government control has been carried and the hotels have beer bars and so for the present, at least, you can't do a thing about it. It's here and it's going to stay. You did all you could to defeat both of these. Everyone knows how you feel about it, but if you will lay off now, we'll vote for you, for you're a good straight-shooter and we like you. We even like to listen to you—on any other subject. We think you are a good member in the House, and with the exception of one or two in our organization, we all feel the same way. You have some good friends among the hotelkeepers."

I was touched by his words and I told him I would always appreciate his coming.

"My quarrel has never been with the hotel people," I said. "I know that most of you do your best to run good houses. But the evil is in the stuff itself, no matter who handles it. Alcohol no doubt has a place in medicine, but as a beverage it is a racial poison. It lowers a man's standard of conduct and makes the user pay a heavy price. Every one of you hotel men could run your houses without it, and make money, too, and you would be happier in your heart. Some day humanity will outlaw it just as slavery was wiped out. That took a long time, and this will too, but I cannot promise that I will ever 'lay off.' I thank you for coming and I hope you will tell the other men how I feel."

We shook hands and parted with mutual good will.

From the angle of human interest, defeat is more attractive than success, inasmuch as it is a more common experience. The average reader can contemplate with considerable fortitude the sorrows and disappointments of someone else. I have refreshed my memory of that time by re-reading what I wrote about it when it was fresh in my mind. I can see that the meeting in the committee rooms after the polls were closed and the returns were coming in was not exactly a cheerful one, although we tried hard to keep up our spirits, and told each other gamely that it was anybody's election. We had proportional representation, and that, of course, took a lot of counting. I did very well on the Number One votes and stood third, but did not get enough of the second and third choices.

By ten o'clock we knew that one of our party was elected, one was defeated, and I was hovering between life and death. By eleven o'clock I decided to call it a day and leave my political fate in the hands of the scrutineers. So I came home and went to bed and to sleep.

I slept until I heard the clip-clop of the milkman's horses. Then I got up and stood at the window to see the sunbeams slanting low across the lawn. It was a comforting scene with the big trees throwing long shadows on the grass.

Then I turned on the radio and got the final score. I was down by sixty votes, and that account was closed. Just for a moment, I had a queer, detached sensation, a feeling of bewilderment, and then I knew I never really believed I would be defeated, but that moment passed and I thought of the two boys. They were at the age when it is slightly embarrassing to have a mother, and especially one who goes out and gets herself defeated. We all made a fine show of cheerfulness at breakfast. After all, it's just as well to admit the presence of a stone wall. The two lads played up well and said they were glad I was going to be at home now, and that it had been no fun to have me away so much, and I appreciated that, but there must have been some root of bitterness in me for I was seized with a desire to cook, and I wanted the kitchen all to myself.

No woman can be utterly cast down who has a nice bright kitchen facing the west, with a good gas range and a blue and white checked linoleum on the floor, a cook book, oil cloth covered and dropsical with looseleaf editions. I set off at once on a perfect debauch of cooking. I grated cheese, stoned dates, whipped cream and made salad dressing and I let the phone ring. It could tear itself out by the roots for all I cared. I was in another world—the pleasant, landlocked, stormless haven of double boilers, jelly molds, flour sifters. The old stone sugar crock with the cracked and handleless cup in it seemed glad to see me and even the marmalade tins with their typed labels, sitting in a prim row, welcomed me back and asked no questions. I patted their honest flat heads and admitted that the years had been long; reminding them, too, that I had seen a lot more wear and tear than they had.

I'm ashamed to have to tell it but I got more comfort that day out of my cooking spree than I did from either my philosophy or my religion, but I know now, when the smoke of battle had cleared away, that I was the beneficiary of that great promise which assures us "that the rivers of sorrow shall not overflow." We often get blessings that we do not recognize at all, much less acknowledge, but God is not so insistent as we are about having all gifts acknowledged.

I do not think I could have endured it that day if my cooking had gone wrong, but nothing failed me and no woman can turn out an ovenfull of good flaky pies with well-cooked undercrusts and not find peace for her troubled soul.

The next day I wanted to get out. I wanted to look away to the mountains, blue in the distance, with ice caps on their heads, so I went to Earl Grey Golf Course and played all morning. The game was not entirely successful. I was too conscious of the Elbow Park houses below me, some of them vaguely resentful, others leering at me with their drawn blinds, like half-closed Conservative eyes. I got on better and did some splendid driving by naming the balls and was able by that means to deliver some pretty powerful pokes.

When one door shuts, another one opens. I remembered what Basil King said when he spoke to us at the Arts and Crafts Club in Toronto in 1921. He had been an Anglican clergyman, but suffered a physical misfortune which made it impossible for him to continue his work.

"On the day I learned the bitter truth that I could no longer continue my work as a pastor," he said, "I bought a typewriter."

I remember the next few years with great satisfaction, for I returned in earnest to my writing. I wrote a short story a week for a syndicate as well as magazine articles, and found no difficulty in finding material. It was all around me. It walked the streets, it came to my door, it even came in with the letters. My difficulty was in choosing, not finding.

The published stories made two volumes, *Be Good to Yourself* and *Flowers for the Living*. The unwritten stories would have filled another two. Some of the most poignant I could not write.

A woman came to me one day, with a tale of neglect and cruelty which was hard to believe. She was a Ukrainian woman with six children, four at school, and her man was a mechanic in the C.P.R. shops at Ogden. Her man was anxious to get rid of her and the family. He had another younger woman ready to take over, and decided he would starve out the family. The mother was afraid to let the neighbors know for he might kill her. He wouldn't pay the light bill so there had been no light in the house for two months, and very little food. Her boys were beginning to steal bread from the baker's wagon. She was afraid the police would get after them and take them from her. She was a pitiful creature, nervously exhausted.

I gave her a hot meal and got some warmer clothes for her, then drove her home to the North Hill and went to see some of the neighbors. I wanted to be sure that she had told me the truth. Some of the neighbors would not talk at all, the selfish ones, who told me they believed in minding their own business. (They belong in all strata of society.) But there were others more courageous, who corroborated her story. One woman told me the children had been coming to her house to do their homework and she said they were good children if they had half a chance. All this I set down on paper, and decided I would see the Chief of Police. I had heard the Chief speak at a child welfare meeting, and liked his voice and his manner. David Ritchie was a Scotsman from Glasgow and I could see that he was much more than the head of a Police Force. Or, rather, I should say he was the ideal head for these guardians of the law. So I laid the matter before him without delay. He listened carefully and assured me the case would have his attention.

In a week I had two visitors from the North Hill, two women with domestic troubles, seeking a solution.

"Why do you come to me?" I asked in surprise.

"Oh, missus, you fix Mrs. Korski's man so good! He get light in house right away—so kwick! Bring home meat, clothes and boots for kids, get new coat for his wife. She say you do it all!"

I knew who had wrought the miracle, but I kept that to myself. I thought it better for Mr. Korski's morale if the truth concerning his reformation were not known in the neighborhood.

When I submitted the new cases to the Chief he told me the story of Mr. Korski's return to good behavior.

"I sent one of my men in uniform to the Ogden shops. He interviewed the foreman first, who had the mechanic brought into his office. Then the sergeant brought him here, and by that time he was thoroughly frightened. They are all frightened of the law. To them a policeman is an enemy. He sat there where you're sitting, white as chalk, and I told him how we deal with men like him in this country, and I told him what I wanted him to do. He was ready to promise anything. One of my men will make a visit there every week, and I don't think we'll have any more trouble. He is a good mechanic and gets a big salary, so he's well able to support his wife and family, and we'll see that he does it. There is a great satisfaction in dealing with wrongdoing before it happens."

That was the beginning of a series of cases (not all from the foreign quarter) where family problems told to me were unsnarled by the wise intervention of Chief Ritchie.

Life reveals whole stories sometimes in a flash, perhaps a sentence heard in a telephone booth, or a chance meeting in a railway station where the tide of humanity comes and goes. The "stuff" of life is all around us.

I remember seeing once in the Railway Station in Calgary a quiet little pale-faced woman in rusty black, sitting beside a battered valise and eating out of a paper bag. Her skirt was too long, her shoes were run over at the heel, and her gloves did not match. As she ate her sandwiches she was reading a small book with a red and black cover, and what attracted me to her was that she was not only reading it, she was studying it with intense interest, moving her lips as she read. No doubt she was getting some little crumb of romance from its cheap pages. My curiosity was so great that I moved over to see just what was absorbing her, and I read, over her shoulder, the caption:

"Directions for Swallowing a Sword."

I wanted to talk to her. There was surely a story here, but unfortunately I had to go out on the platform to meet someone. I looked back at her before going out through the big doors and I noticed that the front of her battered felt hat held a strange device made of silver wire, some sort of ornament. I had to come back to get a closer look and I found it was letters about three inches high and the word they made was "Whoopee."

I couldn't write the story of these years without mentioning the beautiful young Hungarian girl who came to us not knowing one word of English. I shall call her Elsa, though that was not her name. I taught her to read and I know she toils through everything I write, and she might be shocked to see her name in a book. Elsa deserves to have a whole book written about her, for her courage and her uprightness and her desire for knowledge. Her brother, who had come to Canada three years before, had sent her the money for her ticket, but sent no money for expenses, so she arrived in Montreal and boarded the train for Calgary without a cent in her pocket, and without a word of English on her tongue. Stricken with hunger and huddled in misery, she sat in the corner of her seat, afraid to make any outcry. She knew that sometimes people were sent back to the Old Country. When her train left Winnipeg, a kindly conductor noticed her. She was crying then from hunger, and he quickly brought relief from the diner and saw to it that she was taken care of for the rest of her journey. When she learned enough English she told me this and told me, too, that some of her fellow passengers had given her three dollars and she knew then that Canada was a good country.

It was my good fortune to be in touch with the Employment Bureau a day or two after Elsa had arrived. I mentioned to the manager that I would be needing help at the end of the month and had no objection to taking a girl who knew no English. Then he told me about the lovely girl that he had in the office, and how anxious he was to get a good position for her. He said she was as bright as a dollar and as pretty as a picture, and that described her, and so it happened that Elsa and I began the study of Basic English that very day, and a friendship began which has never grown dim. When she found that we had no objection to Hungarian cooking she decided to show us the culinary art of her people. She often assembled a dish of chopped meat, onions and peppers rolled in cabbage leaves and fastened with skewers and baked in the oven and served with boiled rice which became a great favorite. I never could say the name of the dish or even spell it. Her apple pies and chicken goulash are epic memories as were the buns and biscuits and pickled fish which she seemed to always keep on hand.

At first she suffered from loneliness, but one day she came in with a new light on her face. She had found a nice Hungarian family, good family, complete with boarder. Our medium of exchange was very limited at this time, but with the use of the English-Hungarian dictionary she showed me that "boarder" worked in a restaurant and had produced ice cream from box at friend's house.

In a week he appeared and took Elsa for a walk. He was a good looking, tall young man and could speak some English. He brought her back in a very short time and it was two weeks before we saw him again, and again he took her for a walk, time consumed about thirty minutes. There was no lingering and no visit; he said he had to get back to the restaurant. This went on for a couple of months, and then Elsa showed me her dictionary and pointed to the word which meant "marriage," but this was accompanied by much shaking of the head. I gathered he had not mentioned marriage and Elsa, accustomed to the direct ways of her countrymen, was wondering why. I searched through the dictionary and found the word which meant "wait." Meanwhile, of course, our lessons went on every day and Elsa was able to tell me more. Not a kiss, not even a squeeze of the hand—no sweet word. When Christmas came he presented her with a small chain and locket, but still no talk of marriage.

Several months went on and then another factor entered which I thought would quicken the pace of this slow-moving courtship or perhaps end it altogether. The new factor was called Rosie, who had been three years in Canada and who knew the tall young man. Rosie was beautiful, with red lips and high heels, and, by her own testimony, "could spik Inglis parfek" and had never gone to night school. Elsa went to night school two nights a week and was doing very well, but Rosie recommended lighter joys than night school. Night school was the bunk. Never got a girl nowhere. Come to dance to meet fella, said Rosie. Rosie had so many fella she could give Elsa one. All Elsa would need was silk dress, slippers, parfume; fella not care about girls spik Inglis. Laugh and dance and be good sport!

One visit from Rosie was as upsetting to my pupil as a Rodeo is to the Indians, but I had Mike, the young man who took her walking every second Sunday, on my side. Stick to night school, said Mike, and night school it was. And so the battle for the guardianship of Elsa went on.

Every time Rosie came she left Elsa disturbed, and I wished I knew some way of getting rid of her. We called her "the bit of bad news."

One night she came in so radiant I knew she had something to tell Elsa, something particularly unpleasant. She had a bristling air of importance and she had brought one of her numerous young men with her, and he, too, was in the secret, I could see.

I took them into the den and called Elsa. I had a feeling that I had better stay, for I suspected that Rosie knew something that I had learned a few hours before. Something which I had been deputed by Mike to tell Elsa, but I had not had time yet to decide just how I was going to do it. Mike had called me from the restaurant that afternoon, speaking so low over the telephone I could hardly hear him. He must see me, he said. And he could not come to my house. Would I come to Maple Leaf where he worked? Soon, right away, quick.

Having put my hand to the plow I could not turn back now. So I went to the Maple Leaf Cafe and it was all very mysterious. Mike gave me a telegraphic glance which meant: "Hold everything," and he brought me a dish of ice cream and the noon paper. I knew I would have to wait until the other customers had gone.

At last he was free and handed me an envelope, unsealed and addressed "To Whom It May Concern." It contained a testimonial to the character of one Jose Michael Bellagi who had faithfully discharged his duty for the space of three years in a restaurant in Winnipeg. He watched me as I read it, then handed me another one. His method of presenting these testimonials was unique. They came with a circular motion of the arm which was impressive but puzzling. Surely he's about to ask for Elsa's hand in honorable marriage, I thought.

Then Mike spoke.

"It is about Elsa. She is a nice girl. Good girl. Sometime I take her for walk. Just walk. Never did I speak of love. No kiss, even. I lift my hand to God. Do you believe me?"

"I do," I said.

Mike grasped my hand eagerly.

"I did not fool her. I am an honest man. Do you believe me?"

I did, and then again we shook hands.

"Will you tell her no more I come. She must not feel bad. I cannot tell her. You do better. Make her understand. Tell her nice."

"I'll tell her," I said, wondering what had happened. No doubt another girl, and my first thought was of Rosie, but I asked no questions. I did not get a chance to tell Elsa and now here before me were the messengers of gloom, ready to shout it at her. So I stayed in the room. I knew Rosie couldn't hold it long.

"Oh, Elsa," she began, "I got big news. Telegram came yesterday for Mike, Maple Leaf Cafe. Mike's girl from Winnipeg is coming tomorrow on the train and they are going to be married tomorrow night, in church. Ain't that nice, yes? Hungarian boy read telegram and told me."

Her face beamed as she said it. It was a big moment in her life. I wanted to choke her; she was so glad to see Elsa hurt.

Then I got a surprise. Elsa's face showed no emotion and I thought she hadn't yet taken it in.

"Oh, sure," she said in a voice that deceived me completely. There wasn't a trace of sorrow in it, or even surprise. "I'm very glad for Mike. He is a good fella. Friendly to me when I come here strange. I will get nice present tomorrow. Very kind of you to come and tell me, Rosie. I did not know she come so soon!"

Rosie's big shell had not exploded after all, so she and her young man departed somewhat crestfallen.

When they were safely off the premises I told Elsa how proud I was of her, and then I told her what Mike had told me that afternoon, but she wasn't listening. Her face had gone small and white, and I could see the lips quivering. I tried to comfort her. I told her that Mike had not deceived her.

"But why did he come?" she kept saying. "Why did he give me present? He must have like me a little bit. I liked him so good!"

Her teeth were chattering and her whole body shook. I tried to explain that boys and girls could like each other very much and still not want to marry. Mike would always like her and be her friend.

"No," said she bitterly. "I don't want him for my friend if I can't have him for my man."

For two weeks Elsa went around with a dead face. She did her work mechanically, but grew thinner and paler. She could not eat or sleep and I was afraid I was really seeing what old-fashioned novelists delighted in portraying—the broken-hearted maiden dying for love.

One morning when I was having a late breakfast she came in and told me it was all over now, she was all better in her mind and would never think of Mike again, and thanked me for not scolding her when she burned the potatoes. We shook hands on that, drank a cup of coffee and felt that a crisis had been safely passed.

Elsa lived with us for five years and was married in our living room to a railway mechanic who had "master papers" from Buda Pest. She had a white satin dress with veil and orange blossoms, a diamond ring and a seal coat, and outsize photographs to send back to Hungary. The master mechanic had money in the bank, but Elsa persuaded him to buy a big house so she could keep roomers. I think that was the cleanest rooming house in Calgary. Following the depression she and her husband bought a beautiful house in Mount Royal, but after six months' trial of living on the "right side of town," they sold the big house with the circular driveway and went back to the neighborhood they had left and bought another rooming house.

"Feeling better now," she told us, when Wes and I were having dinner with her the last time we were in Calgary. (And what a dinner that was, with chicken goulash and raspberry pie!) "More like home for us among working people and I like keeping rooms clean and nice for people so they can rest when they come home and not have to sweep and wash dish-towels, and we like having them come down sometimes for real good dinner. People who cook on two rings like good meal. Up on Mount Royal every person had lots of time. They had plenty good stuff in their homes, good clothes, good pictures, books, pianos, everything. No one needed me, and that's all right, too. Nobody's fault."

I looked at Elsa with admiration. How wise she was to know that she was happier with her own kind and to arrive at that conclusion without any resentment or bitterness.

Elsa was one of the five girls to whom I taught English when they lived with us. Teaching them was no labor and they paid me back a hundred fold in devoted service, the service that cannot be bought with money, but even apart from that, I had great pleasure in seeing their minds unfold, with that spark of illumination which every teacher craves. After Elsa had learned to read English quite well I gave her a copy of Sara Teasdale's poem:

"They brought me with a secret glee
    The news I knew before they spoke,
And though they hoped to see me riven
They found me light as oak leaves driven,
    Before the storm that splits the oak."

I was delighted to see how it affected her. She saw herself in it and she saw more than that. She saw she was not alone. Other people had had to stand up to the ordeal of false friends. She committed the poem to memory and in trying to explain to me how much she liked it, she said:

"These words fit me like this," locking her hands together.

Women as a rule are not good employers; indeed they are notoriously poor employers, but I believe this current shortage of domestic help is having an influence. People are learning to know each other. I hope that even now some haughty dames are learning wisdom in the sweat of their brows and in the smarting of their chapped hands. Wisdom is often costly but it is always worth the price.

Housework is not in itself dull and disagreeable and it would appeal to the average girl who has an aptitude for it but for the cold stupidity of the mistress of the average home. They are the people who have pushed housework down to the bottom of the list and have driven out of the ranks of homemakers many bright girls who would have served them well. The average woman has been afraid to break the pattern—the pattern which says that the maid must wear a cap, use the back door, cheerfully give up her afternoon and evening, if necessary, and efface herself except when she is needed. She must be diligent, capable, amiable and serene at all times and know her place! What this program lacks is a recognition that the maid is a human being, not a robot, and has ambitions, desires and sensibilities of her own and must be allowed a certain amount of liberty so that she can have a life of her own. She needs friends and relaxation.

I always liked to know how my girls were spending their leisure time and so made their friends welcome and did not expect that the friends should be entertained in the kitchen either. It is good for a girl's morale to have the use of a den or some other pleasant room where she can forget the washing of dishes or the peeling of potatoes; and I would not expect my girls to go around by the back door when a young man brought them home. They had their own key to the front door and there was always a verandah light burning for them when they were out and they knew they were always welcome to bring their friend in for a cup of coffee. Little privileges like this help a girl to know that she is a person of importance with the protection and dignity of a family and a home.

My girls had a party at least once a year when their friends were invited and the living room rugs could be taken up for dancing. I like to remember how glad and gay they were with their own dances, folk songs and games. I remember particularly the Swedish parties, when Anna Swanson, Elsa's successor, presided over our culinary arrangements. Anna sang in the Swedish choir and many of her friends were excellent musicians. How the house rang with laughter and song and the dining room table was replete with braided cardamom bread, pineapple cake, pickled fish, which was eaten with rye bread. They referred to their refreshments as "smorgasbord," which seemed to cover everything, even the coffee. Wes and I were on hand to welcome the guests, but when that duty was performed we faded away and left them to their fun. And never once was this privilege abused.

My association with the girls from Europe gave me a chance to know something of the minds of their employers and some of this knowledge was painful, but revealing. No wonder girls prefer to work anyplace rather than in the kitchen. One of Anna's friends told me her mistress said she could not allow her to use the bathtub. Mary would have to have her bath at the "Y," which was about a mile distant. Mary took the news quite cheerfully, saying she would like that very well. It would be a lovely walk, but would it not take too much time every day? The lady exclaimed in horror:

"Not every day. One bath a week is plenty for you, and you can take it on your day out."

But Mary politely declined to use her precious time every Thursday in this way, and besides wanted a bath every day. She stuck to it, too. No bath, no work. She won, and I hoped she splashed and sang in the tub!

The mistress in this case was the wife of a University professor and the first time I saw her after hearing this story, she was reading a paper to a Woman's Club on the subject of Canadian Unity.

The matter of money and prompt payment of wages was another pressure point, and that brings up the story of Mareska, who decided to leave her place in Elbow Park. There was a matter of forty dollars coming to her when she left, for which her mistress urged her to take an old fur coat in payment. Mareska did not want the fur coat. She came to stay with Elsa for a week's rest before she went to another place, and that is how I came to know about her difficulty in collecting her money.

I felt sure I could collect the money from the lady who lived at Elbow Park, and whom I knew. I could not believe that she would do anything mean, so I phoned her and found her very apologetic. She said Mareska had gone away so suddenly she didn't know where she was. She would bring it over the very next day.

She did not come the next day. Several days passed and I phoned again but there was no answer. Then I phoned her neighbor and asked her to tell Mrs. W. to phone me on a matter of importance, and still there was no response. Then I went over and met her coming out of her house. She told me she had been sick and was just now going to the bank to get the money. A few days after this I decided I would get in touch with her husband who worked in one of the departmental stores. But before I did that the collection of Mareska's debt came about in another way.

Mareska had told her troubles to another Hungarian girl, who had a room in the home of a fiery Scotswoman from the Clyde. Mrs. Jean McCalmon was well-known and feared by the aldermen of the city, for she was a frequent visitor at their meetings, and always a dissenter. She wrote letters to the paper on many subjects, for Jean had the gift of words, not always pretty ones. To Jean McCalmon any fight was better than no fight.

When my phone rang I hoped the delinquent employer had decided to pay the money, but the voice on the phone was not her voice.

"Is that you, Nellamaclung?" came in Jean's unmistakable contralto. She always called me this, spoken as one word. "And do you ken whose speaking?"

"Aye, I ken," I said. "I never could mistake the voice of Jean McCalmon. There's no anither like it this side o' the Clyde."

She laughed in high good humor, and I knew she had won her fight with someone.

"You're quite a smart woman in your own way, Nellamaclung, but you'd better stick to your writing. For from all I can hear you're a ——— poor collector. I have ye beat there."

"How did you do it?" I asked.

"That's what I want to tell you. You ken Charlie, Charlie is a policeman who has a room here in my house; so when Charlie came in this evening, I says 'Charlie, I want a favor. Drive me over to Elba Park. There's a bit of unfinished business over there.' I often take Charlie wi' me when I need a bit of scenery behind me, like a man in uniform. So we drove over and Charlie came up the steps wi' me, and we rang the bell wi' a good loud clatter . . . Now mind ye, I didn't get rough wi' her. I remembered I was a lady, even if she wasn't, and when she opens the door and sees me and Charlie, she looked like a sick cat. But I spoke low and sweet, just as nice as you would yoursel' and all I said was:

"'You dirty hell-cat, do you no intend to pay that decent girl her money?'—And she turns and runs up the stairs like something that was shot out of a gun and she comes back with four ten dollars bills in her hand. So will you just tell Mareska to come over tonight and get her money."

28

Travellers' Joy

W HEN THE WAR IS OVER, and we begin to pick up the pieces, I hope that every facility for easy travel will be accorded us. Our relations with our neighbors are bettered as we go out among them. Visits keep friendship in repair. Many of the happiest memories of my life have for their background the open road. No wonder the song "Don't Fence Me In" rings a bell in many a heart.

The joy of the traveller cannot all be captured in words. It is elusive as the perfume of violets wet with dew and as hard to describe as the elation of soul which comes when the sunshine suddenly fills a room. One of the very happy memories of my life goes back to a day in January, 1938, when Wes and I sat in a Greyhound bus in Vancouver Bus Depot with return tickets for San Antonio in our pockets. Twice we had driven our own car on long trips with great enjoyment, but this time our anticipation was even keener with no responsibility, no parking problems, nothing to do but sit and ride. Wes and I have diverse tastes in many directions. He has always been a lover of sport, but has fought shy of grand opera, political meetings, and courses of lectures in which my heart delighted, but in the matter of travelling and seeing new places we have certainly been good companions. Travellers' joy—the freedom from routine, the liberating sense of being foot-loose, not knowing what the turn in the road will disclose, lifted our souls that day.

There are the sudden little scenes of beauty which flash out of the gray commonplace. On a busy crossing in Seattle we saw an old man feeding pigeons, while the traffic divided and circled around him and his flock; a sign over an auto camp "These Cabins are Either Clean or Closed"; a waitress in Portland who was able to serve a whole circle of customers, wiping away the debris with one hand, making out a bill with the other, watching the toast, frying eggs, and carrying on a conversation all at the one time. Only once did she stop, and that was when her wise-crack elicited no comment. Holding everything, she reproved her public with:

"Folks, I'm talking to you!"

And when we had made a suitable apology the wheels of commerce turned once more.

In Oregon we passed chicken houses ablaze with light at night to deceive the hens into believing that this was another day, to the end that more eggs might be produced, and that we felt was an infringement on the private life of the hens, who as a class have never shirked their public duties.

There are critics of our present day tendencies who say that standardization will catch up to all of us sooner or later and lay its icy hand on our individuality. We could see evidences of this in our own way of travelling; here we were contented to let the big motor bus carry us, instead of being independent with our own car, but it was all so pleasant that we refused to be disturbed over anything. We saw Mt. Shasta white with snow, winding and unwinding a scarf of mist around her head and Black Butte standing out clear and majestic and close at hand. When we asked the people of Dunsmuir, where we spent the night, how far away Black Butte really is, we found in their answers much the same spread as there is in the opinions of the Gordon Head people on the question of how far it is across the straits to the island of San Juan.

Certainly there were no signs of dull standardization in the people we met. There was the man from Alaska who complained of the cold when we stopped at Redding, California. He shivered in his big coat as we walked up and down on the platform and said this dampness might be all right for people who were used to it.

When we travelled through the California country that had just come through one of the worst floods in its history we heard a story that bore no traces of any weakening of the endurance of the people under trial.

The woman who told the story sat behind me and fortunately had a penetrating voice which carried her words easily above the sound of the wheels. She was sitting with a man who thought he knew something of floods and their evil workings, but she convinced him that he, with his trifling report of a ruined crop, was not even qualified to sit on the platform when real flood stories were being told. "Now listen to me, stranger!" I heard her say, and I was glad she talked him down for he was one of these stuffy, low-voiced people, who cannot be heard even one seat away!

"My folks," began the lady narrator, "were the Violses." She paused there dramatically and I knew that a good story was on its way to us. "I guess if any of you listen to your radios you know that name. You should. All that night, December the eleventh, when the water was at its height, the radio was hollering it—'Won't someone go out in a boat and find the Violses? The Violses are adrift in their house. Won't someone go out and get them? They are somewhere in the flood. We can't let the Violses drown, folks!'"

She had a good listening audience then, up and down the aisle, and she told her story with the eloquence of simplicity.

"Mother and Jim were alone. Jim said it never would come over the knoll, but Jim was wrong. It came over the knoll, with a lick and a swish and lifted the house as if it had been a match box and that was right about nine o'clock on Saturday morning. The house is strongly built and it rode the waters pretty good. It is a new house and it only has a canvas roof. It caught on a ridge at last, and that was all that saved them, but they knew if the waters got higher it would float off the ridge and go down the canyon. Mother said the night wasn't so bad at first, for the moon was bright and there was great big stars looking down at them and Mother said the moon was awful pretty, but before morning the moon clouded over and the stars went out and the cold water was harder to bear in the dark. The water was so deep they couldn't sit down. It was right up to their armpits. Overhead they could hear the planes huntin' for them, but they had no way of signalling . . . At two o'clock on Sunday afternoon a man got in his rowboat and rowed right over an almond orchard to get them and took them off. Mother said she was so stiff she didn't feel she'd be able to bend again and she was afraid all this standing in the water might bring on a cold. Mother is seventy-four years old, and she was thirty-two hours in the water. After they got her out of the water it was four hours before she got any attention. It sure was funny to see Mother lying in bed, for a full week, mind you. But she's thankful they're all alive and she doesn't complain. Course they lost their cows and the chickens and all their stuff, but they'll get back on the land and get it planted this spring, and this'll probably never happen again."

I walked up the aisle to get a good look at the speaker. She was her mother's daughter all right, fearless and resolute. She, too, had the proud look of a survivor.

"This country is safe," I said to myself, "as long as it has a good percentage of these imperishable ones. Long live the Violses, long live the spirit of the old lady of seventy-four, who standing in cold water up to her armpits could still think that the moon looked "awful pretty."

We went into Mexico as far as Cuernavaca and had a wonderful eight days in this country where for the most part, time seems to have stood still. Changing money at Laredo and receiving three pesos for every dollar gives the purse a fine bulging appearance and the owner a feeling of wealth, false, but flattering. "Lettuce money" is the name given to these green bills which look like money and feel like money, but lack the full authority of money when they reach the market place. However, the prices asked for food and lodging were not excessive.

One of the most comfortable places we stayed was at Lenares, between Laredo and Monterey, where the words "Canada Courts" drew us like a beckoning finger. There we had an auto cabin with tiled floor, many windows, easy chairs, Durango pine wood-work—shining like satin, a reading light over the bed, plenty of hot water, sandalwood soap, and a home-cooked supper of roast beef, sweet potatoes, frijoles, and cauliflower, with lemon pie and the best coffee we had in Mexico, and all this for nine pesos per person. The cabins have orange trees at the front door, orange trees in bloom and in fruit, and we crossed a clear, swiftly running stream on our way to the dining-room; a wide cool room with a concrete floor, and adobe walls a foot thick, where the cool breeze from the open windows was comforting after a hot afternoon of driving.

"Canada Courts" are owned and run by a Winnipeg man and his wife, who are the only English-speaking people in the town of Lenares. Their three children can speak Spanish now fluently, though they have been in Mexico only a year and a half. I asked the twelve-year-old girl if she were lonely when she first went to school, and she said the Mexican children showed her how to play their games, and the language was easy. Isn't it great to be young and adaptable?

The cabins are named for the provinces of Canada and we were torn between Manitoba, Alberta and British Columbia, but it was no time to hesitate, for other cars were driving in. After supper we talked with our hosts about the Collegiate Institute on Kate Street, E. Cora Hind, Dr. W. A. McIntyre, Neepawa and Minnesota, and after we had gone back to our cabin the little girl brought us copies of the *Free Press*, which we read from the editorials to the obituary notices!

Mexico is not only a strange country, but it seems to belong to another century. Men plow the fields with oxen, long-horned, and the plow is made of wood. Patient women with Old Testament faces walk the highways, wrapped in black mantilloes with sandals on their feet or nothing at all. Even the long-horned cows have sorrowful faces and the same ageless expression.

The highway from Laredo to Mexico City had been open twenty months when we drove over it. When the road was opened I remember reading a story written by a newspaper man and his wife who made the trip, and their chief difficulty on the high places in the mountains was to get the burros to move off the road. We encountered the same problem, perhaps this stubbornness is the burros' only form of exaltation, for he is certainly a poor, burdened little creature in Mexico. He carries everything that can be piled on him—wood, straw, charcoal, ore. And even when the driver sits behind the load the little burro trudges on without complaint. Perhaps his fortitude is explained in Chesterton's fine fancy—that every donkey remembers that great hour of his ancestors: "When there were shouts about his ears and palms beneath his feet."

In Mexico everyone carries something. We saw groups of women carrying pottery in baskets, and one had a green parrot riding on her head. In Mexico City we saw one man carrying a chest of drawers and four chairs on his back, and a woman with live chickens swung around her neck and waist, and even strapped on her forehead. She came through the traffic safely, a moving mound of feathers, heads and claws, advancing on two bare feet.

In Cuernavaca, forty-seven miles south of Mexico City, we stayed at the Borda Hotel which was once the Royal Palace of Emperor Maximillian and his wife, Carlotta. Cuernavaca is the place where the elite of Mexico City have their homes, and it was a dream of loveliness that spring day in 1938, with its glowing bougainvillea in purple and crimson, bermudja in fiery red, bridal bells in white, and many other blossoms never seen by us before. We were delighted to see many geraniums and even the humble nasturtium.

In the palace we ate on the wide piazza, looking into the garden with its fountain and great swimming pool now dry and cracked. In a high-ceilinged drawing room behind us, we saw Carlotta's grand piano, inlaid with gold and mother-of-pearl, now closed and silent, and heard again the story of the hapless man and woman who had been sent to Mexico by Napoleon to defeat the efforts of the Mexicans to set up their own government. Carlotta had died shortly after the Great War, mercifully oblivious to all her troubles and believing to the last that she was still the Empress of Mexico.

Now her palace is thronged day by day with tourists like ourselves, who buy postcards and eat enchalatos and tortillos on her wide verandahs, and look out into the garden where the amber Mexican sunlight falls on the neglected walks and broken statuary. Though the grand piano is silent, a lovely song called "Annitzia" sung by Seniorita Ruis came in on the radio and following the song came the newscast telling of an uprising in San Luis County, led by General Cedillo, in which twenty people had been killed. So the old Mexican drama was going on just the same, with its music and beauty, its hatreds and sorrows—the old drama in which only the actors change.

There are two pictures seen in Mexico which will ever live with me, though I know that no outsider can understand their significance nor adequately describe them in words, for in both of them the past beats through the present, and the future stands, an unknown actor in the wings, ready to make entry. The first one is the whole wide picture of the countryside, with the fertile valleys which lie between the mountains, far below the highway, with their tiny cultivated fields, which not only cover the valley, but run up the mountainside, in squares of greens and browns in great variety of shade, according to the crop. Corn, beans and coffee are the staple crops and surely no one but a native could do this perpendicular work. The people dress in a white cotton cloth, which they make themselves and it must take a lot of washing to keep it clean. The Mexicans are not concerned about the future. Their needs are simple. A coffee dealer told us that the natives who raise coffee bring down only enough to buy what they need and let the balance of their crop rot in the fields. Every third day in Mexico is a feast day and then the people walk on the highway to the market towns, carrying their wares on their heads with the pride of creation. Some places we saw them spinning the fibre of the manguey as they walked. Out of this they make ropes and baskets. They answer every salute with a smile and a wave of the hand. They are not burdened with a sense of poverty. They are not obsessed with any feverish desire to improve their condition.

Is this too primitive an existence? It would be for us. But I believe they are happier than many people you and I know, dogged by a fear of the future, and bitter because someone else has more. The Indians have their handicraft, their love of mystery, the joy of planting and reaping, great sweeping valley-floors, green and abundant below them, mountain peaks shouldering the sky above them. There are sweet fish in the rivers, berries on the bushes, guajolotes (wild turkeys) in the woods, wild orchids and blossoming shrubs everywhere; color in the fields and color in the rocks; no one has any more than another. Their work is their pleasure. The Indian demands nothing of life, but he has many of the things we break our hearts to acquire!

There is another picture, the Shrine of Guadaloupe, which is a few miles northeast of Mexico City, built on the spot where it is reputed the Holy Virgin appeared more than three centuries ago to an Indian, Juan Diego. This was the Virgin's first appearance in the New World; and she left her picture, by a miracle, on the robe the Indian was wearing.

The Virgin's picture, framed in gold, hangs high above the beautiful altar, and to bow before it came the faithful from all over Mexico every twelfth day of December. The Lady of Guadaloupe is the Protector of Mexico. We went to see the shrine the first day we spent in Mexico City. The church, one of the largest we saw, is open at all hours, and many pilgrims were there that day. Some of the little groups had walked many kilometres, to bring their sick to the Virgin's attention. The pilgrims made their way to the altar on their knees, carrying silver trays of oranges, and tomatoes, lighted candles, and one little girl had a charcoal burner sending up a cloud of smoke. A poor woman, with a tired and pitifully sick baby tried to get her little son of five or six to kneel with her as the procession slowly crawled down the aisle, but he broke away, and ran down to the front of the church, thereby endangering her chances of getting relief for her sick child. Her distress at his action was pitiful to see. However, the little prodigal returned and knelt beside her, and the procession crept on. A blind boy played on his violin, as weird and terrible a tune as I ever heard; one, the guide said, which had never been written, but was known to every Indian of the tribe. The procession stopped at a shrine halfway to the altar, and fervently prayed; the violinist redoubled his efforts, an old lady with tattered gray locks took the charcoal burner from the little girl and swung it in front of the Virgin, and the mother held up her suffering child, oblivious of everything but her child's sore need. Ahead of them gleamed the altar, set with many a jewel and gleaming with gold. The alabaster candlesticks, man-high, were lighted from within and glowed in the semi-darkness. The magnificence of the altar and the poverty of the supplicants in their tattered rags made a terrible picture.

The guide hurried us on to see another altar whose railing was of solid silver, and told us proudly how many tons of silver had been used in the church. Then he took us upstairs to the sacristy and showed us the table where the treaty was signed between Mexico and the United States. "Without hard feeling," the guide said. He asked us as we were going up the stairs to observe the picture gallery on the wall, of home-made drawings, each recording a miracle. Here was an auto, just escaping a train, a woman undergoing a Caesarian operation. The pictures were crude and seemed to show the same hand but there was a passionate reality in them.

Outside, on the steps of this great cathedral, dozens of vendors were selling charms and tokens, forcing them into our hands or trying to pin them on our coats; deer's eyes on scarlet strings, holy sweetcakes, rosaries of carved wood, glass or silver medallions with the Virgin's picture. An old woman, with the toes out of her shoes, tried to sell us lottery tickets, telling us it was all for charity, and to buy from her would bring us luck, for she was blind in one eye. Troops of shrill-voiced children pursued us to our car and made us very glad to get away from the cathedral, even though the guide told us it was the richest church in North America and the religious centre of the world.

One of the most distressing details of this picture was the face of the woman who brought her sick baby to the foot of the Virgin. She was so poor and wretched and yet believing. I hope her prayers ascended far beyond the cherub-sprinkled roof and were recorded some place. Out of faith like hers surely will come a regenerated church in Mexico, dominated by the true spirit of Him who said: "I came not to be ministered unto, but to minister."

Very different in character was the next religious institution we visited. On our way home we spent a few days in Los Angeles and I went to the Hollywood Temple.

I first saw Aimee Semple McPherson when she was twenty-eight years old. She had come to Winnipeg to hold services in the old Wesley Church. That was in 1920. Every night people were turned away, and then as always, there was a wide difference of opinion about her. I liked her the first time I saw her, and felt the impact of a great personality. Surely no woman ever received more admiration and loyalty on the one hand, derision and persecution on the other. If Aimee had been a homely woman dressed in rusty black, with her hair pulled tightly back unbecomingly, and carried on her mission-ary work down a back street in unattractive surroundings she would have passed into history as a great saint. But Aimee was beautiful and knew how to dress and did not let the passing of the years destroy her beauty; she was also a great showman and a great financier and so the world in general found it hard to forgive her success.

I regret to have to record that she was bitterly criticized by many of the "good" people who failed to see that she used all her talents and all her powers to spread the Gospel of the Lord. She educated missionaries and supported them in India and China. It is true she attracted people to the Temple by her dramatic and spectacular methods, but she never disappointed them when they came, nor did she ever cheapen or soft-pedal her message. She preached to her congregation the words of life.

The last time I heard her speak she read the story of the Pente-cost for the scripture lesson and took her text from it.

"There was the sound of a rushing wind." When she read these words she stopped and smiled at her congregation. Then she leaned over the desk and said confidentially:

"I like sound. I'm not one bit afraid of sound, even in a church service. It is a good thing to make a joyful noise unto the Lord."

We had good seats in the front row of the gallery, and so had the pleasure of seeing the congregation arriving. The galleries filled first, and I was a bit disturbed at all the empty seats on the ground floor, but at five minutes before the hour of opening the regulars began to come down the sloping runways in formation, eight hundred young people, the students of her Bible school, with jaunty little boat-like caps of different colors. They had gone upstairs first to make this spectacular entry from the front and sides of the auditorium. Meanwhile the surpliced choir filed into the two choir lofts, one on each side of the pulpit. The orchestra, in the pit below the pulpit, strikingly robed in Russian blouses of bright blue with sashes of yellow, were playing one of Sousa's marches under the direction of a slim young person with a head of curly blonde hair.

When Aimee came in the great congregation broke into applause. She was dressed in white, with a rippling cape of blue lined with white. Her golden hair shone with the sheen of ripe wheat and her whole personality radiated health and happiness. She carried a sheaf of crimson roses which she laid on the pulpit. The morning sunshine poured in from eight stained-glass windows, four on each side of the pulpit. A crucifix stands high above the pulpit, with three women in postures of grief at the foot of the cross. Above that is a beautiful mural of the Sower who went forth to Sow.

The service lasted from 10:30 to 12:30, and held everyone's attention every minute. No one seemed to know what was coming next. The choir sang; the orchestra played; an Episcopal minister visiting the city sang "The Lord's Prayer." The sermon lasted for forty minutes and it revealed Aimee at her shining best. She was defending the Four Square Gospel against the criticism of some church which had issued a pamphlet warning its people not to attend Angelus Temple on pain of expulsion. The point of disagreement seemed to be a matter of timing: Did the gift of the Holy Ghost come with conversion or at a later period? The church pamphlet was strong in its belief that God's children got all that there was for them at conversion. Aimee said "No." Conversion came first, then sanctification, and the fruits of the spirit. She ran through the Gospels to prove it, with the speed of a race horse. Her audience laughed and exulted with her and loved her as she covered the church's criticism at every point. There was no malice in her words. Everything she said glowed with good humor. She closed the service exactly at twelve thirty, leading the congregation in the old hymn "Revive Us Again," and surely the Temple was filled with the sound of a rushing wind.

Aimee was a conductor of great ability. She understood the effect of sound and movement upon people. She knew that when people clapped their hands, when they sang, it loosened something in their hearts.

The woman who sat beside me was a staunch Presbyterian whom I had known in Manitoba. She told me she had been a member of Aimee's Temple for eight years. When I asked her what had led her away from John Knox she said she had been attracted to Aimee because of the great work she was doing for the young people of Hollywood.

"This Temple," she said, "is not only a great church auditorium. It is a Bible school, a college, a settlement house and a relief centre. It is open every night of the week and no needy person is ever turned away from its door. The young people come here because they have good fun and wholesome recreation mixed with instruction. Times change you know. John Knox's methods would not do for Los Angeles in this year of 1938. Churches here have to meet the competition of moving picture shows and dance halls. Aimee inspires people, gives us a vision, and makes us all feel important. She makes us work, but she works harder herself than anybody else. Aimee has Power"—and I knew by the way she said it it had to be spelt with a capital.

My memory of that service will ever be the rapt and worshipping faces of the young people to whom Aimee Semple McPherson was guide, friend and high priestess!

29

Nova Scotia

SOME YEARS IN OUR LIVES stand out like mountain peaks. Life can go on at the same level for long periods of time, then suddenly the chart shoots up to a high level of activity. 1938 was such a year for me.

In July I was invited to attend the Silver Jubilee of the Women's Institute in Nova Scotia, and had the great privilege of visiting many parts of the province, due to the kindness of my good friends, Miss Annie M. Stuart, of Grand Pré, and Miss Helen Macdougall, Superintendent of Women's Institute. The Department of Agriculture in sending me the invitation to become the Convention speaker told me that they would make a visit of the whole peninsula part of my program. That was a generous invitation which no one could refuse.

No part of Nova Scotia holds more interest for the tourist than the little village of Grand Pré with its tragic memory of the Expulsion of 1755. I first made the acquaintance of Longfellow's "Evangeline" at Northfield School in Manitoba, when this narrative poem was part of the course of studies. Evidently there was no fear in the heart of "our betters" then that this story would undermine our love for the British Empire, even though our hearts burned with indignation when we read of the peaceful Acadians and the sorrows which came to them. Longfellow, who never saw Grand

Pré or the Gaspereau River, told his story well. He took seven years to think about it, and must have had a clear picture of that beautiful country in his mind. The long metre he used seems exactly right for this abundant scene, with its rolling hills and undulating valleys.

One of the questions on a teacher's examination when I was a student was: "To what do you attribute the charm of 'Evangeline'?" and a lad from the prairie, who has since become a writer, wrote in reply:

"The charm of this poem lies in the long, lingering melancholy sweetness between the subject and the predicate."

I hope the examiner recognized the glimmer of genius.

On my first Sunday in Grand Pré we attended the United Church service in the Old Covenanters' Church, built in 1804 of hand-sawn boards and hand-made nails. It has the high pulpit and sounding board, and the box pews, each with its own door. We sat in the Stuart family pew, with its old footstool, which has served the family for a hundred years. In the last generation Sunday School began at 9:50 and the preaching service followed. Two o'clock was the time for dismissal. So the people of that day took their devotions in heavy proportions.

But on this Sunday the service lasted one hour. The church was gay with flowers, the choir was made up of young people, and after the service laughter was heard around the tombstones. A Chicago car drove up as we stood around in groups and the driver asked if he might photograph us, and had it done before we had even begun to look pleasant. He said he was getting pictures of the places of inter-est. He had the Dionne sisters, Niagara Falls, the Reversing Falls, and Evangeline's Monument. He told us he had just two weeks for his holiday, but he was covering a lot of ground. Then wiping his beaded brow—for the day was hot—he vanished down the road.

But no one else in Grand Pré was hurrying. A Sabbath peace rested on the woods and down the shady roads and paths where the people wandered leisurely homeward to their Sunday dinner of baked shad, from the River Avon, green peas and cherry pie. At least, that is what we had, served on lovely old china taken from a corner cupboard.

Evangeline's monument stands in a park just north of the railway station. Beautiful French marigolds circle around it, and the clover sod was, that day, damp with the recent rains. Evangeline clasps her distaff, and turns her head towards the river. I asked about this but no one seemed to know. She should, we thought, be looking up the hill towards the home she was leaving forever.

The old church, which was built on the site of the one where the Acadians worshipped, and where the proclamation was read to them on that fateful Sunday morning, is now a museum where we saw a series of pictures, which tell the story of the expulsion. The scene at the seashore is full of misery, where the people sit with their pathetic little treasures in their hands, waiting for the boats to take them away.

At the gate we saw Evangeline's willows, gray with age, and listing to leeward, gnarled and twisted old warriors that have bent before many a bitter blast from the Atlantic, but have somehow survived the buffetings of time. Still they stand and put forth their leaves each spring. Somehow they moved me more deeply than any of the treasures of the Acadians, or the pictures men have drawn of their sorrow, for in their battered trunks and twisted branches they seem to hold the unconquerable spirit of the men and women of that tragic time.

The visitor to Nova Scotia is always advised to see the South Shore. President Roosevelt had spoken of the "unhurried ways of the fisherfolk." Ramsay MacDonald had called it "the land of heart's desire" wondering why he had missed it for so long.

A woman, to whom I had been speaking on the train, a Lunenburg woman, looked at me enviously when I said I was on my way to Nova Scotia—for my first visit.

"I wish I could see Lunenburg harbor for the first time," she said, "when the ships return and the masts stand up like a forest."

She told me something about the coastline, with its indentations, and its coves, and creeks, and the ways of its people.

"The paved road has done a lot for the people," she said. "I am not one that wants to keep the fisherfolk as primitive as they are in some places, just to make the tourists stare and rave about them. I want them to have some comforts, too, and now they are getting them, even radios and tablecloths."

"There are places along the South Shore where the people once lived on fish and potatoes," she went on, "never bothering with any other vegetable, but with tourists coming and wanting meals, they began to make gardens, and live better, in every way. The women work in the hay fields with the men. Mary, my maid, whose home is on the South Shore, says she won't take her holidays until the haying is over. Her two sisters work in Boston, and have learned American ways, but when they come home they do what father says. When father says 'We'll make hay', they make hay, and they daren't talk back to him. The heavy father who can rule his household may have gone from other parts of Canada, but he still rules in some of the fishing villages on the South Shore."

We motored from Windsor to Chester, through upper Falmouth, following the Avon river, until we saw where it had its source. The streams here, no longer subject to the tide, are clear, but dark, as if the color of the trout had dyed the water. The road we travelled is winding and narrow in places, but in good condition, and well made. Drinking troughs along the way reminded us that much of the transportation has been done by ox-teams, though we saw only two or three of these bringing out loads of hay.

We passed some beautiful orchards before we reached the heavily wooded country, and I was interested to see that the space between the rows of trees was planted with buckwheat, now in bloom. This will be cut and left on the ground for a mulch. I wondered why the ground was not cultivated, but the cover-crop is in favor now, and appears to be successful, for the trees are well set with fruit.

At Chester we went to the Lovatt House, where travellers have been fed and sheltered for more than one hundred years. In the low-ceilinged dining room, with its brown walls, and floor and great carved sideboards, we had a good meal of liver and onions (at least that's what I had). I knew I should eat fish in Chester, but I could not resist my two old friends.

The pictures on the walls are of royalty: King Edward the Seventh with Queen Alexandra and their eldest child, King Edward the Eighth in his young boyhood, and the present King and Queen. The lights above our heads came from lanterns. Under our feet were hooked mats whose patterns were growing dim with the heavy-footed years. We met people, at the next table, who were going over to an island nearby, which they own now and have planted with potatoes, making an experiment of growing a red potato much favored in Jamaica.

We hurried through the meal to get out to see the bay, while the daylight held. It was all I had hoped, and more. Peace lay on the water, and on the islands which lead the eye step by step to the open sea. It was all so sweet and calm, it was hard to believe that this haven of rest had been the scene of robbery, pillage and murder. I wondered about the Payzant Island, where poor Marie had seen her husband fall across the doorstep, shot by the Indians who carried her and her four children away nearly two hundred years ago. One of her descendants in Wolfville had told me the story, and given me Dr. MacMechan's book—I thought of Marie Payzant, too, as we passed through Upper Falmouth, where she had found sanctuary after her tribulations and where members of the family still live.

The island of mystery, four miles from Chester, Oak Island, draws everyone's interest. Here it is supposed that Captain Kidd buried his ill-gotten treasure. We heard the story of the dying sailor who confessed that he had been one of Captain Kidd's crew, who buried two millions of money on a "secluded island east of Boston." A queer pit has been found on Oak Island, and many attempts have been made to recapture the treasure, but the pit fills with water, and nothing has been found yet. I was interested to hear the story of Captain Kidd who began his career as a recognized English trader, but chose the career of a pirate, robbing any ship he met, English or French. This was in 1696. In 1698 he arrived in New York, loaded with spoil which he buried on Gardner's Island. He was arrested by the order of the Governor of Massachusetts, sent back to England, tried, and hanged in 1701. The loot of Gardner's Island was found and amounted to something like sixty thousand dollars.

But the people who live on the South Shore today are more interesting to write about than the pirates who roved its waters years ago, robbing and killing.

After leaving Mahone Bay we saw many berry-pickers, offering baskets of blueberries for sale. There were stands beside the road where lovely waterlilies in crocks could be bought. Signs told us that hand-made rugs and quilts were ready for us, and in support of this, we saw samples on fences and verandahs, and about this time we began to notice that we were crossing the railway track very often. That is true of the whole South Shore. The highway and the railway track cross and recross, seeming to vie with each other in showing the traveller everything that is to be seen. No one can see it all, but we drove slowly and did our best.

Little sheltered coves, with canoes at anchor, beaches of pure red sand, where people lay in the sun; a party of picnickers, opening their baskets; a woman on the verandah of a lovely white house, shelling peas; two women driving by with a horse and covered buggy. (I am sure they had a laprobe embroidered in chain stitch); a white house, with rain barrels at each side, painted white, too; fish drying on the shore in front of Frolic school; cobblestone houses at Dublin Shore; and always the sea with its fishing boats, steamers, fuel barges, and at least one lovely yacht with gleaming sails, a stranger, a painted lady, among the hard-working craft!

At Liverpool, we stopped for supper at a neat little restaurant where tourists with bandanna handkerchiefs on their heads sat at the next table. We wanted to reach Lockport for the night, but a fog settled in from the sea, and we stayed at White Point Beach, where the great rollers of the Atlantic threw spray on the rocks, and filled the air with a sound so much like a heavy rain that every time I wakened I had to resist the impulse to get up and shut windows all over the house.

We agreed that the Pubnico villages should be seen—there are so many of them, all in a row, on both shores of Pubnico harbor. There

is Lower West, Middle West, and West Pubnico, and the same number of East Pubnicos, and at the head of the harbor Pubnico itself.
They are on the map. In reality there are Mids and Centrals as well.
We had a good lobster salad with the Amiraults there, I think it was
at Mid East Pubnico in a neat little restaurant which displayed a sign
that "no intoxicating liquor would be tolerated in the premises."
The dark-eyed proprietor told us liquor "makes plenty trouble," and
we agreed with her. The highway department is with her, too.

We went to the little shop which advertises Acadian Handicrafts,
and there we learned about Pubnico.

Seignior Philip d'Entremont, first Baron Pubnico, settled there
in 1651, with his tenants. In 1755 the people of this settlement were
deported with the rest of the Acadians, but they were allowed to
return in eleven years, the only Acadians who were thus favored.
Their holding contains 1,500 square miles, and is now the oldest
Acadian settlement in the world.

The folder, given to us, tells that the "d'Entremont family, des-
cended from the highest nobility of France and Savoy, are related to
the royal family, and this nobleness has been transmitted by marriage to most of the Acadian families of Digby and Yarmouth, as
well as many of New Brunswick and Quebec."

The window of the little handicraft shop is made into a winter
scene, with salt for snow, and little houses made of bark, and ox-
teams carved from wood, drawing loads of logs. Inside the shop there
are pictures made by a needle instead of a brush, with wools instead
of paint, and with carved frames. We saw two of the Amirault family
here, who told us these handicrafts are carried on by the women in
the winter, the designs handed down from mother to daughter.

On the road from Sidney to Glace Bay there is a small mining
town called Reserve Mines, made up largely of Company houses.
These houses are dull little dwellings on rutted streets. They have no
trees or flowers and the outlook is somber. The floors of the houses
are laid on the ground, and the earth works up through the cracks in
the boards, making a continual dust in dry weather and dampness
when it rains.

Great things have happened in this little town since then, for Father Tompkins, the priest of the parish, had a vision of better things for his people and he brought his people together in groups to study the whole question of co-operative housing. According to Father Tompkins' philosophy "ideas have hands and feet." So no wonder something happened.

It was our great privilege to see the first of the co-operatively built houses. There were eleven of them built in a long semi-circle, and each had an acre of ground. Each contained six rooms and was fully modern.

Miss Mary Arnold, who had been for eighteen years connected with co-operative enterprises in New York, came to Nova Scotia to spend the holiday, and fortunately for Nova Scotia and the co-operative movement there, she decided to stay.

On the Sunday afternoon we spent at Reserve Mines, we met many of the people who will live in these houses when they were finished and heard from them how the idea had grown and what it was going to mean to them to have their own vegetables and flowers and a decent place to live. All the pride of ownership was shining in their faces, and with it the joy which comes to the builder, for these men and women had done almost all the work on their houses, under the direction of one experienced carpenter. They told us that in addition to the initial payment of one hundred dollars they were paying a rental slightly less than the ten dollars they had been paying for the dull little Company houses, and best of all, in twenty-five years the house would be clear. The monthly rental covered insurance too.

The story of the co-operative movement in Nova Scotia and how it has spread all across Canada is well known now. It has brought joy and hope to many who saw no way out of their financial difficulties. It has nothing to offer to the speculator who hopes to get rich quick by some lucky chance, but it does make a great appeal to men and women who have the will to work together. To them it is a great demonstration of how man can help his fellow man and himself at the same time. St. Francis Xavier University at Antigonish will always be held in grateful memory for the great assistance its staff has given to the working people, not only of Nova Scotia but of all Canada. Father Tompkins gave me a book when I visited him at Reserve Mines, and the name of the book is *The Lord Helps Those Who Help Themselves*. It contains the history of this movement and the title takes on new meaning as the tale unfolds. It goes back to the good father's philosophy "that ideas have hands and feet," and might well have had as its foreword that dynamic poem of Ella Wheeler Wilcox:

"I gave a beggar from my well-earned store
Of shining gold. He took the precious ore
And went and spent and came again,
Still hungry as before.
I gave a thought and from that thought of mine
He found himself, the man, supreme, divine.
Clothed, warm and crowned with blessings evermore,
And now he begs no more."

30

The League of Nations, 1938

O N M Y W A Y H O M E from Nova Scotia in August I received a wire from the Prime Minister, informing me that I had been appointed one of the Canadian delegates to attend the League of Nations to be held in September, and asking for an immediate acceptance. I received the wire just before we got into Blue River and hastily wrote my acceptance. Then I began to wonder what I would say to my family. They had put up with a lot from me, and I had already been away from home five weeks.

I did not break the news the first day, and when I did I found they were all ready to accept it with good grace. I had about a week to get ready. There were so many things to think of, but I had good helpers and at last I was ready to leave, my suits were cleaned, my trunk packed, and I had a new evening dress. I had one great regret and that is that I had not followed the meetings of the League of Nations more closely, though I had always been a member of the League of Nations Society. I felt so ignorant and inadequate.

However, the Government had thought of that, and I was given a portfolio with the full history of the League in it, and I did put in some hours on the sea voyage acquainting myself with its contents. When, after a very pleasant voyage and train journey, we reached Geneva, I found many other delegates who were also there for the first time, and who were struggling like myself to grasp its significance.

The League of Nations was a world within a world and no doubt will go down in history as a great stride forward in humanity's long and painful journey. It grew more amazing to me all the time I was there. Much time was spent in the first few days in getting the committees set up. Setting up committees seemed to be a complicated business, accompanied by much formality. The chairman is proposed by someone who dilates on the choice he is making. Someone "seconds the motion," and tells of his pleasure in so doing. Then the senior delegate of the country from which the chairman has been selected gives tongue at some length thanking all those who have spoken for the honor they are about to bestow on his country by making Monsieur ———— their chairman, and finally the proposed chairman voices his appreciation and deep humility in accepting this honorable office, and knows the compliment is one to his country and not to himself, but will endeavor to carry out his duties as well as his limitations will permit. If there are no objections (and there were none), and after everything had been translated and duly applauded, the chairman of the committee is declared elected. And time wore on!

The League had forty-seven countries in its membership in 1938, and its income was derived from its members. This was the first year that all the meetings were held in the beautiful new building overlooking Lake Geneva. It has a commanding position with a view of Mt. Blanc, and gleams white on a terraced slope, flower beds in strange combinations of colors heighten the sheen of the green lawns. The building is of stone and many of the floors are of marble and the corridors are wide. The glass doors are so clear and flawless that a secretary walked through one, absent-mindedly. This was told to us the first day as a warning. The Assembly Room has a system of lighting which makes a perpetual daylight. The rostrum has three levels. The seats are of walnut, upholstered in cream cloth. There are deep galleries on three sides of the Assembly Hall, giving a seating capacity for perhaps a thousand people. One of the most astonishing things about the League was the skill of the translators. When a speech was being made in some language other than English, by a device on our desks we were able to hear it in English by the use of earphones. Each speech had to be submitted in manuscript beforehand, to give the translators the opportunity to familiarize themselves with it. We could watch the speaker, but the voice that we heard was the voice of the translator. After the speech was concluded the English or French version was given from the platform for the benefit of the galleries.

We soon found out that it makes a great difference to a speaker whether he has something to say, or has to say something. This was particularly true in the first few days when the Chief Delegates of each country, who were not willing to put sanctions against the aggressor countries, presented their reports. The reasons were all in the same vein. No longer have we universality in the League. We have suffered many withdrawals. In order to be effective sanctions would need to be imposed by all nations. No country wants to offend its neighbor. We are peaceful people. We cannot take the risk of another war.

Lord de la Warr, speaking for the United Kingdom, used these arguments, and I do not think he enjoyed the position in which he found himself, but he had to say something.

There were three men who had something to say and they rent our hearts as we listened. The Spanish delegate, Alvarez del Vayo, scored the League for its callous indifference to the fate of his country, and deplored the disappearance of Austria as an independent state. "One looks in vain," he said, "in the Secretary-General's report for one word of condolence or farewell to our sister nation which has been swallowed by an aggressor. The aggressors know now that they can do this with impunity, as far as this League is concerned. But the Spanish delegation would like to direct to the spot once occupied by the Austrian delegation a glance of indignant protest."

The General Assembly observed a moment of embarrassed silence. Then the Spanish delegate went on, pleading with the League to take action now! It was still strong enough to impose sanctions if it would. "Are the western democracies going to wait until half the nations represented here have disappeared, before they take action? Do we not still believe in collective security? Nothing that has happened has weakened Spain's determination to fight on for a vigilant, strong and self-assured League of Nations."

The day that Dr. Wellington Koo spoke to the Assembly, many Chinese people gathered in the galleries. Beautiful women in their slim straight gowns with lovely furs, and what a speech they heard from their gifted countryman! He made us all hang our heads in shame and bitter repentance for our share in his country's griefs. He reminded us that China had been a member of the League from its beginning, and that the League had declared Japan to be the aggressor nation, and although the League had the machinery in its framework to deal with aggressor nations, through Article 16 which deals with the whole question of sanctions, yet not one member of the League had put an embargo on Japan. Japan has been able to buy as much war material as she wants. Dr. Koo spoke without bitterness, but with a stark simplicity that stripped away every excuse.

The other speaker who had something to say was Mr. Litvinoff who spoke for the Soviet Union. His country, he said, had not been a member of the League at first, and had come in after long doubts and hesitations, but having entered the League, it had been unfailingly loyal to the League, and was ready to perform all the decisions of the League, which were directed to conserving peace, and combatting the aggressors, irrespective of whether those decisions coincided with Russia's immediate interest as a state. He compared Article 16 to a fire brigade which was evidently set up in the innocent hope that by some lucky chance there would be no fires. Unfortunately fires have broken out, very bad fires, and the action of the League seemed to be that we must at once dissolve the fire brigade—of course, not forever, he added sarcastically, but merely temporarily. Directly the danger of fire disappears, we shall re-assemble the fire brigade without a moment's delay.

So the nineteenth assembly of the League of Nations began, in a spirit of fear and distrust, regret and recrimination.

I thoroughly enjoyed having a seat on the Fifth Committee, which dealt with social legislation of all kinds. There was something here to be proud of—the work among refugees, the great efforts that were being successfully made to stem the evils of narcotics and bring to nought the designs of evil men, the work of health organizations, nutrition and housing, and securing better labor conditions, the prevention of epidemics by international co-operation. I learned much about these and could see that in these and in kindred matters, the League had abundantly justified its existence. The League may have failed as a police court, but as a research bureau and a clearing house of ideas it was succeeding.

But even in the Fifth Committee the movement was slow, and I thought they wasted much time in paying compliments to each other, and being tediously careful that all due credit be given. Arguments would run on for half an hour at a time about trivialities. One day I made bold to tell them that I thought that if nobody cared who got the credit, much more could be accomplished, and for this I was reprimanded, privately, by one member of the Canadian contingent, who told me I did not understand how important it was not to offend any of the delegates. I said I could not understand grown-up people being so sensitive. I knew there were people here who had worked long and earnestly, but that surely was no reason for them to act like the young mothers at a baby show!

Three women on our committee were outstanding, Irene Ward, M.P., of the United Kingdom; Madam Alexandra Kellontay of Russia; and a Scandinavian woman, Madam Kesselgren. Madam Kellontay was then and is now the Soviet minister in Sweden, and I was attracted to her the first day our Committee met. From her I learned much about the Soviet Union, and the great pride they have in their young people, and the great plans they have for their development. She convinced me, if I needed any convincing, that the Soviet Union wants nothing but peace and good will, and a chance to develop their own resources.

She told me something of the conditions in Russia before the Revolution, and what a struggle it had been to bring education to the people after the long dark days of misrule under the Czars.

The tension in the League grew as the political situation in Europe grew more threatening. Even in our Committee the speeches deteriorated. They crackled up and down the tables like conversations at a funeral. We could not give our whole mind to "an international signalling at low level crossings" or consideration of "stateless persons released from prison" when we knew we might all be stateless persons unless the signs were changed.

It was a long stretch from Monday to Friday in the last week in September, measuring time by heart beats. On Monday night we heard Hitler speak from Berlin. His fiery words were punctuated by the hoarse cheers of his listeners, as he screamed his intention of marching into Czechoslovakia on October the First if his demands were not met. On Tuesday night we had a blackout, when every blind was drawn, and every light in the street extinguished. We had supper that night at a restaurant, two blocks from the Hotel de la Paix where we stayed. The two Swiss girls in the party said their worst fear was that French troops would march across Switzerland, and the Swiss would have to resist them. "And France is our friend, but in war there is no sense or reason." The Hon. Ernest Lapointe, who was the leader of our delegation, was recalled by a cable to Canada, and called us in to say good-bye. I remember we were comforted by his words when he said: "There will not be war, I think, at least for a year. But we must be ready for anything. Hitler means business!"

Every day there were less people at the League as the delegates were called home, and from the Swiss people I gathered there was a feeling that Hitler would begin his offense by bombing the League of Nations' buildings to show his disrespect for law and order. The day we travelled to Paris the train was crowded to overflowing. Baggage was piled in the corridors and every available inch was taken in the train. There were not seats for everyone so we took our turns at standing up, and holding on to the rail, we looked out at the flying Savoy landscape, beautiful with the sunshine of a perfect day. The blue Rhone ran below, cattle fed on the meadows, blue-smocked men were at work in their fields, one man holding the plow and one man leading the horse, just as their ancestors did in 1870.

Civilians, with rifles, guarded the stations, and we passed companies of cavalrymen, trains tore by at frequent intervals, crowded with people, and we read in the papers that two million people were being evacuated from Paris.

We stayed at a small hotel, the Burgundy, just off the Rue de Madeleine in Paris and all night there were sounds of feet on the street below and the beat of horses' hoofs, for mobilization was carried on at night. I got up to watch the street activities and could see below me men with bundles hurrying, women saying good-bye. It was a weird scene at three in the morning in the dimly lighted street.

The next day came the news that the men at Munich had arrived at a settlement, and Paris relaxed. We were sitting outside the Cafe de la Paix when we heard it. An American woman who had lived in Paris since 1907 came over to our table and told us. "I was here on the night war was declared in 1914, and last night I stayed until everyone was gone. I am the only one left of the old crowd, and the boys wanted me to stay."

That afternoon we stood in the crowd which lined the streets to see the triumphant arrival of Daladier, who had flown back from Munich. The steps of the Madeleine were filled with people. Every window, every doorway, every balcony above the street. Policemen with white batons directed the traffic, and the big trucks and busses shoved the people out of their way like snow-plows. But there was no confusion, or shouting. Everyone smiled and chatted. Children with candy sticks, held on "papa's" shoulders to see; old and young, rich and poor, mingled happily. A Frenchwoman, leaning on a cane, complained of her ankles—then laughed, and said, "I should not think of them. I am happy enough now to forget my pain . . . We are grateful to your Chamberlain, and to the King of Italy. Did you know he refused to sign the order for mobilization? Yes! Mussolini ordered it, but Victor Emmanuel said no—he would not send Italian soldiers to fight against their good friends—he would abdicate first. So you see, sometimes it is good to have a king."

A half hour grew into an hour, and still the crowds gathered. Still more crowds came in quickly from side streets, policemen on motorcycles cleared a narrow path, and in a flash an open car sped by heavily guarded on all sides. Everyone waved and a few cheered. Daladier smiled and bowed and in a flash was gone.

The Frenchwoman said: "Now I can think about my ankles. Maybe this is a great moment in the history of Europe. Anyway, I can say my prayers now and go to bed. The last few nights have not been good for sleeping, even for a tired old woman, who lost everything in the last war."

I shall always be glad I saw the League of Nations, that gleaming white palace, built by many nations, and made beautiful by their arts and crafts. I feel I was privileged to see the actual working of that great experiment to bring peace by discussion and arbitration— that great experiment which almost succeeded.

If the first act of aggression, Japan's invasion of Manchuria, had come earlier, when the dread of war was fresher in men's minds, and if the United States had been there in full power, the history of the League might have been entirely different, and the history of mankind, too.

In 1988, the beautiful white palace, with all its facilities, its far-reaching communication system, its clever and efficient people, experts, advisors, diplomats, its great Library of 240,000 books, its wealth of knowledge, its reports and surveys, everything in order and available, and the personnel in every department, down to the last filing clerk, filled with a sincere desire to serve . . . It was a sight to make the angels weep. It was so beautiful, so efficient, and yet so tragic!

It was like a magnificent house, furnished with exquisite taste and fitted with every device known to man for his comfort, pleasure and safety, air-conditioned and insulated, beautifully designed lighting system, with all modern improvements for cooking and cleaning, elevators from every room, nothing over-looked or forgotten— except one thing. There was no electricity.

The League lacked power and I am not now referring to an armed force to carry out its will, I mean the compelling constraining power which comes into men's hearts when they love their neighbors as themselves, and know that what concerns one concerns all. Dr. Wellington Koo struck this note when he said to the Assembly, in pleading for sanctions to be put against Japan:

"Perhaps you think it does not matter what is happening in China, which is far away from the homes of many of you. I tell you, cruel, unprovoked aggression is like blood poison, and the human family is like the human body. If there is poison in the foot, the hand is not safe."

The sterility of the League smote my heart with a sense of helplessness, as these words fell on the Assembly. Listening to them were representatives of at least three-quarters of the world's population and every one of us wanted peace. Surely some way must be found to release all this potential good will.

I knew there was a way and I have no doubt many people in that Assembly knew it too. Before going to Geneva, I had been for ten days at Interlaken, attending a world conference of the Oxford Group. There were people there from forty-five countries, rich and poor, bishops and communists, coal miners and university professors, all united in one purpose—to know the will of God and do it.

I heard strange stories, some of which sounded like Saul's conversion on the road to Damascus, told calmly and convincingly. I heard a British leather manufacturer tell how he had hated his rival in business until one day this new Way of Life came to him. Then he saw in a flash how small and miserable he had been in his outlook on life, and in the light of that experience all the satisfaction he had had in outwitting his competitor was gone, and in its place came a great desire to set the back-stakes of his life straight. He sought an interview with the other man, expecting to be thoroughly rebuffed, but to his surprise he found the other man was ready to take his share of the blame. As a result both firms benefitted and were able to make better shoes and sell them at a lower price to the public, at the same time paying better wages to their employees. Then he told us what had moved him to make this change in his mental outlook. He said his secretary had given him the challenge one day, when she came in to tell him about a mistake she had made. He was struck by the girl's honesty, and asked her why she had told him. Then she told him that she was living by a new standard and had to be honest in everything, even if she lost her job.

I heard many stories like this and saw for myself that these people had an illumination in their souls which was irresistible. They were released and happy, free from self-consciousness and afraid of nothing. They had evidently received that strange "warming of the heart" which John Wesley experienced at Aldersgate.

I had heard much criticism of the Oxford Group and their house parties, the angle of criticism being that they put up at the best hotels, dressed for dinner, and had a very good time generally. It is quite true that they have a good time, but it is not the jollity of idleness. It is the high fellowship of a great crusade.

They have other points of resemblance with the Wesleyans. They have class meetings, too, but they call them "quiet times," and they tell their spiritual experiences, but they call that "sharing", and they care nothing about money. They believe, like the Wesleyans, that if they do God's will, God will provide for their needs. The leader, Dr. Frank Buchman, is of Swiss origin, and was a Lutheran pastor in an American city. No man in modern times has been more slandered than Dr. Buchman, yet he goes his way with nothing but love in his heart for all mankind. He is a simple man in his tastes and commands the devoted loyalty and affection of people in every country of the world.

Much of the misunderstanding and criticism of the Group comes from the fact that they do work with people in high places, not exclusively of course, but the majority of their contacts are with labor leaders, employers of labor, manufacturers, statesmen and other people of wide influence and there is a good sound reason back of this policy. A man who controls the destiny of hundreds of his fellow men can make their lives happy or miserable. Moral decay of the leaders in any country brings swift destruction as we have already seen. But we can understand this criticism for there are still many people who believe that God's children should ever be poor and humble and somewhat apologetic.

There is nothing apologetic about the Oxford Group. They believe the promises, and they know that the power of God is as real in the spiritual world as electricity is in the physical world, but like electricity it has to be "piped" into human hearts. God's power flows through the humble and the contrite heart. The Oxford Group is not a denomination, nor does it enter into competition with any other form of religion. It is a permeation, a warming of the heart, a quickening of the soul.

It was my privilege to work with the Press Committee which sent reports from this great ten-day gathering, this unofficial league of nations, and I certainly found myself in good company. One of the newspaper correspondents was Fredrik Ramm of Norway. I had heard of him in connection with Amundsen's flight over the North Pole. He had accompanied the intrepid explorer. When the Oxford Group visited Norway in 1934, Mr. Ramm was changed and wielded a mighty influence in the Scandinavian countries.

In July, 1940, he was arrested by the Germans and thrown into jail. Knowing his great influence with the Norwegians, the Quislings were afraid to keep him a prisoner and presented him with a document which would have won for him his liberty. They asked him to declare that he would carry on no religious or political activity. Fredrik Ramm tore up the document, but so great was his influence that he was released for a time. But the next year he was arrested again and sentenced to life imprisonment as a leader in the Oxford Group, which the Germans had disbanded, declaring that it was an "arm of the British Secret Service." Quisling, the arch-traitor of Norway, declared that the Group had "poisoned the soul of Norway."

Fredrik Ramm was locked in solitary confinement in Hamburg's worst concentration camp because he refused to make armaments for the Nazis. As a result of his ill-treatment he died in November, 1943.

The story of his life lives on in a play, written by some of the friends who knew and worked with him. The name of the play is *And Still They Fight.*

I hope the League of Nations has contributed something to the great San Francisco meeting, which will have taken place when these words are printed. D-Day had to have its Dieppe, costly and heart-breaking, but military experts say the price was not too high for the lessons learned. The League went down to defeat because each nation was trying to save itself at all costs. In spite of all its formalities, its eloquent preambles and graceful compliments, its secret slogan was "Me First" and we know now, or we should know, that that policy is not only wrong, but self-destructive.

When the United Nations build a permanent home, and we in Canada are hoping that some part of our country will be honored as their place of residence, I would like to see these words, which are the soul and essence of our Christian philosophy, carved above the portal of this House of Hope:

"He that seeketh to save his life shall lose it; and he that loseth his life for My sake, shall find it."

31

The Way of Words

"WORDS ARE THE ONLY THING that live forever."
So spoke Winston Churchill thirty-seven years
ago at a writers' dinner in London. Looking
back, as I am doing now, trying to untangle the threads of life, and
weave them into a pattern, I see how true this is.

People utter words without knowing their full power. When the
barons at Runnymede put the pen in King John's grubby hand and
forced him to sign the Magna Charta, they thought they were speaking only for themselves in that great document in which these words
are written:

"To no one will we deny; to no one will we delay; to no one will
we sell justice."

But as the years rolled on, and the barons and King John returned
to dust, these words gathered strength and power far beyond the
meaning the gentlemen of Runnymede intended.

Prior to the first Great War we thought we were firmly set on our
way to peace and prosperity. Everything was coming our way. If
our souls are like the boles of trees, that period will show a thick
smooth ring, good to behold. We were a simple-minded, hopeful
people, and Alfred, Lord Tennyson, was our poet. We believed there
was an inherent quality in the Cause of Right which would give it

the victory and that was a pleasant doctrine which went well with chenille hangings, Axminster carpets, plumes in our hats, interlined skirts and good crops.

But let no one accuse us of sitting back in rocking-chairs waiting for the Golden Hour. We dreamed great dreams, but strove mightily. It was a clean new country we were living in then. We had no weeds, no rats, no fifth column, no unemployment and no Jew-haters.

I remember vividly the first time I was brought face to face with the horror of Anti-Semitism. It was in the pages of a book called *Little Citizens* by Myra Kelly. Miss Kelly was a young teacher in New York's Eastside, and she wrote about her pupils, many of whom were Jewish. One family was expecting a little cousin to arrive from Russia, and great were the plans made for her arrival. The whole school was aglow with expectancy. There was some jealousy, too, in the children who had no little cousin coming on a big ship. One day the little cousin arrived, but no one could see her. She was too sick. Then the story came out, bit by bit. Told to teacher with bitter tears. The little cousin was all that was left of her family, her papa and mama and baby brother six months old had been killed in a pogrom . . . Even on her little body was still the open wound where a cross had been cut by a "Christian."

Myra Kelly died young but her words live on. Since then we have heard and seen much of Anti-Semitism and know that it is a sure sign of moral decay.

I wonder why the whole Christian world has not risen against it, but somehow it did not seem to penetrate our optimistic souls. It seemed fantastic, unbelievable and far away. It couldn't happen here. We "somehow hoped" with Tennyson, "that good would be the final goal of ill."

Words again!

Hitler knew the power of words, and so wrote down for all men to read, if they would, his whole plan of attack on humanity. In it he said that people would believe anything if they were told over and over again, and the bigger the lie, the better. He began his work of degeneration by teaching very young children to hate and despise the children of other races. Nursery rhymes breathed death and desolation. He tried to stamp out Christianity and destroyed whole libraries in his plan for darkening the souls of the German people, and the deluded young Nazis screamed with joy, and danced "in the light of burning encyclopedias." It was the dance of death but they did not know it.

It has taken us a long time to understand that all this concerned us, and there are still among us many people who have not grasped its full significance. We are all proud of Canada's war effort, but our great concern now is how are we going to match it in our efforts for peace? It is much easier to make a great effort as a nation than to perform even small acts of sacrifice as individuals. It is easy to get cooperation when we are under the threat of aggression. I have heard people say quite frankly: "It is better to give generously now than let our enemies come in and take everything." Without this driving force of necessity mixed with fear there is a grave danger that as soon as the fear is removed we will revert to our former selfishness.

We see this in attitude to those stricken, desolate people who have been torn out by the roots by the cruelties of war. We are very sorry for them, of course, but they need more than sympathy and they have a right to expect something from us, the people of Canada, with our abundance of land and wealth of resources. In making an appeal on behalf of these homeless people we get a more sympathetic audience if our appeal is based on the level of profits.

Already in Canada we have seen what refugees can do. They have brought to us new skills, and instead of taking away jobs from our people, they have given them profitable employment. New industries have come to Canada, potteries, glove-making, new methods in agriculture and lumbering, and the record is growing. But my heart is heavy for my country, if it is true that we can be moved to generosity only by the hope of material reward.

Have we lost the spirit of our fathers? Are we afraid to venture anything for righteousness' sake?

The First Methodist Church in Ontario, now the magnificent Metropolitan in Toronto, was built by the faith of a man who mortgaged his farm to make the initial payment! Have we really to see the balance sheet and the gilt-edged guarantee before we will risk our money?

I do not mean to insinuate that there is anything inherently wicked in prosperity. Christ wanted everyone to have the abundant life. Poverty, which some religions have vainly tried to glorify, is, I believe, a cursed thing in this world of abundance. God intended us to have light and heat, comfort and beauty. It is only in the denial of these good gifts to others that the sin lies.

Canada, blessed among nations, must not close her gates to the homeless and desolate! We will impoverish our own souls if we do!

There is a great opportunity at this time, when the destiny of mankind is hanging in the balance, for inspired writers and speakers, people who know the power of words. We will never know what we owe to Winston Churchill for the fighting words he has put into our hearts. In the last war, David Lloyd George threw us many a life line in his mighty phrases. Let us be thankful, too, that the President of the United States has the apt word at his command. We are an articulate people, who delight in clarity of thought. No leader would dare to tell us "to think with our blood," which is a dark mysterious phrase, according well with what Matthew Halton calls "the muddy depths of the German soul."

Let us rejoice that we are rich in the treasury of great words, spoken by great men on great occasions, words made to be carved above doorways and on mantels, in schoolrooms, and colleges, in railway waiting rooms and on the archways of great bridges.

Speaking of bridges, someone surely blundered when an inscription was chosen for the new Burrard Bridge in Vancouver. It is a magnificent structure, and beautiful in design. No one can approach it without a throb of pleasure. Proudly it spans an arm of the Pacific Ocean. Above it the lions keep perpetual guard, and the Sleeping Beauty dreams the centuries away. There are ships in the harbor, and the famous skyline is etched in ivory on the blue horizon. Over its broad trafficways go the people of many nations, but on its middle-span is carved these meaningless words, with nothing in them but a prideful boast:

"On land and sea and in the air we prosper."

There is nothing in that to inspire, guide or comfort, nothing to bind the hearts of men in fellowship. Not even a word of gratitude.

Some Babbit did this!

There is something about words carved in stone which makes them more than words. Their permanence seems to give them authority. I noticed this many years ago in a simple sentence above the entrance of Harriet Island, a delightful spot where the people of St. Paul enjoy their summer evenings. These are the words:

"The health of the people is the wealth of the nation." Some day I hope someone will compile a book of Canadian inscriptions suitable for all our buildings. There is a beautiful poem entitled "The Song of the Wheat" by Knox Munson, which would look well inscribed on a grain elevator at the head of the Lakes, or in the corridor of some public building in Regina. Wheat has made Saskatchewan the richest province in the Dominion according to the 1944 revenue, and the Saskatchewan people would do well to honor it in enduring stone. Here are the words of Mr. Munson's song:

"Blow fitful winds, blow through my limber strands
O life, waving in undulating rows,
And exercising me with your magic hands.
Come gentle rain, I am the one who grows
The gold of strength, come play your tunes on me—
Whirling your songs of dampness to my feet;
I have the mouth to feed, and energy
Flows deep within the pellets of my wheat.
Blow wind, come playful rain, I cannot wait
Too long—I have important work to do.
Come nourish me or I will be too late,
For starving tongues depend on me and you."

I was glad to see that the Saskatchewan Co-operative Producers, when tendering a complimentary dinner to the Canadian Federation of Agriculture, paid tribute to one of our poets by using a verse on the menu card; under the picture of a grain elevator were these words by Edna Jaques:

"What precious treasure does this temple hold?
Great bins of wheat stored up like miser's gold,
Bread for a hungry world, the fruit of toil,
The blessed alchemy of sun and soil,
A golden heritage of wealth and power
Holding the skyline like a shining tower."

Over the Research Building in Ottawa there is an inscription which has always seemed to be very beautiful and appropriate, and when I inquired about its origin I found it was taken from the First and Second Book of Esdras in the Apocrypha, and reads as follows:

"Great is truth and mighty above all things. It endureth and is always strong. It liveth and conquereth forever more. The more thou searchest the more thou shalt marvel."

To the present Prime Minister of Canada, Mr. Mackenzie King, belongs the honor of having chosen these strong words and caused them to be graven on a lintel where everyone can see.

32

Conclusion

I T IS NOW TWO YEARS since I wrote the introduction to this book, which is a long time to have a book on the loom. The whole face of the world has changed since then, and is still changing. Even today will not hold still long enough to have its picture taken.

In sharp contrast to this perplexing world, I can see from my window a lovely spring day, and a peaceful countryside. English meadowlarks are singing over Mr. Edward's green fields, though Mr. Edwards himself with his boyish step no longer drives the horses up and down the furrow. A red tractor does the work there now, and the crop has been changed from daffodils to cabbages and cauliflower, but the beautiful arbutus tree still stands out in the middle of the field, as perfect in outline as the tree which once stood in all its beauty on Page One of the *First Manitoba Reader*, over the unadorned sentence: "This is a tree." The cabbages and cauliflower in their ivory white perfection are satisfying to the eye, and if we could forget their predecessors, the dancing daffodils, which in other years made a golden carpet down to the sea, we might go the whole length and say with Selina Peake that "cabbages are beautiful."

Under the mellowing influence of this warm April sun, the physical world that lies before me is bursting with gladness. Brown bulbs have turned to blossoms of every hue, and the bare branches which groaned and rattled in the winds of winter are now filled with pink rosettes. The buds on the lilac are swelling and the peach tree outside the kitchen window shows little points of pink against the stucco.

The birds are agitated over the housing problem. There are not nearly enough bird houses, they are crying, as they bitterly complain that no one appreciates what they are doing for the war-effort. Birds are notoriously bad tenants, as we all know. They would rather move than clean house. I do not believe that the birds have as much fun as they had before the planes usurped their domain. They had enough enemies before, the natural enemies, whose plan of attack is known—hawks, crows, stray cats—without these huge monsters in the skies. And yet they survive, these little helpless balls of feathers, by sheer weight of numbers they survive, and still they sing as if their little hearts would burst if they could not lift that song of ecstasy.

In the two years since I began this book, I have done much sitting in a sunny corner, sheltered by a hedge, with the pleasant heat of the sun on the back of my neck. Often I have seen older people sitting, as I am now, and I have been sorry for them, but there really is no need for sorrow. Every season of life has its compensations, and there is a mental activity which does not depend on motion. It is often true that those who sit in the wings can see more than the players. I know many people with whom I would like to share this peace and quiet. I wish I could hand over some of it to the women who are doing two jobs, and who come home tired at night, yet have to do another day's work before they can sleep, the women who have to face dirty dishes in the sink, no fire in the stove, and hungry children waiting to be fed. If we have any sympathy to spare, let us feel it for the young people of these brittle days, whose young lives are spent in anxiety and fear.

They need our prayers and our loving sympathy. They are the brave young ships laboring through life's heavy seas, in danger from above and below. Let us give them our loving thought, but let us not waste even a shred of sympathy on the battered old ships, safely anchored in a peaceful haven.

Speaking as one of the old craft, riding at anchor in a safe harbor, I am glad to record that even these hard years bring certain satisfactions. I am proud of the way women have taken their places in many departments of public service, and of how the attitude towards women has changed for the better. Many women have broken new trails and hold their positions with dignity, asking no favors and receiving none, remaining good humored and dignified at all times. These are the women who dress modestly, keep their hair neat and their voices low, and never try to win approval by lowering their standards of conduct, I like to remember the "seniors" among the women workers—Miriam Green Ellis, whose agricultural writing is unsurpassed; Claire Wallace in radio, to mention only two.

We are proud of the young ones too. A few days ago I listened to an interview on the radio with a young entertainer named Peggy Anderson, who had been singing and dancing for the American troops in Italy and elsewhere. She was interviewed by Mrs. Barlow, who asked Peggy how she could do so much travelling and dancing and still remain in perfect health. Peggy replied: "We are all trained well before we start out, you see, and we never drink. The boys would not like us if we did, for they want to respect us, as well as admire us."

I wish every teen-age girl could have heard that!

When I wrote in the Introduction to this book that I was about to "summer fallow" my mind, the figure of speech was more apt than I knew. Surely the whole world has undergone a plowing and a harrowing which no mortal mind can fully grasp. The skies of the world are darkened by the black wings of sorrow, and no country and very few homes have escaped their sinister shadow. Nationally we have had sore losses—the Archbishop of Canterbury, Wendell Wilkie, and now President Roosevelt. These great men have been taken from us, leaving us bewildered and lost. We think of Lincoln, who was taken before he had achieved his purpose, and of Wilson, who planned, but was not permitted to fulfill his mission. Is it possible that we depend too much on our leaders?

In our own family we suffered the first break in 1944. For forty-six years we had an unbroken family circle. Then came the reeling blow and our eldest son, our beloved Jack, was gone—gone like a great tree from the mountain top, leaving a lonesome place against the sky.

The first few days of shock bring a merciful anesthesia, when time stands still and the world seems to have ended. You know then why people stop the clock and draw the blinds, and you have a better understanding of why Miss Haversham ordered the wedding feast to be left on the table when her world broke down. It is a pathetically futile, but human, attempt to hold back the desolation which has come upon you.

But that passes, and you know that life goes on, and you must stand up to it. Besides, there is the family, drawn closer in the community of sorrow. Thank God for the family!

Wes and I were like the two sad disciples who travelled the road to Emmaus, sorrowing for the One whom they loved. They had seen Him die, and their hopes had died with Him. Suddenly they were joined by a third traveller, a stranger, whose sympathy brought out the whole story. It comforted them to tell him their sorrow, and when they came to their house, they begged him to stay with them and be their guest for the night. As they sat down to eat there was something about their new friend's way of breaking bread which opened their eyes. The record says simply: "They knew Him in the breaking of bread."

This is an old, old story, but no one ever really knows its meaning until they walk that sorrowful road, and find their hearts suddenly comforted as the Great Truth breaks over them in light and hope.

Death is not the end. It is but the portal to a brighter, fairer world. Life is a circle. We see only a small jagged segment of it here, and even that small part, we see through a glass darkly. The part we see with our mortal eyes does not make sense; it is like the fragment of a story you read in a torn magazine—you know there must be more of it. W. M. Letts' beautiful sonnet has comfort in it:

"When I consider Life and its few years—
A wisp of fog between us and the sun,
A call to battle and the battle done
Ere the last echo sounds within our ears;
A rose choked in the grass; and hours of fears;
A burst of music down an unlistening street;
The waves that past a darkling shore do beat;
I wonder at the idleness of tears!
Ye old, old dead, and ye of yester-night,
Chieftains, and bards, and keepers of the sheep,
By every cup of sorrow you have had,
Loose me from tears, and make me see aright
How each hath back what once he stayed to weep,
Homer his sight: David his little lad!"

The overflowing kindness of friends bring vibrations of comfort and strength. There are letters from friends and some from strangers. "He was good to me when I needed a friend" . . . "He helped me to regain my self-respect" . . . "It did me good just to see him" . . . "A nod from Jack brightened my day" . . . "He was filled with the joy of living, and had a way of imparting it" . . . "I never knew anyone who had so many friends" . . . "Man and boy he served his country well" . . . "He will be long remembered for his compassionate heart."

As the days went on I found myself holding on to that simple sentence: "They knew Him in the breaking of bread." It throws a gleam of light across the desolation of this troubled world, where the whole creation is groaning under intolerable burdens. The breaking of bread suggests something we can all do; something we all must do. Work is more than mere activity—there is healing in it!

From this sheltered spot I see people working on the land; there are girls in bright overalls and sweaters, with gay handkerchiefs on their heads, picking flowers; there are men putting fertilizer on the cabbages which are being raised for seed. I wonder if it sweetens their labor to know they are contributing to the needs of their fellow men? Who knows how far this seed may travel? Or what bit of scorched earth it may restore? I like to think that the men who were spreading on the fertilizer have this in mind.

On the other side of Mount Douglas there lives a Manitoba friend of ours who has now arrived at the age when people usually develop high blood pressure and cease from their labors. But this man did nothing of the kind. He came out here, bought some raw land, put it under cultivation and began to raise vegetable seeds. He went at it scientifically, with the help and blessing of our Agricultural Department, and has achieved success. Last winter, when his farm duties were over for a month or so, he worked for a seed house in Vancouver, lived in a boarding house, carried a lunch, worked long hours, travelling both ways in darkness, but was happy because he was weighing and packing seeds for Europe. He was helping to rebuild the waste places. He saw his work in the seed house, not as work which makes an old man's muscles tired, but as a chance to do a bit of world building. This man has the vision. He sees his Lord in the breaking of bread. He did not tell me this. I saw it in his face.

If I were young again—and I wish I could go back—I would spend my life as a teacher of young children, doing all in my power to give them a vision of the dignity and glory of being builders and planters, makers and menders. Children are great idealists, until the stupidity of their elders puts out the fires of their aspirations. We have seen, to our sorrow, how the heart of Nazi youth was betrayed and turned to evil. Surely we should put our energies into the battle for man's redemption with equal fervor.

In the next few years Canada, as one of the most fortunate nations in the world, will be called on to give, and I have faith in my country that we will give generously, and I hope we will give gladly. It is not enough to give of our abundance and then sit back and wait to be thanked. Charity has always been given. Good works and alms deeds have been faithfully performed for the poor and the needy, and the poor have remained poor and often bitter. This time we must give in a different spirit. We must remember that man cannot live by bread alone. We must give ourselves with the gift. The breaking of bread has in it the suggestion of many kindly gracious deeds which we can all perform. We have here in Canada people of many races, but unfortunately, some of them are smarting under our rebuffs, our lack of courtesy and understanding.

It does not take much to make people happy, and by the same token, it does not take much to make them bitter; a few insults, and the damage is done. The fourteen hundred Hindus who live in this province, British Columbia, are intelligent, law-abiding people, and they are British subjects, and yet they were denied the rights of citizens by a vote of our elected representatives just the other day. Surely this is a great blunder, and all the greater because it comes at a time when the free people of the world are making a mighty effort to unite against the powers of barbarism. As a people we lack imagination. I have no doubt that Christ was referring to imagination when he said: "I came that they might have Life, and that they might have it more abundantly." I am sure that the "more abundant life" referred to the quickening of all our senses, and until that quickening comes in the hearts of people, they will continue to make costly mistakes. Without any mental effort on our part, we can see that the German people lack imagination, and that is one cause which has lead to their downfall. But strangely enough we fail to apply the lesson.

When we look back over our lives we can see most of our mistakes have come by not entering fully into the minds of other people. Sometimes this happened because of diffidence, sometimes from lack of interest, and sometimes it was plain, ordinary stupidity. I believe it is this lack of imagination on the part of good people which has given the church a black eye and a reputation for being "stuffy." Sometimes their good works are done grudgingly, and so cease to be good works.

I remember one time a woman gave me a pair of pillow covers that she had embroidered herself. They were beautifully done and wrapped in white tissue paper with silver ribbon. But this is what she said: "Now I do hope you will appreciate this gift, for I spent many an hour on this embroidery when I really should have been sleeping."

I did not know what to say. I wanted to tell her I was sorry she had ever thought of them. They were certainly no joy to her in the giving, and no joy to me in the receiving. She made me feel that I was accepting the product of sweated labor. This was a gift with a sting!

As this is the last chapter in the book I find it hard to end it. I am one of these irritating people, who hang on to the door-knob after they say good-bye, and will neither come back nor go, always remembering something else which must be said, and here it is:

Do not look for safety in this world. There is no safety here. There is only balance. This is what Christ meant when he said: "As a man thinketh in his heart—so is he." We have not much choice in the mechanics of our lives—the house we live in—the family or race we belong to—the color of our eyes or skin. But in one respect we have liberty and that is in our attitude to life. Many a busy woman has truthfully said that her life is a never-ending round, a steady grind, but if she has in her heart this spiritual balance, she can make her life a spiral round, by giving it that Other Dimension, which is the greatest thing in the world.

THE END.